Identifying the Mind

PHILOSOPHY OF MIND SERIES

Series Editor
David J. Chalmers, University of Arizona
This series provides a forum for work at the cutting edge of the philosophy of mind.

Self Expressions
Minds, Morals, and the Meaning of Life
Owen Flanagan

The Conscious Mind
In Search of a Fundamental Theory
David J. Chalmers

Deconstructing the Mind
Stephen P. Stich

The Human Animal
Personal Identity without Psychology
Eric Olson

Minds and Bodies
Philosophers and Their Ideas
Colin McGinn

What's Within?
Nativism Reconsidered
Fiona Cowie

Purple Haze
The Puzzle of Consciousness
Joseph Levine

Consciousness and Cognition
A Unified Account
Michael Thau

Thinking without Words
José Luis Bermúdez

Identifying the Mind
Selected Papers of U. T. Place
Edited by George Graham and
Elizabeth R. Valentine

Identifying the Mind

Selected Papers of U. T. Place

Edited by
George Graham
Elizabeth R. Valentine

OXFORD

UNIVERSITY PRESS

2004

OXFORD

UNIVERSITY PRESS

Oxford   New York
Auckland   Bangkok   Buenos Aires   Cape Town   Chennai
Dar es Salaam   Delhi   Hong Kong   Istanbul   Karachi   Kolkata
Kuala Lumpur   Madrid   Melbourne   Mexico City   Mumbai
Nairobi   São Paulo   Shanghai   Taipei   Tokyo   Toronto

Copyright © 2004 by Oxford University Press, Inc.

Published by Oxford University Press, Inc.
198 Madison Avenue, New York, New York, 10016

www.oup.usa.org

Oxford is a registered trademark of Oxford University Press

Library of Congress Cataloging-in-Publication Data
Place, U. T. (Ullin Thomas), 1924–2000.
Identifying the mind : selected papers of U. T. Place / authored by U. T. Place;
edited by George Graham and Elizabeth R. Valentine.
p. cm.—(Philosophy of mind series)
Includes bibliographical references and index.
ISBN 0-19-516137-8
1. Mind-brain identity theory. 2. Philosophy of mind.
I. Graham, George, 1945–
II. Valentine, Elizabeth R.
III. Title   IV. Series.
B105.M55P58   2004
128′.2—dc21   2003041939

1 3 5 7 9 8 6 4 2

Printed in the United States of America
on acid-free paper

Acknowledgments

We gratefully acknowledge considerable assistance from others. We wish to thank David Chalmers for encouraging us to put this collection together and for his help with a range of editorial decisions including suggesting the book's title. Robert Miller of Oxford University Press was also an invaluable source of help and encouragement, always ready to answer detailed questions. Place's son, Thomas, played a crucial role by making available to us indexed, electronic files of Place's papers. Place's widow, Peggy, supported us in many ways, in particular by giving us an indirect sense of Place's own involvement in our project and of how much it would have meant to him—and does to her—to publish with Oxford University Press.

Other people have helped us in a variety of ways. They include (in alphabetical order) David Armstrong, Veronica Askew, Hanoch Benyami, John Bickle, Tom Dickins, Owen Flanagan, Harry Lewis, William Lycan, Dave Palmer, Matjaž Potrč, Antti Revonsuo, Teed Rockwell, Mark Slocombe, Jack Smart (Place's close friend and intellectual colleague, and author of the foreword), Dorothy Smith (Place's sister), Danilo Šuster, and Jason Wheeler Vega.

Thanks are also due to our families and colleagues for their encouragement and support. Special thanks are due to Patricia Graham, George's wife, and to John Valentine, Elizabeth's husband.

We are grateful to the following for permission to reproduce material in this volume: chapter 4, "Materialism as a Scientific Hypothesis," reprinted from *Philosophical Review*, 69, 101–104, 1960, © 1960 Cornell University, by permission of the publisher; chapter 5, "Consciousness in Psychology," sections 3 through 6 from a paper published in the *Proceedings of the Aristotelian Society, supplementary volumes*, 40, 101–124, 1966, reprinted by courtesy of the editor of the Aristotelian Society © 1966; chapter 7, "Thirty Years On—Is Consciousness Still a Brain Process?" reprinted from the *Australasian Journal of Philosophy*, 66, 208–219, 1988, by permission of the Australasian Association of Philosophy and Oxford University Press; chapter 8, "Token- versus Type-Identity Physicalism," reprinted from *Anthropology and Philosophy*, 3, 21–31, 1999, by kind permission of the editor and publisher; chapter 9, "The Two-Factor Theory of the Mind-Brain Relation," reprinted from *Brain and Mind*, 1 (1), 29–43, 2000, © 2000 Academic Publishers, with kind permission of Kluwer Academic Publishers; chapter 10, "The Causal Potency of Qualia: Its Nature and Its Source," reprinted from *Brain and Mind,* 1 (1), 29–43, 2000, © 2000, Academic Publishers, with kind permission of Kluwer Academic Publishers; chapter 11, "Consciousness and the 'Zombie-Within': A Functional Analysis of the Blindsight Evidence," reprinted from *Beyond Dissociation: Interaction between Dissociated Implicit and Explicit Processing*, edited by Yves Rossetti and Antti Revonsuo, pp. 295–329, John Benjamins, Amsterdam, 2000, by permission of the publisher; chapter 12, "On the Social Relativity of Truth and the Analytic/Synthetic Distinction," reprinted from *Human Studies,* 14, 265–285, 1991, © 1991 Kluwer Academic Publishers, by kind permission of Kluwer Academic Publishers; chapter 13, "The Role of the Ethnomethodological Experiment in the Empirical Investigation of Social Norms, and Its Application to Conceptual Analysis," reprinted from *Philosophy of the Social Sciences*, 22, 461–474, 1992, © Sage Publications, by permission; figure11.1, The ventral and dorsal streams (from Milner, A. David and Melvyn A. Goodale, 1995, *The Visual Brain in Action*. Oxford University Press, figure 3.1, page 68), reprinted by permission of Oxford University Press and the authors.

Foreword

Ullin Place was in my opinion the true pioneer of what became known as the identity theory of mind (though Herbert Feigl deserves mention). His paper "Is consciousness a brain process?" emerged after discussions with me and C. B. Martin at the University of Adelaide. At the time, I was trying to argue against Place from the point of view of Rylean behaviorism, but in the end Place converted me. Place came to the department of philosophy of which I was head, as lecturer in psychology. He introduced scientific psychology and got a laboratory going. He paved the way for what after his time became a large and excellent department of psychology led by Malcolm Jeeves, whose approach was more physiological. Ullin Place continued to think of himself as a psychologist but I think that his true greatness was as a philosopher. The fact that he published his two seminal articles in the *British Journal of Psychology* delayed the recognition of his ideas by the philosophical community, but recognition did come. The present collection of papers will help to widen appreciation of his work, much of which was published in journals other than the most mainstream philosophical ones. Ullin did continue to think of himself as a psychologist, no less than a philosopher.

It was a great loss to the University of Adelaide and to Australian philosophy when Ullin decided for personal reasons to return to England. (I had first known him when he was an undergraduate and I a research fellow at Corpus Christi College, Oxford.) He became a lifelong friend, and on visits to Britain I enjoyed visiting with him and Peggy and walking with him to the North Yorkshire moors. It gives me great pleasure to write this preface and commend this volume of some of Ullin's papers and also to express my thanks to George Graham and Liz Valentine for their work as editors; they deserve the thanks of the philosophical and psychological public at large.

Melbourne, Australia   Jack Smart
June 2002

Preface

This book is comprised of what we regard as some of the best papers written by Ullin T. (U. T.) Place. Many of the central ideas found their original expression in "Is Conscious a Brain Process?" in 1956. However it was the publication over more than four decades of papers on consciousness and mentality, on the one hand, and brain and behavior, on the other, that permitted Place systematic development and expression of his views.

Most of Place's papers were, however, in relatively inaccessible journals and scattered in spatial and temporal diffusion. This book is the attempt to rectify that—to make the inaccessible accessible and to eliminate the diffusion. Since the papers in this collection appeared over a span of many decades, containing uneven levels of productivity and periods of minor refinement and reorientation, it was no mean task to decide what to include and in what form. The topic of consciousness is regularly Place's target, but his sights focused on mind more broadly and on topics outside philosophy of mind about which his philosophical views on mind and consciousness required him to speak and write.

This book is the product of complete and total collaboration between the two of us as coeditors. The listed order of our names is alphabetical (arbitrary).

Work between us on the project began in response to inspiration from a variety of sources, including the recognition that near the end of his life Place had wished to compose one or more books. He discussed possible book projects with professional friends, former colleagues, and possible publishers. The diagnosis of terminal illness, however, prevented him from bringing these plans to fruition.

Why us? How did we become interested in the project?

The first named of us, George Graham (GG), initially became personally acquainted with Place while he (GG) was editor of *Behavior and Philosophy*, which in the 1980s published a number of Place's papers on B. F. Skinner. GG, though not a Skinnerian, was interested in the philosophy of the experimental analysis of behavior. Various philosophers including Charles Taylor (in an earlier philosophical life), Jon Ringen, and Daniel Dennett had written seminal material on either B. F. Skinner or psychology in the experimental tradition, and GG conceived of *Behavior and Philosophy* as, in part, a means to encourage more such work. Place, meanwhile, was looking for philosophers who were willing to discuss behaviorism without scowl or embarrassment. Place considered himself a *behaviorist* of sorts (see editorial introduction and chapter 1, pp. 27–28, for clarification). GG was delighted to publish Place's attempts to nourish the journal with his reflections on Skinner's analysis of verbal behavior.

Place and GG became friends. To GG, Place was a model of an empirically informed and deeply committed philosopher. His creative allegiance to figures in twentieth-century philosophy of mind (foremost Gilbert Ryle) that by the 1980s had fallen out of professional favor GG interpreted as an act of intellectual courage to be admired.

Elizabeth Valentine (EV) had known Place for almost twenty years, largely through the History and Philosophy Section of the British Psychological Society. They had common backgrounds and interests in philosophy and psychology; and both became founding members of the Section when it was formed in 1987. Place gave a paper at every annual conference, convened symposia on the Section's behalf at national conferences, and served on its committee for a period. EV (like many others) came to appreciate Place as a friend and mentor, always able and willing to provide help and advice.

Our pairing of interests, GG as philosopher of mind, EV as a psychologist with interests in its philosophy and history as well as consciousness, matched many of Place's most central intellectual concerns. After his death, each knowing of the other through Place, we approached one another about collecting some of his best papers in a manner that would suggest, by virtue of its thematic organization, the type of book that Place himself wished to compose. This would be a book that represented the sustained and systematic nature of his thought. GG met over lunch with David Chalmers, the philosopher of mind and editor of the series in which this book appears, and Robert Miller of Oxford University Press to discuss such a book. In David and Robert, GG and EV therein found two persons eager to encourage the production of this collection.

In preparing the papers for this volume, we have made minor editorial alterations and corrections, aimed at clarifying the text. We have retained the use of the masculine pronoun in the earlier papers, largely for reasons of simplicity; Place was not averse from using the female pronoun when usage changed, as is evident from his later papers.

Birmingham, Alabama   G. G.
London, England   E. V.
October 2002

Contents

Editorial Introduction: Place in Mind and Mind in Place
George Graham and Elizabeth R. Valentine   3

1   From Mystical Experience to Biological Consciousness:
A Pilgrim's Progress?   14

2   The Concept of Heed   30

3   Is Consciousness a Brain Process?   45

4   Materialism as a Scientific Hypothesis   53

5   Consciousness in Psychology   56

6   The Infallibility of Our Knowledge
of Our Own Beliefs   63

7   Thirty Years On—Is Consciousness Still
a Brain Process?   70

8   Token- versus Type-Identity Physicalism   81

9   The Two-Factor Theory of the Mind-Brain Relation   90

10 The Causal Potency of Qualia: Its Nature
and Its Source   104

11 Consciousness and the "Zombie-Within":
A Functional Analysis of the Blindsight Evidence   113

12 On the Social Relativity of Truth
and the Analytic/Synthetic Distinction   138

13   The Role of the Ethnomethodological Experiment
      in the Empirical Investigation of Social Norms
      and Its Application to Conceptual Analysis   155

14   Linguistic Behaviorism as a Philosophy
      of Empirical Science   165

      Appendix: Publications of U. T. Place   185

      Notes   191

      References   201

      Index   211

Identifying the Mind

Editorial Introduction
Place in Mind and Mind in Place

George Graham
and Elizabeth R. Valentine

Ullin Thomas (U. T.) Place can justifiably be described as the pioneer of the modern identity theory of mind, according to which mental processes can be identified with processes that go on in the brain. He was the author of the first of the trilogy of papers[1] that established the theory as a defensible philosophical position.

Place offered at least two estimations of his paper's impact. One is humble; the other is uncharacteristically immodest. The one (Place 1988; chapter 7, this volume) is that his paper was an ancestor of the materialism that has become an establishment view in contemporary philosophy of mind. The other (Place 2002; chapter 1, this volume) is that the paper marked a watershed in philosophical discussions of the mind-body problem whose impact was comparable to that of Descartes's *Meditations*. In our judgment there is no doubt that the paper constituted a watershed, helping to set the agenda in the philosophy of mind for the next half century. So its impact has been much more than just ancestral, if less than the volcanic force among philosophers of mind of the *Meditations*.

Although almost all philosophers know this classic paper "Is consciousness a brain process?" (hereafter ICBP), published in the *British Journal of Psychology* in 1956,[2] much of the remainder of Place's work is little known, for a variety of reasons. He wrote no single-authored book, many of his articles were not published in mainstream journals, and he often espoused unfashionable causes. Place was more concerned to pursue the truth as he saw it than to court favor or publicity. This book brings together a selection of some of his best papers.

Ullin Place: The Person

Place was born (on October 24, 1924) and lived most of his life in North Yorkshire, where he farmed sheep and had an intimate knowledge of local archeology and place names; he was also an expert on edible fungi and a model-railway enthusiast. He won an Open Scholarship to Corpus Christi College, Oxford in 1942, but his studies were interrupted by the war, in which he signed up as a conscientious objector and worked in the Friends' Ambulance Service (his mother's ancestors were Quakers). On his return to Oxford after the war, he became one of the first cohort of the new honors school in philosophy, physiology, and psychology, graduating in philosophy and psychology in 1949. The following year he took a diploma in anthropology, for which he was always grateful for its adding a social dimension to his thinking. Formative influences from this period were logical positivism and its heir, ordinary language philosophy, under Gilbert Ryle, J. L. Austin, and Paul Grice. Place taught psychology at Adelaide, South Australia, in the 1950s, served as a clinical psychologist in the British National Health Service in the 1960s, and taught clinical psychology and then philosophy at Leeds University in the 1970s. He retired from teaching in the early 1980s, devoting himself to full-time philosophic research until his death from cancer on January 2, 2000.

Place was an inveterate conference-goer (typically staying in a camper and cycling to the conference venue). As Phil Reed (2001) recalls, he would take on anyone anywhere anytime in debate. He was generous toward younger and intellectually less able students and was always calm, tolerant, and courteous. His work showed great independence, originality, and informed scholarship. The equanimity and stoic courage with which he faced his final illness showed him to be a true philosopher. Ullin Place was a man of the highest intellectual and moral stature.

Place and Mind-Brain Identity Theory:
A Short Historical Overview

The modern identity theory of mind is a version of materialist monism about the mental. Its central claim is that the mind (and its properties and activities) is nothing but the brain (and its properties and activities). By this is meant not the brain *simpliciter* but the brain in psychological operation. This means (among other things) that conscious events (pains, itches, mental images, and so on) are brain processes. They go on in the brain. It also means that we can learn about mentality through sciences such as neurobiology and neurophysiology, despite the logically independent descriptions of mind in ordinary language and of brain in neuroscience, as well as different methods of verification in those contexts. The theory is sometimes referred to as central state materialism or as the psychoneural identity thesis. These are apt labels, since mental operations are identified with neural processes.

Although materialism dates back to classical times and reappeared periodically from the sixteenth century onward, it was essentially blocked historically by the influence of Descartes's postulation of an independently existing mental substance. Place (1990) attributes the first formulation of the 'identity theory' to Boring (1933). However, a number of other philosophical developments were required before the identity thesis could be accepted. Crucial among them was the later work of Wittgenstein, Herbert Feigl's analysis of sense and reference, and Gilbert Ryle's logical behaviorism.

Place's (1956) statement of the theory, prefigured in Place (1954), was formulated as a result of discussions with J. J. C. Smart, C. B. Martin, and D. A. T. Gasking, which took place at the University of Adelaide in 1954. Feigl's (1958) view was developed independently, based on an earlier paper (Feigl, 1953). Smart later became converted and published a defense of mind-brain identity theory the following year (Smart, 1959).

Place's version of the identity theory restricted the theory to mental events (discrete occurrences in time), such as sensations and mental images, and formulated the notion of identity in terms of constitutional or compositional identity. Place claimed that brain processes constitute mental events in the sense that mental events are made up of nothing but brain processes. On his view, mental events described in ordinary language are described and explained scientifically in terms of brain processes. Brian Medlin (1967) and later D. M. Armstrong (1968) extended the scope of the mind-brain identity claim to all mental states (including enduring and nonconscious attitudes or dispositions), such as beliefs and desires (a move that Place opposed). Although a range of objections have been leveled against the identity theory (epistemological, violations of Leibniz's law, multiple realizability), the identity theory continues to exert its influence.[3]

The theory's influence operates at two levels. The first, metalevel, influence concerns how best to conduct the metaphysics of mind and is independent of actual acceptance of the identity theory. Partly because of ICBP's pioneering role, it is widely believed that scientific evidence is relevant to philosophical questions about the mind. Just how relevant is open to debate, but if one's goal is a physical science of mind, which was indeed Place's goal, it is assumed that the processes responsible for behavior are amenable to physical scientific description. ICBP's claim for mental event–brain process identity facilitated the search for descriptions of brain and behavior that permit entities characterized in two different vocabularies (mind and brain) to count as descriptions of the same entity. The journey from such characterizations to a physical science of the mind is complicated and contentious, but ICBP confronted some of its major challenges and argued they are not as damaging as once thought to be.

The second influence is at ground level—the level of ontological commitment at which it is asked, What is the *best* metaphysics of mind, assuming that some version of materialism is true? After a period of popularity in the 1960s, mind-brain identity theory was largely superseded in popularity by a position known as *functionalism* (Putnam, 1973). One of the main reasons for the development of functionalism was the claim that mental processes are multiply realizable. If the same conscious or mental events may be realized in various different kinds of minds, including alien mind forms and artificial minds, then they are likely to be physically realized in different ways, including nonneurally. Hence, mental processes cannot be identical to brain processes.

ICBP did not anticipate, because it could not anticipate, the popularity of functionalism. Nevertheless, Place claimed that it was empirically plausible or scientifically reasonable to assume that mental processes are identical to neural processes. The goal of defense of this hypothesis, he noted, is to ensure that it is not dismissed on logical grounds alone and to identify the hypothesis as able to be confirmed by further empirical research. The identity thesis thus became a source of inspiration as much as a letter of doctrinal metaphysical law and provided a basis for its own self-refinement and continued development. A number of philosophers (Kim, 1992; McCauley and Bechtel, 2001) recently have argued, for example, that the multiple realizability commitment of functionalism is compatible with embracing an identity thesis. The route to this conclusion is argumentatively complicated and not without dissent (see Graham and Horgan, 2002), but such features are characteristic of Place's original defense of the identity thesis. ICBP urged that the metaphysics of mind pay attention to scientific evidence—even if such evidence is complicated and contentious to interpret.

Although Place launched mind-brain identity theory, he was not, as noted above, a full-scope mind-brain identity theorist. ICBP helped to found a theory whose later developments he did not fully accept. This irony needs to be explained. Place was a mind-brain identity theorist about all and only mental phenomena best described as discrete datable occurrences and as in the head or inner (i.e., not necessarily manifested in overt behavior), for example, pains and itches. He referred to such phenomena as events. Place was not an identity theorist about what he referred to as states, such as beliefs or desires. He was a materialist about the mental, certainly, but a promoter of central statehood just for internal mental events. In the case of mental states, including, for him, propositional attitudes such as believing, wanting, or intending, Place was a disposition-behaviorist. He made this clear in his 1956 paper: "In the case of . . . concepts like 'knowing', 'believing', 'understanding', 'remembering', and volitional concepts like 'wanting' and 'intending' . . . an analysis in terms of dispositions to behave is fundamentally sound" (p. 44; chapter 3, this volume). He repeated his unwillingness to generalize the identity thesis from events to states on numerous occasions (see, e.g., Place, 1988; chapter 7, this volume).

Place never abandoned a behaviorist interpretation of states (or attitudes). Periodically throughout his career, he paid respects to Ryle, Wittgenstein, and B. F. Skinner for inspiring his behaviorist sympathies if not for the letter of his construal of behaviorism. Place contended that, although dispositions of a behavioral sort depend, causally, upon the brain, dispositions should not be identified with central states. In this he differed from Armstrong (1968, pp. 85–88) and resisted endorsing expanded-scope mind-brain identity theory (a thesis that became known as central state materialism). "Mental processes," he wrote near the end of his life, "just are processes in the brain. Dispositional mental states, on the other hand, are not, in my view, states of the brain" (Place 2000a, p. 30; chapter 9, this volume).

Armstrong insisted that behavioral dispositions can and should be identified with their microstructural basis in the brain. Place counterargued that insofar as the neural basis of a disposition of a mental sort (together with its evoking stimuli or disposition partners in the world) causes the manifestation of a disposition, a disposition cannot be identical with its neural basis. This is because causes cannot be identified with their effects. Causes and effects must, as Hume taught, have distinct existences. So, a disposition described as unmanifested, as a type of neural state (as above) cannot cause or help to cause the very same disposition or state as manifested. In short, Place favored a species of what may be called a Divided Account of the Mind. The domain of the mental has two kinds of components: (1) mental events (conscious events and processes), which are brain processes; (2) mental states or attitudes (such as beliefs), which (for him) are dispositions to behave.

In Place If Not in Step

Though some of the specific positions that Place advocated are out of step with current philosophical thinking about the mind, in general his positions are not out of place. His preference for a divided account is one example, the general spirit of which is in keeping with some currently popular philosophical views. It is quite common in contemporary philosophy of mind to adopt a divided account of the mental.

One influential divided or two-component account consists in distinguishing between an aspect of the mental sometimes known as the phenomenal and an aspect known as representational or Intentional. 'Representational' refers to the aboutness of the mental. The belief that snow is white, for example, is about the fact or proposition that snow is white. Additionally, sometimes, as in the case of the philosophy of phenomenal consciousness known as representationalism, advocated by Michael Tye (1995), Fred Dretske (1995), and a number of other philosophers, the phenomenal is understood as a certain sort of representational content. Phenomenology is said to possess Intentionality or aboutness. To illustrate: consider the perceptual visual experience of red when part of consciously perceiving a red balloon. For a representationalist like Tye or Dretske, this perceptual experience is understood as representing the balloon (conceived as something external) as red. The representational content of the state is that of a red balloon. Phenomenal or conscious experience is said to embody a particular form of representational content. Sometimes this is called 'phenomenal representational content'. Redness as perceived in the red balloon is (part of) the phenomenal representational content of the red balloon perceptual experience.

Central to the most popular version of representationalism (that of Tye and Dretske, and known as externalist representationalism) is the additional proposition that phenomenal representational content is one and the same as external, real-world properties. Phenomenal representational content is not in the head. Phenomenal representational properties are those that conscious experience depicts objects as possessing and that help to causally explain the occurrence of conscious experience of those very same properties. So, as the externalist position contends, in perceiving the balloon as red, the property of redness is an external, real-world property of the balloon—a property that helps to causally explain the represented presence of red.

Place would have endorsed some (but not all) of this. He would have agreed that mentality consists of two aspects or components. He would have agreed that one of these aspects is representational and the other consists of conscious or phenomenal awareness. He also would have agreed that representational content is not in the head. A major component of Place's divided account of the mental consists in emphasizing the nonneural location of representational content. Place claimed that states of mind represent, but he also claimed that representational content resides in dispositions of the body, and relations between special sorts of dispositions (foremost, dispositions to verbal behavior) and the social and natural environment. He did not—as noted above—equate dispositions with brain states. Place distinguished between states of mind (such as beliefs) that are representational, on the one hand, and mental events that are phenomenally constituted by the way in which they appear in experience (conscious events), on the other. He dialectically toyed with the idea of interpreting conscious mental events (such as sensations of pain) in terms of his category of the dispositional-representational, but he rejected this possibility. "Dispositional properties," he wrote, "exist prior to and in the absence of their manifestation." Sensations, however, "are not like this. They make themselves felt from the very moment" of their existence (before they dispose to behavior). It is partly for this reason that they are best understood as "one and the same thing as the brain processes . . . with which they are correlated" (Place, 2000b, p. 190–191; chapter 10, this volume).

Ironies with respect to Place do not end with the fact that he was not, fully or strictly, a central state materialist. Although Place conceived of the identity of the mental and the physical as contingent, in the theory as originally formulated, be believed that this identity could become analytic at a later stage. A contingent identity is, modally speaking, for Place, an identity that it is not self-contradictory to deny. (Place was not a friend of possible-world semantics, so he did not characterize contingent identities as identities that are true in some but not in all possible worlds.)

To understand Place's account of identity, one must be familiar with his philosophy of language and interest in sociolinguistics. An important feature of his theory of linguistic meaning and representational content is the claim that statements of identity of the type-type sort, expressed by a claim like "Sensations are brain processes," possess a conventional or socially relative component and must be contextualized to speech conventions and linguistic communities. Type-type identity statements are true (or false) depending, in part, on how the general (type) terms in the identity statement are conventionally understood by competent speakers. Suppose, for example, we propose that water is H_2O. If the proposal is made before competent speakers adopt the general convention of talking of water in terms of its chemical composition, such a claim as "Water is H_2O"

expresses a contingent identity. It is not self-contradictory to deny the identity. However once the convention is adopted of speaking of water as H_2O (and various other conditions are met) the claim expresses a necessary identity: the identity statement becomes a necessary (and in the language of philosophy, analytic/ conceptual) truth. Nothing then counts as water without counting as H_2O. The process whereby contingent type identities become necessary identities depends, in addition to linguistic convention, on extralinguistic reality (the "various other conditions are met"), including cumulative empirical discoveries.

A number of philosophers, including Matjaž Potrč in correspondence with Place, objected to his claim that there are conventional elements in statements of type identities. The protest is that it confuses the question of the presence or absence of type identities (an ontological issue) with the question of how linguistic conventions change and affect classifications (a semantic-developmental issue). Place's reply to this objection is that it reflects a misunderstanding of the proper semantics of both identity statements and general terms like 'water' or 'sensation'. There was a time when "Water is H_2O" was a contingent type-identity statement. At that time it was not self-contradictory to suppose that a sample of water might be discovered that did not have the chemical composition H_2O. However, once the identity statement becomes accepted as a matter of fact, it becomes a necessary truth that water is H_2O: being H_2O becomes part of the meaning of the general term 'water'. For Place, the necessity/contingency of the identity of types or kinds of things (such as water or sensations) is a matter of what it is or is not self-contradictory to deny, given existing general linguistic conventions plus empirical discoveries.

Of course, positing a role for linguistic conventions in the proper classification of theoretical identities must seriously complicate Place's overall conception of the role of science and empirical discovery in determining and describing the identities that really do obtain between things in the world. We normally think of identities between types of things (say, between water and chemical composition) as nonrelational or intrinsic facts about those things. This is especially the case in examples of what philosophers refer to as natural kinds (like water). Place pictures type identities (including type identities for natural kinds) as, in part, relational or extrinsic facts that essentially involve classes of things not considered on their own but whose kind or type status is dependent upon how sentient and verbal organisms (like persons) respond to and reinforce categorizations of them. If there is more to the modality of water's chemical identity than water itself determines, and this includes contingent (changeable) social conventions for general terms, then not just the necessity of the relevant identity but, arguably perhaps, its fully objective or mind-independent existence seems to be called into question.

In the end, Place is less interested in the 'intrinsic vs. extrinsic' tension than in how to devise a plausible semantics for type-identity statements. There is, for him, a dynamics working at the level of classification that puts a theory of reference and meaning alongside an appreciation of the social nature and evolution of language.

The Empirical Side of Place

The philosophical relevance of empirical discoveries, and the mix of these with social conventions, occupied Place throughout his theoretical life, which, although he was a professional philosopher, began as an experimental psychologist and always included a strong social-psychological or empirical component. Although famed for his work in philosophy rather than psychology, Place held positions in both disciplines (sometimes concurrently) throughout his career, maintaining what Lewis (2000) referred to as a "dual commitment to philosophy and science." He was a Chartered Psychologist and was proud to be a Fellow of the British Psychological Society. In his first post as lecturer in psychology within the department of philosophy at the University of Adelaide, he developed work in experimental psychology, establishing a psychological laboratory (procuring electrical relays from military surplus stores, for opening and closing gates in rat mazes) and laying the foundation for the subsequent formation of an independent department of psychology.

Although Place published no strictly empirical papers, he carried out a number of experimental studies early in his career, during the six years he spent working as a clinical psychologist in England. One investigated the use of behavioral techniques for the treatment of enuresis, in which he employed a caravan as a portable consulting room. In another, he tested Skinnerian and Rylean accounts of the relation between mood and motivation (operationally defined in terms of rate of responding) in a sample of manic-depressive psychotic patients. Pressing a key in the presence of a green light incremented a counter, whereas pressing it in the presence of a red light decremented the counter. The counter acquired reinforcing properties from the associated cash payments made at the end of the experiment. Place's results showed a positive relationship between mood and motivation (responding being higher in elation and lower in depression) under conditions of positive reinforcement, consistent with both the Skinnerian and Rylean accounts, but a reversal (responding being lower in elation and higher in depression) under negative reinforcement, consistent with Ryle's but not Skinner's position. In a recent conference paper (Place & Wheeler Vega, 1999), these data are used to support Place's behavioral theory of emotion, originally developed in the 1970s and seen as anticipating Apter's (1982; 1989) reversal theory. Place's theory offers an analysis of emotion in terms of two dimensions: hedonic tone (pleasant-unpleasant) and arousal (high-low) plus a third factor, the 'performative impulse', reflecting the environmental contingency.

Place was impatient with philosophers' habit of unnecessarily prolonging debate and engineering the insolubility of philosophical problems. True to his background, he saw philosophy as a scientific linguistic enquiry, the investigation of scientific language using conceptual analysis. Place (1996a; chapter 14 of the present volume) discusses his view of conceptual analysis as an empirical endeavor, the empirical investigation of linguistic conventions.

His claim in ICBP was that the statement that consciousness is identical with a brain process is an empirical thesis. Throughout his life he pursued the issue of the neuroanatomical basis and adaptive function of consciousness, keeping informed of scientific discoveries. As late as 1991 he was Visiting Fellow at the Neuroscience Institute' in New York. Place (2000c; Chapter 11, this volume) represents the culmination of this work. Shortly before his death, Place was asked by the musician and philosopher Teed Rockwell whether he would be willing to classify himself as a neurophilosopher. Place replied that he preferred to resist the label, claiming that his last papers on consciousness and the brain (three of which are reprinted in this collection) helped to make him a neuropsychologist rather than neurophilosopher.

Place's Self-Presentation

A good position by any other name should still be as serviceable. Given that Place had long since ended his career as an experimental psychologist, "neurophilosopher" would have suited him. However, he typically did not choose labels in a manner that would assist in his own self-promotion or sweeten his reputation. He described his approach to the philosophy of empirical science as "linguistic behaviorism" and made efforts to derive insights into language from B. F. Skinner. He offered himself as a fan of Oxford ordinary language philosophy. As noted, he advocated partial conventionalism about modality (identity and necessity) or statements of modality.

These labels and others he sometimes used are unpopular. At least a few also mislead about the actual character of positions. His admiration, for example, for ordinary language philosophy was not an admiration for armchair conceptual analysis of the sort that is designed to sidestep or (worse) limit the explanatory scope of empirical science. Quite the contrary, as he explains in Place 1992a (chapter 13, this volume), for him what makes a particular analysis correct is empirical facts about the semantic norms of speech communities. If the analysis captures those norms, it is correct, otherwise not. Such norms, as the above remarks about identity indicate, have conventional and thus changeable components. However, for Place empirical science also helps to modify the semantic norms of speech communities. It prompts and reinforces changes in speech conventions. So, conceptual analysis is doubly empirical: it aims to unearth empirical facts about language use and these facts themselves change empirically under pressure from science.

When asked, shortly before this death, to name an overarching theme uniting his work—to describe what was distinctive about his approach to the range of issues in the fields of philosophy, psychology, and linguistics on which he had written Place wrote as follows:

> The dominant influence that pervades my thinking in all these areas is the later philosophy of Wittgenstein and its progeny, Oxford ordinary language philosophy. It is often supposed that the preoccupation with the way people talk in ordinary nontechnical contexts, which is characteristic particularly of the latter, makes this tradition antipathetic to the scientific enterprise and the conceptual innovation that it re-

quires. My contribution, such as it is, has been to try to rebut that allegation by showing that its philosophical method, conceptual analysis, is part and parcel of the empirical scientific enterprise and can lead us through a rehabilitated picture theory of meaning to important new scientific insights in such fields as the metaphysics of the causal relation, the mind-body problem, a reevaluation of traditional behaviorist objections to mentalistic explanation in psychology, and to an approach to linguistics that emphasizes function in the context of utterance as the determinant of structure. (Personal communication, 19 October 1999)

How This Book Is Organized and May Be Read

The papers in this book are grouped into two quantitatively unequal sets. After the first autobiographical essay, the first set, which runs from chapter 2 ("The concept of heed") through chapter 11 ("Consciousness and the zombie-within"), consists of temporally sequenced contributions to central issues in the philosophy of mind. A central preoccupation of these is Place's argument that to achieve an understanding of mind and of how to identify it, it is not enough to understand behavior or dispositions to behavior whereby various states of mind reveal or constitute themselves. One must understand how and why conscious mental events resist behavioral analysis. Chapter 11 comprises Place's most concerted effort to demonstrate the philosophical utility of neuroscience. One of the challenges that Place's identification of conscious events with brain processes faced is how to identify which types of brain processes are types of conscious events. Place argues that to meet this challenge one must understand what the job of consciousness is and where this task is performed by the physical system—the nervous system. Place's proposal is that there are two systems: (1) consciousness, which deals with problematic input and thus is in need of extensive processing, and (2) the "zombie-within," which separates problematic from nonproblematic input, dealing automatically with the latter and passing the problematic input on to consciousness. Armed with this hypothesis, chapter 11 identifies proposed modules with their neurological basis, specific anatomically defined structures in the brain.

The final three chapters of the book constitute the second and smaller of the two sets of papers. Partly because of his divided account of the mental and commitment to an element of conventionalism in the semantics of type identity, Place wrote on topics outside the philosophy of mind narrowly understood. These included the topics of conceptual analysis, reference, truth, and meaning and the theory of dispositions and causal necessity.

Place's views on these topics underwent numerous refinements and revisions over time. This occurred over a period throughout the 1980s and early 1990s in which he wrestled with the theory of verbal behavior of B. F. Skinner and tried to extract from Skinner's framework a picture theory of meaning and correspondence theory of truth. We have not included papers from this period for two reasons. First, they are difficult to read by all but the most informed and appreciative readers of Skinner. Second, Place summarizes the results of much of this work in the final chapter of this volume. This summary represents Place's clearest and most assured convictions concerning language, meaning, and reference as well as causality and dispositions.

One way in which to read this book is to read it as a book from start to finish. This means from papers that reveal a developing and systematic materialism about mind to chapters that explore issues outside the philosophy of mind but raised by Place's version of materialism and divided account of the mental. However, another is just to read selections from within the book, motivated by a reader's personal concerns or interests. For example, chapter 8 discusses the relative merits of type- versus token-identity theory; chapter 12 explores the mixture of external world realism and social conventionalism in Place's theory of meaning, truth, and reference. Chapter 1 offers a revealing self-portrait, although the book itself is a portrait.

We hope the appearance of this collection will serve to draw the attention of philosophers to Place's work and earn him the recognition he deserves. Here at last is the single-authored book—a book by U. T. Place, our deeply admired intellectual colleague and dearly missed friend.

From Mystical Experience
to Biological Consciousness
A Pilgrim's Progress?

The story I shall tell is a piece of autobiography. But it is not, as you might suppose, a record of my own mystical experiences. For I do not claim to have had any. It is rather a record of a thought process that led from a childhood interest in religion, through an adolescent interest in mystical experience as a psychological phenomenon, to the publication forty years ago in the *British Journal of Psychology* for 1956 of a paper titled "Is consciousness a brain process?"

"Is Consciousness a Brain Process?"

In that paper, as I say in the abstract, "The thesis that consciousness is a process in the brain is put forward as a reasonable scientific hypothesis, not to be dismissed on logical grounds alone" (Place, 1956, p. 44). It is widely accepted that that paper marks a watershed in philosophical discussion of the mind-body problem, one whose impact, though confined to discussions of that particular issue by professional philosophers in the English-speaking world, ranks in the magnitude of its effect with that of Descartes's *Meditations* more than three hundred years earlier.

Needless to say, the idea that human behavior is mediated and controlled by the activity of the brain and that conscious experiences are an integral part of that control process was not new. The idea is to be found in the writings of the Greek physician and philosopher Hippocrates of Cos sometime around the turn of the fifth and fourth centuries BC. It appears in the works of the Roman poet Lucretius and in the sixteenth century in the writings of Hobbes and Gassendi. In the eighteenth century it appears in La Mettrie's *L'Homme Machine* and in Cabanis's doctrine that the brain digests sense impressions and excretes thoughts. In the nineteenth century, many physiologists were materialists in this sense. Earlier this century,[1] moreover, the idea that the relation between consciousness and the brain activity with which it is known to be correlated is an identity relation was proposed by the psychologist E. G. Boring (1933) in his *Physical Dimensions of Consciousness*.

In philosophy, on the other hand, ever since the debate between Hobbes and Descartes ended in apparent victory for the latter, it was taken more or less for granted that whatever answer to the mind-body problem is true, materialism must be false. It is this that has now changed.

Since the late 1960s it has been virtually impossible to find a reputable philosopher, in the English-speaking world at least, who is prepared to defend mind-body dualism in the form in which it was defended by Descartes. Although everyone agrees that there is still a problem—philosophers need to keep problems like this alive in order to justify their continued existence as a profession— almost everyone now accepts that some form of materialism must be true. Even in Britain, where the mind-brain identity theory, as it has come to be called, has never had the same following as in Australia or the United States, I know of no philosopher who would be prepared to defend the form of mind-body dualism or idealism that was taken for granted by their predecessors of forty years ago.

Many factors contributed to making my paper the turning point it has turned out to have been, not least the fact that its thesis was adopted and introduced to a philosophical audience by J. J. C. Smart, then professor of philosophy in the University of Adelaide, who had appointed me in 1951 to take charge of the teaching of psychology within his department and who had participated in the debates at Adelaide during 1954 in which the thesis of my paper was knocked into shape (see his "Sensations and brain processes," which appeared in the *Philosophical Review* in 1959). But what made the difference, as far as philosophers were concerned, between this and earlier versions of materialism were two things:

1. For the first time, a clear distinction was drawn between materialism as the claim, which Smart and I rejected, that what the individual is *talking about* when she describes her conscious experiences are processes in her brain, and materialism in the form that we endorsed, which holds that those experiences are *as a matter of fact*, though she doesn't know it, processes in her brain.
2. In response to the objection that conscious experiences have properties or "qualia," as they have come to be known in the recent philosophical literature, which it makes no sense to apply to a brain process, we pointed out that when we describe what it is like to have a particular experience, we are not ascribing any kind of property to the experience itself. We are simply comparing it with the kind of experience that typically accompanies a sensory encounter with an object or situation of a particular kind, the acquisition of a particular belief, or that typically induces a particular type of emotional response. Once we appreciate that such descriptions are only similes, we realize, as I put it in my paper, "that there is nothing

that the introspecting subject says about his conscious experiences which is inconsistent with anything the physiologist might want to say about the brain processes that cause him to describe the environment and his consciousness of that environment in the way he does" (Place, 1956, p. 50).

The Via Negativa

It is this last point that brings me to the topic of this talk. For, although it has other sources that I have described elsewhere (Place, 1989), part of what led me to see how very little we can really say about our conscious experience was the insistence of the mystics on the inadequacy of words to describe *their* experience, an inadequacy epitomized by the so-called *via negativa* in which all that can be said about the intrinsic properties of such experiences is "Not this. Not that."

The Functions of Consciousness

But this is not the only aspect of "Is consciousness a brain process?" which, with hindsight, can be seen to have its roots in the story I shall tell. Another feature, curiously enough, which has its links with my adolescent preoccupation with mystical experience is the conception of consciousness as part of the biological equipment, not just of human beings, but of all warm-blooded creatures and perhaps some cold-blooded ones as well, which has evolved by virtue of its function in controlling the behavior of the organism in ways that would not be possible without it. This issue of the functions of consciousness in the control of behavior is not specifically discussed in "Is consciousness a brain process?" It is, however, discussed in an earlier paper titled "The concept of heed," published in the *British Journal of Psychology* in 1954, to which "Is consciousness a brain process?" was intended as a sequel.

In "The concept of heed" I criticized Ryle's attempt in his (1949) book *The Concept of Mind* to extend the dispositional analysis of our ordinary mental concepts from verbs such as 'knowing', 'believing', 'wanting', 'intending', and 'being vain' or 'intelligent' where it makes no sense to talk of someone spending time doing these things, to a group of mental activity verbs which he refers to as "heed concepts," verbs such as 'looking', 'listening', 'watching', 'savoring', 'paying attention', 'concentrating', 'studying', 'enjoying' and 'trying', which one can quite properly be said to spend time doing. Ryle's contention is that when we say of someone that they are paying attention, we are not referring, as was traditionally supposed, to an internal mental activity of monitoring what is going on: we are saying that he or she is doing whatever else he or she is doing with a particular disposition, with a disposition to succeed, which an inattentive performer lacks. In the paper I defended the internal monitoring theory of attention by pointing out that paying attention to what one is doing, though in most cases a necessary condition of successful performance, is not sufficient. Not only must one have acquired the skills involved, one must also pay attention to, and thus become conscious of, the right features of the task. In order to succeed in a game such as tennis, attention must be focused on such things as the trajectory of the ball coming toward one and on the intended trajectory of one's own shot. Acute consciousness of the kinesthetic feedback from one's muscular movements would be a fatal distraction.

In addition to this emphasis on the role of attention and consciousness in the performance of a motor skill, a function that is needed as much by an animal as by a human being, I also drew attention in the paper to two other functions of consciousness that are exclusively human—that of providing the internal stimulus without the occurrence of which a speaker cannot give a first-hand description of what is impinging on his or her sense organs at the time or give a first-hand report of that event on some subsequent occasion in the future.

This functional account of consciousness, which, as I shall try to show later, can be much elaborated and refined in the light of recent neuropsychological evidence, stands in sharp contrast to doctrines such as epiphenomenalism and psychophysical parallelism, which seek to protect dualism from empirical disconfirmation by depriving consciousness of *any* causal role in the control of behavior. Put that way, you can perhaps appreciate how someone who was attracted to the idea of mystical experience by the possibility it offered of transforming the individual's behavioral dispositions in a more ethically acceptable direction should feel that if the only way to preserve dualism is to deny the causal efficacy of consciousness, dualism must be rejected.

My Father's Influence

But so much for the endgame. Let us now go back to the opening moves.

I was born in 1924 in Northallerton, the county town of what was then the North Riding of Yorkshire. My father was the second of five sons of a joiner and carpenter in the village of Langton-on-Swale, a few miles to the northwest of Northallerton, who with the help of his sons had built up a successful business, buying, felling, processing, and selling home-grown timber. My father's role in the business was to buy the standing timber, and this gave him the experience and contacts that enabled him after the end of the First World War to acquire a considerable fortune by speculating in the purchase and resale of the large country estates that were then coming onto the market all over the country, partly as a consequence of the introduction of death duties by Lloyd George in his 1911 budget and partly as a consequence of the decimation of what in those days we referred to as The Great War.

By 1930 when I was five, he had made enough money to purchase a converted farmhouse in the country four miles south of Northallerton, where we lived cocooned and insulated from the harsh realities of the post-Depression years, surrounded by what, by present day standards, was a veritable army of servants: a housemaid, a parlor maid, a cook, a kitchen maid; a nanny, a governess, and a nursery maid looking after us children; a secretary and an accountant looking after my father's in-house office; and outside two chauffeurs and two gardeners.

My father was already 52 when I, his eldest child, was born. His health was already showing signs of wear and tear. He suffered from chronic bronchitis due to heavy cigarette smoking, a duodenal ulcer, and heart trouble. He was already well on the way to achieving his three life ambitions: to own a Rolls-Royce, to send his children to public schools, and to devote as much as possible of his plentiful spare time to his passion for fly-fishing for trout.

Although he was a man of considerable moral integrity, with a strong sense of public duty—he was a magistrate, a county alderman, and chairman of the Finance Committee of the North Riding County Council—he was not when I knew him a religious man. The only occasion on which I can remember him attending a church service was in the chapel at my preparatory school when he and my mother were waiting to take me out on a Sunday morning. He had had a religious phase in his youth. As a teenager he had been befriended by the local vicar and given special tuition, which meant that he was much better educated and more widely read than would have been expected from someone who had left school at the age of fourteen. Not surprisingly, this tuition included a significant element of religious instruction. Shortly after, as a young man, he became interested in the works of Annie Besant and her Theosophy movement. I only discovered this *after* I had already become interested in mysticism myself. So any connection between the two episodes must be a matter of genetics rather than parental influence. In any case, he had put these religious interests firmly behind him when he settled down to the serious business of earning a living and making his way in the world. His philosophy of life, to use that hackneyed phrase, was a version of the popular Darwinism of his day. Based on his experience in business, he saw and conveyed to his children a picture of life as a desperate struggle for survival in a cruel world. The nightmare image of nature "red in tooth and claw" surfaced repeatedly, particularly when he overindulged on his regular whisky nightcap.

This picture of the world that awaited us in the future was in sharp contrast to the comfort, affluence, and apparent security of life as we experienced it at home. Moreover, my father increased the sense of anxious foreboding by constantly reminding us that he was an old man in none too robust health, who would not always be around to protect and provide for us. The angst that this created was exacerbated by the mystery surrounding the way he made his money. He emphasized our dependence on his ability to make money and the fragility of what he had created, but he offered no guidance as to how we in our turn were going to survive in the dangerous and hostile world he described.

Preparatory School and the Discovery of Religion

My first experience of that dangerous and hostile world beyond the safety and comfort of home came when, at the age of eight, I was sent to a boarding preparatory school for boys two hundred miles away in the northern outskirts of London. That traumatic experience coincided with my first significant encounter with religious belief, religious language, and religious ritual. I have no doubt that my enduring fascination with the last developed as a response to the anxiety generated by the first. My preparatory school was somewhat unusual for institutions of its size in having its own private chapel, a neat brick building in the Early English Gothic style, where we attended matins and evensong according to the rite of the Church of England every Sunday, with Holy Communion for those qualified to take it once a month, and, once a year for some of the older boys, a service of confirmation by the Lord Bishop of St. Albans complete with miter, cope, pectoral cross, and pastoral staff. For the first time I had my own copies of the Christian Bible, the *Book of Common Prayer* and *Hymns, Ancient and Modern*. These I devoured avidly, particularly the obscurer recesses of the *Book of Common Prayer*, such as the service of Commination and the Athanasian Creed. To this experience and the reading it inspired, I owe a love of church music and medieval church architecture, a fascination with medieval monasticism and with ecclesiastical vestments, particularly as represented on the monumental brasses of the medieval period.

But there was also a more intellectual concern. I was scandalized by the existence of differences in religious belief; and I can remember, sometime around the age of ten, resolving that when I was older I would organize a congress of the leaders of the different sects and faiths and compel them to resolve their differences and decide the issues once and for all. A naïve idea no doubt, but one that, as I hope to show, foreshadowed what was to come. But to explain what led me to that thought, I need to say something about my mother's religious background.

My Mother's Influence

As with my father, religion played no great role in my mother's life. She would occasionally drag the family off to attend a service in our local parish church, but it was evident that this was more from a sense of social duty than from any sense of religious obligation. As children we were brought up to say grace before and after meals and to say prayers for the welfare of the family before going to bed at night; but though these practices were condoned by our parents, the initiative came from the nursery staff, from Nanny, and the governess. Although I did not appreciate its significance until much later, from the point of view of the development of my own religious attitudes the most important fact in my mother's religious background was that through her father she was a direct descendant of Margaret Fell, the Mother of Quakerism, who, after the death of her first husband, Judge Thomas Fell, married George Fox, the founder of the Society of Friends, whose follower and protector she had been since his first visit to Ulverston in 1652. However, the family had been expelled from the Society in the early nineteenth century because one of my ancestors had "married out." Consequently, my mother was not brought up as a Quaker. Though decisively nonconformist in outlook, the family was not affiliated with any particular sect. Partly for this reason, partly because of the Quaker background, partly because when my mother was young the family attended the services of a sect known as the

"Peculiar Baptists" (who, like all Baptists, believed in delaying baptism until the individual is old enough to accept it as a matter of deliberate choice), and partly because of my grandfather's scientific training and outlook, my mother was never baptized. Nevertheless, she thought of herself in her later years as a member of the Church of England with a perfect right to take communion whenever she saw fit—and woe betide any vicar who dared to challenge that right.

Consequently, although both my parents agreed that we as children should be brought up as members of the established church and should attend Church of England schools, my mother refused to allow me to be baptized according to the service of baptism as set out in the 1662 *Book of Common Prayer*. The reason for this was that it contains a statement to the effect that anyone who dies unbaptized must inevitably go to hell. I was, therefore, baptized at home by the local Congregational minister, sadly the only contact I have ever had with that ancient branch of what is now part of the United Reformed Church. By the time my sister was born some eighteen months later, proposals had already been made for a revision of the prayer book. Consequently, her baptism was delayed for some two years in anticipation of that event. Despite the refusal of Parliament to sanction the 1928 prayer book, she was eventually baptized at the same time as the elder of my two younger brothers by an Anglican vicar who was prepared to overlook the lack of parliamentary authority and use a form of the baptism service that omitted the offending statement. These facts about our baptism, which we learned quite early in life, combined with the fact that my mother's brother had, much to her disapproval, married a Roman Catholic and been compelled to allow his children to be brought up in that faith, had made me conscious of differences in religious belief and with the fact that such matters were open to dispute some time before my own interests in religion had been aroused.

A third fact about my mother's intellectual and religious background that is important in this connection was her own and her family's scientific background. Her paternal grandfather was cofounder of a firm of pharmaceutical chemists in Liverpool and was honorary secretary to the Liverpool Gallery of Inventions and Science. Her father followed his father into the business and was himself a trained and meticulous analytical chemist. My mother was given an education that enabled her to enter Liverpool University and later King's College, London, to read for a degree in analytical chemistry, which included physics as well as organic and inorganic chemistry and bacteriology. The idea behind this was that she should eventually assist her father in that aspect of the business. She failed to graduate, not, if her own autobiographical account is to be believed, because of any defect in her final examination performance but because of prejudice on the part of her examiners arising from her well-known activities as a militant suffragette. She was not the only member of the family with scientific training. One of her brothers was a civil engineer, her sister's husband was an electrical engineer, and their son, my first cousin, was, when we were still children, well on the way to becoming the distinguished geologist he now is.

I mention these facts by way of explaining how it came about that despite the fact that my own education up till the age of eighteen consisted of no more than a couple of hours' instruction in science, I became aware at a relatively early age that many traditional doctrines of religious belief, such as those connected with the creation of the universe, had been superseded by scientific research and formed the opinion that such research, offered a way—the only way—of resolving issues that had been debated by theologians and philosophers for centuries.

Puberty and the Discovery of Mysticism

I must now move forward a further five years to the spring of 1940 when I was fifteen and World War II had been going for less than a year. It was then that I discovered mysticism. I was introduced to it through two books that I found on the shelves of the library of the public school[2] where I was a pupil. The first and most influential was *Mysticism* by Evelyn Underhill (1911). The second was a little book called *Protestantism* by the then lately retired Dean of St Paul's, W. R. Inge (1935).

Evelyn Underhill

I was attracted by the idea of mysticism as described by Evelyn Underhill for three reasons:

1. It presented religion not as a set of beliefs and a set of rituals that made sense only in the light of those beliefs but as a personality-transforming psychological process. Moreover, although she did not discuss the mysticism of the oriental religions, Hinduism, Buddhism, and Taoism, it was clear from those she did discuss that mysticism was something that transcended particular religious faiths. Not only were there mystics from all the different sects of Christianity listed in her pages: there were pagan Neoplatonists, Jewish mystics such as Philo, and Islamic mystics such as the Sufis. The different faiths merely provided a language in terms in which what was obviously the same psychological process was described and interpreted.
2. A second feature that attracted me to mysticism was that it appeared to offer a way not so much of controlling as of redirecting into more morally acceptable channels the two deadly sins that were preoccupying my thoughts at that time, anger and lust. I shall not attempt to explain or to justify my belief at that time that anger and sexual desire are intrinsically sinful, except to say that in addition to factors in my own particular childhood experience this view has deep roots in the Christian, if not in the whole Judaeo-Christian-Islamic, tradition. What I now find difficult to justify is the persistence of this view at a time when, as I shall shortly explain, I was already proposing to defend my belief in the virtues of the mystical personality transformation as a biologically adaptive mutation. To suggest that the survival of human species depends on limiting the

expression of sexual and aggressive impulses is one thing. To suggest that it requires a total redirection of desire from the satisfaction of these impulses toward universal compassion and benevolence is quite another. It may be argued that to have a minority of people in whom this transformation has occurred may have advantages in promoting the survival of the social order, but to propose this as an objective for all is biological nonsense.

Of course, in my reading of Evelyn Underhill I had been made aware of the sexual symbolism in the writings of many mystics. I had also come across the idea that she mentions, particularly in connection with the writings of Coventry Patmore (1877; 1895), that mystical experience is very similar to and no doubt psychologically connected with the experience of sexual orgasm. But Coventry Patmore is talking about sexual consummation in the context of a loving Christian marriage, something very different from the grubby homosexuality I was currently experiencing in an all-male English public school of those days.

3. A third feature that attracted me to mysticism as portrayed by Evelyn Underhill was that it appeared to offer a personality transformation that would provide the inner strength needed to withstand all the pain and suffering that my father had led me to expect in the world beyond his protection and whose reality was emphasized daily as news of catastrophe, torture, misery, and death came over the airwaves and in the newspapers as World War II unfolded. How could I, in my unregenerate state, hope to withstand torture at the hands of the Gestapo or the experience of a Nazi concentration camp? Even as the likelihood of those fears being realized receded as the war progressed, there was still the inescapable prospect of the death of my parents and ultimately my own death. But notice that what the mystical personality transformation appeared to offer in this latter case was not any assurance of life after death. It was rather the inner strength, not just to accept but actively to welcome the prospect of one's own personal annihilation. There was nothing in this view of mysticism that was incompatible with the idea that mystical experience is a process in the mystic's brain. There was even less call for a belief in a soul that survives the death of the body than there is in Buddhism with its belief in perpetual reincarnation until the final annihilation of the individual personality is achieved in Nirvana.

Dean Inge and My Quaker Heritage

Had I not already discovered mysticism through Evelyn Underhill's book, Dean Inge's (1935) little treatise on *Protestantism* would not have had the impact that it did. For although he was in his day one of the most outspoken advocates of what Baron von Hügel (1908) calls "the mystical element in religion" and had written his own introduction to the subject in his *Christian Mysticism* (Inge,

1899), in *Protestantism* it is frequently mentioned but not explained. Though Inge was well aware of the mystical tradition in pre-Christian Neoplatonism, having himself written a definitive two-volume treatise on the *Philosophy of Plotinus* (Inge, 1918) and of the mystical tradition within the Catholic Church, in *Protestantism* he presents the mystic's claim to be in direct communion with God in his or her own inner life as one of the motives behind the Protestant rejection of the need for a priest or, for that matter, a long-dead saint, to intercede with God on behalf of the individual. With this bias in favor of mysticism, it is not surprising that the centerpiece of the book is his chapter on Quakerism. For it is in the practices and teaching of the Society of Friends that the mystical element in Protestantism appears in its most pure and unadulterated form. It was my reading of this chapter that led me to investigate my own Quaker roots, to read George Fox's *Journal* from cover to cover, to become an attender at Friends' meetings, getting into trouble at my public school for absenting myself from School Chapel on Sunday mornings in order to do so, to register for exemption from military service on grounds of conscience when called up in January 1943, and to apply successfully to join the Friends' Ambulance Unit the following April. In my submission to the tribunal applying to be registered as a conscientious objector, I conceded that in my present unregenerate state, I could not effectively meet evil with good and hope to prevail, but I believed that with the kind of personality change that develops through mystical experience it should be possible. It was a possibility that I was concerned to keep open, one that I felt would be closed if I were to engage in military activity. Having long since abandoned that aspiration, I find this argument not only unpersuasive but not a little smug. Nevertheless, though I find it difficult to work out a consistent attitude either emotionally or intellectually on the issue of violence, the Quaker peace testimony has left a deep mark.

Rationalism and the Origin of a Research Project

In the same year (1940) in which I discovered mysticism, I first encountered the arguments of the so-called "rationalists," using that term not in its technical philosophical sense but in the sense of someone who puts rational argument and scientific evidence before faith in deciding matters of religious belief. This was in the pages of a book titled *The Churches and Modern Thought* by Vivian Phelips (alias Philip Vivian), first published in 1906, and reissued with corrections and additions by the Rationalist Press in their Thinker's Library in 1931. Needless to say, this was not a book that I found on the shelves of my school library. As the inscription on the flyleaf testifies, it was purchased at a bookstall on Leeds City station on my way back home from school at the end of the summer term in July 1940. This book presents the case for thinking that all the principal doctrines of the Christian religion are either demonstrably false or, at best, unsupported by any convincing evidence of their truth. The case rests on scientific evidence, in particular the Darwinian evidence for the view that biological phenomena are the products of evolution by variation and natural selection rather than products of divine creation and divine purpose, the scientific improbability of miracles and such events as the virgin birth, the resurrection and the ascension, the higher criticism of the biblical record, and evidence for the importation into primitive Christianity of ideas from other contemporary religious traditions. The effect of reading this book was to reinforce my conviction that religious beliefs and the magical rituals based upon them, however attractive and emotionally moving, are intellectually untenable, and that to base one's life on the supposed truth of historical claims that might easily turn out to be false in the light of newly discovered evidence was like building a house on shifting quicksand. But fortified by my reading of Underhill and Inge, I was not persuaded to abandon my faith in religion as such. For they had persuaded me to see it not as a set of doctrines and rituals based upon them but as a personality-transforming psychological process to whose reality the writings and lives of the mystics bear testimony.

Vivian Phelips considers the argument from the reality of mystical experience as a psychological process in his book (Phelips, 1931, pp. 179–184). He deploys two counterarguments against it. The first questions the theistic interpretation of such experiences, on the grounds that there is no more reason to interpret them as a communion with God than as a communion with the Devil or any other supernatural being. The second draws attention to the similarity of such experiences with those reported by persons of unsound mind. You will not be surprised to learn that I found neither of these arguments convincing— the first because I was already familiar through Evelyn Underhill's book with the idea that uniformities in the underlying psychological process transcend differences in the theological or nontheological language used to describe them, and the second because it seemed possible to distinguish between the experiences of the mystic and those of the psychotic by their fruits, those of the mystic being morally and socially adaptive, those of the psychotic morally and socially maladaptive.

It was this book and this section of it in particular that reawakened the idea that, as I have already described, had come to me some five years before, that it was my mission in life to settle the issue of differences in religious belief once and for all. Now however, I conceived it, not as a matter of knocking heads together in some gigantic congress of religious leaders, but as a research project designed to demonstrate the reality and adaptive utility in the Darwinian sense, of the personality transformation induced by mystical experience. In order to equip myself to carry out this project, I would need to study two basic disciplines, psychology and social anthropology, before specializing in the psychology and anthropology of religion and religious experience in general and mystical experience and the attendant psychological processes in particular.

Between January and March 1943, before joining the Friends' Ambulance Unit, I had the good fortune, thanks to a scholarship at Corpus Christi College, to spend a term up at Oxford. As soon as I arrived, I began to explore the possibility of putting this scheme into practice. I contacted the then Nolloth Professor of the Philosophy of the Christian Religion, Canon L. W. Grensted, who had written a book on the psychology of religion (Grensted, 1930) from a broadly psychoanalytic perspective. He was very sympathetic to my proposal but pointed out that psychology was not at that time available as an undergraduate degree at Oxford and that, in any case, in order to go on to psychology at the postgraduate level I would need to have read philosophy. For reasons I shall explain in a moment, that news was very unwelcome. Nevertheless on examining the limited number of courses (known as "sections") that were available in wartime Oxford, in addition to taking a section in English—which I felt duty bound to do, since English had been the main subject offered in my scholarship examination—I decided to take a section in the theory of knowledge with Hume's *Treatise of Human Nature* as the set book. I found the section in English which was on Shakespeare's *Othello* profoundly boring, but I was entranced, contrary to my expectations, by the theory of knowledge. When I returned to Oxford in 1946 I found to my great delight that there was a proposal to introduce a new honors school in which psychology would be combined either with philosophy or with physiology. Needless to say, I was soon queuing up to be among the first batch of undergraduates to be admitted to this honors school when it opened for business in October 1947.

Despite the fact that by this time my interests were moving away from mystical experience toward the mind-body problem and consciousness in general, on completing my degree in 1949 I spent a year reading for the postgraduate Diploma in Anthropology at Oxford with social anthropology as my special subject, exactly as prescribed by the project as I had conceived it in 1943. I shall always be grateful to that experience for adding a social dimension, not only to my conception of religion but to my concept of psychological, linguistic, and philosophical research. But by the time I left to take up an appointment as lecturer in psychology in the department of philosophy at the University of Adelaide in South Australia in April 1951, by now with a wife and a year-old son, although I took my collection of books on the subject with me, the mysticism project was effectively dead.

Philosophy and the Mind-Body Problem

The somewhat jaundiced view that I had formed of philosophy as an academic discipline by the time I arrived in Oxford in January 1943 may seem surprising in view of the fact that the term 'philosophy' has been frequently used from the time of the earliest occurrences of the word in connection with the activities of the pre-Socratics to describe the writings of an essentially mystical character. But this use of the term has little in common with what Gilbert Ryle used to call that "proprietary brand of haggling" that is academic philosophy. The poor opinion that I had formed of academic philosophizing was derived from another book I had purchased a year or two earlier (in October 1941, to be precise), Olaf Stapledon's (1939) *Philosophy and Living*, a two-volume paperback in the Penguin Books Pelican series. The first three chapters of that book are devoted to a discussion of the mind-body problem that Stapledon takes to be the central problem of philosophy around which all else revolves. He expounds the principal theories one by one: interactionism, psychophysical parallelism, epiphenomenalism, and the dual aspect theory, illustrating each with a neat little diagram.[3] The arguments for and against each are rehearsed and examined, but at the end the problem remains unresolved. My reaction to this was to see it as just another case of a theological dispute of the kind that from the age of ten I had seen as my mission to resolve. Now, however, I had a different idea of how that resolution was to be achieved. Endless philosophical haggling over the centuries had plainly got precisely nowhere. The resolution of the problem would come only by applying the methodology of empirical science. Thus it was that the resolution for the mind-body problem through empirical psychophysiological research became a subplot, as it were, to the main research objective of establishing the adaptive function of mystical experience, soon to be moved center stage as the prospect of realizing the mysticism project receded into an increasingly distant and uncertain future.

Logical Positivism

Despite owing my academic reputation, such as it is, entirely to the philosophical community and despite having spent the final twelve years of my working life as a professional philosopher, the jaundiced view of academic philosophy I acquired from Stapledon has remained with me ever since. I am still as impatient as I ever was with the endless logic-chopping and the persistent obfuscation of issues simply in order to keep the debate alive. Nevertheless, as I have already mentioned, I began to take a more favorable view of academic philosophy as a result of my encounter with the theory of knowledge during my one term at Oxford in 1943. What led to this change was the encounter with logical positivism, partly in the form of A. J. Ayer's (1936) *Language, Truth and Logic* and partly from attending lectures on Hume from Friedrich Waismann, one of the founding members of the Vienna Circle who had taken refuge in Oxford after the *Anschluss* of 1938. I was attracted to logical positivism by two things. In the first place, it offered the prospect of ending the perpetual cycle of philosophical debate by showing that all the traditional philosophical problems arose from failure to distinguish matters of fact, which were to be decided by the relevant empirical science, from issues of logic and language, which were to be decided by the application of formal logic to the analysis of sentences. Second, by insisting that religious statements, since they cannot be verified, are literally nonsense, it was congenial both to my rejection of religious belief in favor of religion as a psychological process and with the insistence of the mystics that no words could possibly capture the ineffable quality of the experiences they were struggling to describe.

Ordinary Language Philosophy

When I returned to Oxford in 1946, logical positivism was being replaced by ordinary language philosophy, as expounded by Ryle, Austin, and the man who was later to be my own tutor in philosophy, Paul Grice. At first, the differences between logical positivism and ordinary language philosophy were not apparent, at least not to me, and it appealed for exactly the same reasons. Traditional philosophical debates were dismissed as conceptually confused. Their total liquidation within twenty years was confidently forecast. The same distinction was drawn between empirical and conceptual issues. The philosopher's expertise was again restricted to issues of language.

It was only gradually that I became aware of the differences. Chief among these was the replacement of mistakes in formal logic by deviations from ordinary usage as the source of conceptual confusion in philosophy. Another difference, which I did not appreciate until I heard Austin's "Sense and Sensibilia" lectures (Austin, 1962a) when they were first presented in Trinity term 1947, was the refutation of phenomenalism and with it the subjectivism that had dominated epistemology since the time of Descartes. This made sense of another innovation of which I had been made aware earlier in the same academic year when I heard Ryle give the lectures that were later published as *The Concept of Mind* (Ryle, 1949), the behaviorist analysis of our ordinary psychological language. All these developments, once I became aware of them, were grist to my mill. Never much of a formal logician, I was much more at home with ordinary language. Abandoning phenomenalism, once Austin had demonstrated its absurdity, was like waking from a bad dream. Sentences describing features of the public world, on whose aptness as descriptions of those features all observers agree, appeared—as they still do—a far more secure foundation of empirical knowledge than sentences in a private sense datum language, whose words (as Wittgenstein puts it), "refer to what can only be known to the person speaking" (Wittgenstein, 1953, p. 89). Strange as it may seem, this too I found congenial to my interests in mysticism. For if our ability to communicate depends on our language being anchored to features of the public world, it explains why the mystics find such difficulty in communicating private experiences that have no obvious correlates in that world.

Behaviorism

One consequence of studying psychology alongside philosophy at a time when Ryle, Austin, Grice, and Strawson were creating Oxford ordinary language philosophy was that the acknowledged behaviorism of Ryle and the unacknowledged behaviorism of Wittgenstein, which I learned about from the then newly appointed Wilde Reader in Mental Philosophy at Oxford, Brian Farrell, was to awaken an interest, also fostered by Farrell, in the neobehaviorism of Tolman, Hull, and Skinner whose different formulations were then the focus of theoretical debate within psychology, not so much in Britain, as in the United States. It was through this that I became, as I remain to this day, a behaviorist.

To say that I became and remain a behaviorist is not to say that I deny or was even ever tempted to deny either the existence of conscious experience or the possibility of studying it scientifically. To do that would have been to abandon everything I have ever stood for. To say that I am a behaviorist means that I subscribe to the following principles:

1. Since linguistic communication is possible only insofar as words are anchored to what is publicly observable, it follows that, as things stand, the only way to study the private experiences of the individual is through objective records of what subjects have said when asked to describe them.
2. Since linguistic communication is possible only in so far as words are anchored to what is publicly observable, it follows that the primary function of our ordinary psychological language is to enable us to describe and explain the publicly observable behavior of others. Describing our own private experience is a secondary function, which it does not do very well.
3. Although the primary function of ordinary language is to enable us to describe and explain the public behavior of others, this way of talking contains many features that make it unsuitable as a theoretical language for scientific psychology. Consequently, I endorse the attempt by the behaviorists to construct an alternative to it for scientific purposes.
4. However, I also believe that our ordinary psychological language is the source of important insights into the nature of the states and processes involved in the control of behavior both human and animal. But these insights, I maintain, can only be extracted by the use of the technique of conceptual analysis as developed by Wittgenstein and the ordinary language philosophers.
5. The phenomenon of conscious experience, which appears in the self-reports of human subjects and for whose existence those reports are the objective evidence, is an integral and vital part of the causal mechanism in the brain that transforms input into output, stimulus into response, thereby controlling the interaction between the organism and its environment. Its peculiar properties can be understood only in the light of the distinctive function it performs in that process of input to output transformation.

Postscript

As you will see from this, behaviorism, as I construe it, brings us full circle back to where we started, to the thesis of my 1956 paper. But where does that leave the original project to examine the nature and function of mystical experience from a biological perspective? I have already remarked that by the time I left for Australia in 1951, I had for a variety of reasons both personal and intellectual effectively abandoned the project. Three years ago, realizing that I was never going to get round to studying them again, I decided to make more room on my bookshelves for other things by presenting my collection of some 140 books on mysticism to the Alistair Hardy Trust, Religious Experience Research Centre, at

Westminster College, Oxford. Curiously enough, at around the same time I had begun to take an interest in the work of my old friend Emeritus Professor Larry Weiskrantz, of the Department of Experimental Psychology at Oxford, on the phenomenon of blindsight which develops as a consequence of lesions of the striate cortex, both in man (Weiskrantz, 1986) and, as we now know from a brilliant experimental study by Alan Cowey and Petra Stoerig published in *Nature* (Cowey & Stoerig, 1995), in the monkey. This has enabled me to elaborate my account of the biological functions of consciousness in general and conscious experience in particular in ways that have some interesting implications for our understanding of the nature of mystical experience. To expound that theory and its implications at all adequately would need another paper, but suffice it to say that what the evidence suggests is that the behavior of mammals and probably that of other vertebrates is controlled by two distinct but closely interlocked and interacting systems in the brain, that we may call "consciousness" and the "subconscious automatic pilot," respectively. The function of consciousness is threefold:

1. to categorize any input that is problematic in that it is either unexpected or significant relative to the individual's current or perennial motivational concerns,
2. to select a response appropriate both to the presence of a thing of that kind and to the individual's motivational concerns, and
3. to monitor the execution of that response.

Conscious experience, on this view, is the first stage in the process whereby problematic inputs are processed by consciousness. Its function is to modify the figure-ground relations within the central representation of a problematic input until an appropriate categorization is achieved. The function of the subconscious automatic pilot is to continuously scan the total current input so that it can alert consciousness to any input it identifies as problematic, while protecting it from overload either by ignoring those nonproblematic inputs that require no response or by responding appropriately but automatically to those for which there already exists a well-practiced skill or habitual response.

In terms of this model the practice of contemplation described by the mystics would appear to consist in the switching on of conscious experience but without allowing it to proceed to the next stage, that of categorizing the input. Since there is no categorization, there is no response selection and no response execution. The individual remains keenly conscious but totally impassive and, insofar as the state can be maintained, unmoved by anything happening in the environment. Clearly since it prevents consciousness from exercising its biological functions, such a state cannot be adaptive if it is maintained indefinitely. But it may well have special virtues as a form of recuperation over and above those provided by sleep.

2

The Concept of Heed

Do the words and expressions that the subject uses when he makes his introspective report refer to internal events going on inside him? If they do, it is difficult to see why we should not use the subject's statements in order to formulate and verify hypotheses about such processes. If they do not, it is difficult to see what reason we should have for believing in the existence of the sort of events that are described in the textbooks of introspective psychology. If, as is suggested in this paper, some of them do and some do not, it becomes extremely important for the psychologist to be able to discriminate between the two cases.

Now insofar as the language of the introspective report is the 'psychological' language of ordinary speech, this is the question that has recently been exercising the minds of the philosophers; and in at least one case (Ryle, 1949) the conclusion that has been reached is preponderantly negative. In his book *The Concept of Mind*, Ryle has attempted to show that the traditional view which holds that mental states and processes are private internal occurrences within the individual is mistaken. He does not deny that some of the statements that we ordinarily make about people refer to states and activities of the individual that are 'private', or 'covert', in the sense that only the individual himself can report their occurrence. He would maintain, however, that such statements constitute only a small minority of the statements we make about our own and other people's minds.

I shall argue in this paper that the number of mental concepts that do entail a reference to covert states and activities of the individual is much larger than Ryle is prepared to admit. In particular it will be contended that a reference of this kind is involved in our ordinary use of such expressions as 'being conscious of' or 'paying attention to something', 'observing', 'watching', 'looking', 'listening', 'seeing', 'hearing', 'smelling', 'tasting', 'feeling', 'noticing', 'perceiving' and 'recognizing'.

The Concept of Heed

The key notion in Ryle's account of what is traditionally referred to as our 'appre-hension of the external world' is the concept of 'heed'. As he himself points out (p. 136), this notion of 'heed' or 'heeding' is closely related to the concept of 'con-sciousness', which is the basic concept in all the traditional theories of mind. While heed does not carry quite the same theoretical load as does the notion of consciousness in the traditional theories, it is employed by Ryle in his analysis of a wide range of mental concepts, and a large part of his case against the view that mental concepts entail a reference to covert states, processes, and activities would seem to depend on his ability to show that paying heed is not a covert activity.

Ryle defines the notion of 'heeding' or 'minding' as embracing such concepts as "noticing, taking care, attending, applying one's mind, concentrating, putting one's heart into something, thinking what one is doing, alertness, intentness, studying and trying" (p. 136). Concepts that "entail, but are not entailed by, heed-ing" include enjoying, disliking, pondering, searching, testing, debating, plan-ning, listening, relishing, calculating and scrutinizing (p. 136), looking (p. 232), observing, watching, descrying (p. 207), and recognizing (p. 223). Remembering something, according to Ryle (pp. 91 and 137–139) involves having paid heed to it at the time, while being conscious of sensations in one's body or objects in one's environment is evidently synonymous with heeding or noticing them (pp. 157–158). It will be seen from this that Ryle's concept of heed corresponds more closely to the traditional concept of attention than to that of consciousness. On the traditional theories consciousness is the basic notion of which attention is a special active or conative form. For Ryle on the other hand, it is 'attending' or 'heeding' that is the basic concept, and no distinction is drawn between paying attention to something and being conscious of it.

The Contemplative Theory of Heed

The traditional or, as Ryle calls it, the "contemplative" theory of heed or atten-tion and consciousness, in the form in which I wish to defend it, may be stated as follows. The expression 'paying attention' refers to an internal activity of the individual presumably of a nonmuscular variety whereby he exercises a measure of control over the vividness or acuteness of his consciousness of (a) the sensa-tions to which he is susceptible at that moment, or (b) such features of the envi-ronment as are impinging on his receptors, without necessarily adjusting his re-ceptor organs or their position in any way. In paying attention to something the individual is regulating the vividness of his consciousness of the object or sensa-tion in question and hence the number of its features of which he is conscious. The expression 'being conscious of something' refers to a peculiar internal state of the individual that normally accompanies any reasonably intense stimulation of his receptor organs, the particular form assumed by the individual's state of consciousness at a given moment being determined by the pattern of physical en-ergies impinging on his receptor organs at the time.

Being conscious of something is by definition a necessary condition of the individual's being able to give a first-hand report on that something either at the time or later. It is not, however, a sufficient condition of the individual's ability to make such a first-hand report, since it is possible for someone to be conscious of things that he cannot put into words, without his actual capacity to verbalize being in any way disturbed. Likewise, though here the relationship is probably contingent rather than necessary, the successful performance of any skilled activity depends to a greater or lesser extent on the individual paying attention to, i.e., maintaining a vivid consciousness of, relevant features of the situation and his own activity with respect to it, but the mere fact that someone is paying attention to what he is doing does not entail the performances being adapted to the demands of the task.

Ryle's Objections to the Contemplative Theory

Ryle's first objection to this type of theory (pp. 136–137) is that it leads to a reductio ad absurdum in those cases where we speak of watching carefully or attentively. He points out that it is always possible to ask of a spectator whether he has been a careful or a careless one. In order to interpret this on the contemplative view, he suggests, we should have to postulate an additional process of watching his watching, which is present in the careful spectator and absent in the careless one. This interpretation leads to an infinite regress, since it would always be sensible to ask whether or not this watching of one's watching was done carefully or not. There is, however, no reason why the contemplative view should force us to adopt this particular interpretation. As Ryle himself points out (p. 136), minding can vary in degree. There is, therefore, no reason why we should not say that the difference between the careful and the careless spectator lies in the amount of heed that each pays to the scene before his eyes. The careless spectator is not one who fails to watch his watching, nor is he completely oblivious of what is going on; he merely pays insufficient heed to it. What distinguishes the careful spectator from the careless one are the detailed and accurate reports that he is able to furnish as a result of the richness and vividness of the impressions with which his more active heed-paying provides him.

Ryle's second objection to the traditional theory of attention is that it fails to account satisfactorily for those cases where we speak of applying our minds to some task, such as whistling or driving a car. In this case, he argues (p. 138), we are not doing two things, whistling and minding, driving the car and attending to our driving; we are performing a single activity in a certain way. He points out in support of this contention that we cannot stop driving the car and continue our heed-paying. This argument, however, is singularly unconvincing. The fact that we cannot stop driving and continue our heed-paying merely shows that we cannot continue to pay heed to something that is no longer there to pay heed to. We do not normally lapse into unconsciousness after applying the hand brake; we turn our attention to other things. On the other hand, the fact that one can, if one is sufficiently foolhardy, continue to drive and cease to pay heed to what one is doing would suggest prima facie that there are two distinct processes going on here. Ryle is doubtless right in pointing out that in driving with care one is not doing two things at once in quite the same sense as one is when one is walking along and humming at the same time. In humming and walking at the same time one is performing two distinct sets of muscular movements simultaneously. When heeding and driving occur together, on the other hand, there is only one set of muscular movements, those of manipulating the controls; and in that sense there is only one activity being performed. No one, however, supposes that heed-paying is a separate set of muscular movements occurring alongside the muscular movements involved in driving. Nor is heeding thought of as an unrelated activity going on at the same time as the driving. It is a peculiar sort of internal activity which controls the movements of the driver's limbs, by regulating his consciousness of the stimuli to which he responds.

The Dispositional Theory of Mental Concepts

Although Ryle has failed to produce any conclusive objections to the contemplative theory, it is clear that if he can give a plausible account of the logic of 'heed concepts' that dispenses with the assumption that they refer to peculiar private events within the individual, we should undoubtedly be led to prefer such a theory on the grounds of parsimony. We must therefore examine the account that Ryle has offered of the logic of these concepts in order to discover whether or not it constitutes a satisfactory alternative to the traditional view.

The peculiarity of mental concepts as a class is that in order to determine whether or not someone knows, believes, understands, recognizes, remembers, wants, feels, is enjoying, attending to, or thinking about something, you either have to cross-examine him or else observe considerable stretches of his behavior before you can settle the question with any degree of confidence. This logical peculiarity is traditionally explained on the assumption that these mental concepts refer to invisible states and processes within the individual, whose existence and nature can only be determined with certainty by the individual in whom they occur, although it is usually possible also for an external observer to make reliable inferences about them by observing the behavior to which they give rise.

Ryle's explanation of this logical feature is quite different. He supposes that mental concepts, or at least most of them, refer to what may be called behavioral dispositions, i.e., capacities, tendencies, or temporary dispositions to behave in a certain way. To assert that someone has a capacity or tendency to behave in a certain way on this view is not to say anything about what is going on here and now; it is to assert a hypothetical proposition about how the individual could or would behave if certain circumstances were to arise. Hypothetical propositions of this kind can only be verified by investigating the behavior of the individual under the conditions supposed. The proposition "X can swim," for example, can only be verified by observing X's behavior when in the water. Similarly with the proposition "X knows the date of the battle of Salamis": unless you happen at that moment to hear X say, "Salamis was fought in 480 BC," you would either have to wait for the chance of hearing his reactions when called upon to exhibit his knowledge of ancient history or else adopt the more practical course of testing his knowledge by asking the appropriate question. The reason why it is often necessary to cross-examine the individual in order to discover what he knows is not that knowing is a peculiar internal state or activity of the individual of which he alone is directly apprised; it is that an important part of what we mean when we say that X knows the date of the battle of Salamis is that he can give you the correct date when asked to do so.

With a few notable exceptions, of which 'cogitating', 'visualizing', and 'having sensations' are the most important, Ryle attempts to apply this type of explanation to all the mental concepts treated in his book. In most cases moreover the attempt has proved remarkably successful. To my way of thinking there can be little doubt that the dispositional account that he gives of such concepts as 'knowing', 'believing', 'understanding', 'recognizing', 'remembering', 'intending', and 'wanting' is substantially correct. It is only with his attempt to apply it to such concepts as 'attending to', 'observing', and 'being conscious of something' that I wish to quarrel.

Ryle's Application of the Dispositional Theory to Heed Concepts

Ryle contends (pp. 137–139) that to say that someone is paying attention to what he is doing entails that he has at least two important dispositions: (a) the disposition under favorable circumstances to remember and give a first-hand report on what it is he has been paying heed to, and (b) the disposition to adapt his performance to the various demands of the task as they arise. Now it is quite true that if we are told that someone is paying close attention to what he is doing, we normally expect him to be able to answer questions about his activity and to have made at least a better showing at the activity than if he had not been applying his mind to the same extent. It is also true, as Ryle points out, that we frequently conclude from the fact that someone is unable to answer questions about something that has been said in his presence, or from his failure in certain skilled performances, that he has not been paying attention to what was said or to what he was doing. But it does not follow from this that to say that someone is paying attention entails that he has the disposition to do these things. A schoolmaster frequently concludes from the fact that a boy has got the wrong answer to a mathematical problem that he has set about it in the wrong way. Yet this would not lead us to say that to set about a problem in the right way entails a disposition to get the right answer. We only conclude that the boy must have used the wrong method if we know that his capacities are such that he could not have avoided getting the right answer had he used the correct method. Similarly, we only attribute someone's failure in a skilled activity to lack of attention if we know that his capacities are such that no other explanation of his failure is possible. One would hardly expect someone who had never been near an airplane before to be able to meet the demands of the task of piloting one, however closely he attended to what he was doing.

On the view that I am urging, the individual who pays attention is more likely to succeed insofar as he becomes acutely conscious of those features of the situation that are relevant to the successful performance of the task. Close attention to his own activity will be of no avail to the unskilled person because he has not learned to discriminate between the relevant and irrelevant features. On the other hand, an acute consciousness of the details of his own activity in relation to the environment may actually detract from the efficiency of performance in the case of an individual who has learned to make many of the adjustments involved automatically. Thus we frequently say of someone whose skill is already well developed that his performance suffered because he paid too close attention to what he was doing. It is difficult to see what meaning could possibly be attached to this statement on a dispositional theory of attention.

In claiming that the term 'attending' entails 'being able to say something about what is going on,' Ryle is on stronger ground. It is certainly true that it would be extremely odd to say that someone was paying attention to something but could tell you absolutely nothing about it. But it is arguable that this is merely because one cannot pay attention to something without at least noticing the thing to which one is paying attention. There is no doubt that to say one has noticed something entails that one has the capacity to mention it and point it out, but to say that one has noticed something and to say that one has paid attention to it, are not, as Ryle appears to think, to say the same thing. 'Noticing' is an achievement concept like 'recognizing' or 'perceiving', not an activity concept like 'pondering' or 'attending'. 'Noticing', perceiving', or 'recognizing' are the achievements that result from the activities of looking, listening, and attending. If one looks, listens, or attends, one normally notices or recognizes something or other, but one can also attend and fail to notice; one can look and fail to see, listen and fail to hear. When we say that we have failed to notice anything, what we really mean is that we have failed to notice anything remarkable or anything additional to what we have already noticed. You can hardly be said to have paid attention if there was nothing at all that you noticed as a result of your attending. But it does not follow from the fact that A notices more about the situation than B that A was paying closer attention. The man who pays closer attention usually notices more, but the relationship is contingent rather than necessary.

Ryle's Account of the Logic of Heed Concepts

The expression "paying attention to something" exhibits the distinctive logical characteristics that are normally associated with words and expressions that refer to activities. The fact that it is perfectly good sense to speak of someone being engaged in paying attention to something, while it is nonsensical, for example, to speak of someone being engaged in knowing or understanding something, clearly shows that 'paying attention' or 'heeding' is an activity expression in contrast to dispositional verbs like 'expect', 'know', 'like', and 'believe', or achievement verbs like 'understand', 'remember', 'recognize', 'perceive', and 'infer,' where such a combination would be nonsensical.

It might be objected that 'attending' differs from those verbs that unquestionably refer to activities in that it is not sensible to use it in conjunction with adverbs like 'quickly' or 'slowly.' We can say, "he slowly began to pay attention to his surroundings," but not, "he paid slow attention to his book for five minutes and then rapid attention to the blackboard." There are, however, a number of expressions that can properly be described as 'activity verbs' of which the same is true. For example we can say, "He slowly took hold of the hammer," but not "He held the hammer slowly for five minutes." The analogy between 'attending' and 'holding' seems generally very close.

In support of his contention that 'attending' is not an ordinary activity verb, Ryle draws attention to the curious fact that it is always possible to replace a 'heed verb' by a 'heed adverb'. We can speak, to use his examples, of 'reading attentively', 'driving carefully', and 'conning studiously' just as readily as we can of 'attending to the page in front of one', 'taking care in one's driving', and 'applying one's mind to the task of translation' (p. 138). Ryle contends that the adverbial form is the more accurate way of expressing what is meant when a 'heed concept' is used. To say that someone is doing something heedfully, he maintains, is merely to say that he is doing it in a certain way or in a certain frame of mind, i.e., with a disposition to adapt his performance to the various demands of the task as they arise and to answer questions about it.

On this theory the fact that 'paying attention' behaves like an ordinary activity word is explained on the assumption that the phrase "paying attention to something" is analyzable into two parts: (1) a categorical statement that a certain activity is taking place, and (2) a hypothetical or dispositional statement about how the individual in question would behave if certain contingencies were to arise. Ryle calls it for this reason a "mongrel categorical statement." The categorical part of the statement from which it derives its logical characteristics is, however, extremely uninformative. It asserts merely that some unspecified activity is being performed. In order to discover the nature of this activity we must find out what it is that the individual in question is paying attention to. As Ryle points out (p. 143), to say that someone is paying attention is an incomplete statement, unless we are told or unless it is obvious from the context of the remark what it is that he is paying attention to. On this view the part of the supposed meaning of the phrase that refers to the performance of an activity is strictly speaking redundant, since it must always be supplemented by a specification of the activity that is being performed.

In his lengthy discussion of 'mongrel categorical expressions' (pp. 140–147), Ryle is at pains to try to explain how it is that the fact of attention or inattention can be used to explain the failure or success of the individual in the activity he is performing. He shows convincingly enough that we can explain the bird's flying south by saying that it is migrating, without implying that migration is an additional process superimposed on the activity of flying south. The statement that the bird is migrating explains the behavior of the bird by bringing the particular behavior in question under the general rule that birds of certain species change their habitats at certain times of the year. Unfortunately he does not explain how the analogy is to be applied in the case where we explain the failure of an individual to complete a task satisfactorily or to give an adequate report on what was happening by saying that he was not paying sufficient attention. It is difficult in this case to see what the general rule involved could be, unless it is the rule that if you don't pay attention you won't be able to carry out the activity you are performing satisfactorily or give an adequate first-hand report on what went on. On Ryle's analysis of attention this general proposition reduces to the tautology "unless you are disposed to give a first-hand report on what is going on and to carry out what you are doing satisfactorily, you won't be able to give a first-hand report on what is going on or carry out the activity you are performing satisfactorily."

The Objection to Ryle's Account of the Logic of Heed Concepts

Although Ryle fails to produce any conclusive reasons for adopting his theory of 'attending' in preference to the traditional account, it is difficult to produce any decisive arguments against it as long as we restrict the discussion to the special case where we speak of someone paying attention to what he is doing. His case breaks down, however, once we try to apply it to those cases where we are said to pay heed to an object in our environment, or to some feeling we have, without being engaged in any other activity with respect to it. Ryle castigates the traditional theorists for "misdescribing heed in the contemplative idiom" (p. 137), but in developing his own theory he himself overlooks the important cases where paying heed to something is purely a matter of watching, listening, observing, or contemplating. Ryle explains the fact that 'attending' exhibits the usual characteristics of an activity verb, rather than those of a dispositional verb, on the assumption that verbs such as 'attending' and 'heeding' assert the occurrence of the activities that are being performed attentively. There is no special activity called 'attending'; there is only the attentive performance of an activity. The logical consequence of this theory is that the individual's own activities are the only sorts of things to which attention can be paid. If Ryle's theory were correct it should be nonsensical to talk of someone paying attention to anything other than an activity that he himself is performing. In fact, of course, we can speak with perfect propriety of the paying attention to any kind of object, phenomenon, or sensation that is visible, audible, tangible, or otherwise perceptible. In such cases there is no activity that is being performed attentively or heedfully. To attend in such cases is merely a matter of contemplating or observing the object or phenomenon in question. We cannot say that when we pay heed to something we are watching it, listening to it, observing it, or contemplating it heedfully, since as Ryle himself points out (pp. 207 and 223), words such as 'watching', 'listening', 'observing', and 'descrying' already entail that heed is being paid. These expressions do not refer to activities like driving a car, which can be performed with or without heed; they refer to special forms of the activity of heed-paying itself. It makes no sense to say that someone was observing, watching, contemplating, or listening to something without paying any attention to it, whereas it makes perfect sense to speak of someone driving without paying any attention to what he is doing.

The inadequacy of Ryle's account appears most clearly when we examine the account that he gives of expressions like 'being conscious of', 'observing', 'watching', and 'listening'. To be conscious of the sensations in a blistered heel, according to Ryle (pp. 157–158), is to pay heed to them; but what is the activity that is being performed attentively or heedfully here? It would seem from his long discussion of 'observation' (chapter 7) that for Ryle to say that one is observing something is to say that one is paying heed to the sensations derived from it, and 'watching' and 'listening' by the same token refer to the paying of heed to visual and auditory sensations respectively. But we cannot say that 'having sensations' is the activity that is being performed heedfully in these cases, since to have a sensation itself entails paying at least some heed to the sensation. We can speak of failing to notice the sensations that one would have had if one had paid attention to them; but to say that one had a tingling sensation in the left toe without noticing it is nonsense. Ryle accuses the traditional theory of being unable to provide a sensible account of the difference between a careful and a careless observer, but his own theory, while giving a plausible account of carefulness, fails to explain the activity of observing.

The Dispositional Theory Restated

Although Ryle has failed to provide a satisfactory account of consciousness, attention, and observation in terms of the dispositional theory of mental concepts, it would be unwise to conclude that such an account cannot be given. Ryle's account fails mainly because he overlooks the fact that our own activity is not the only sort of thing to which we can pay attention. The possibility of providing a plausible dispositional theory that takes account of our consciousness of and attention to objects, phenomena, and sensations is not ruled out. Indeed it is not difficult to suggest the form that such a theory might take.

We have seen that although paying attention to what one is doing does not entail being prepared to meet the demands of the task in hand, it cannot be denied that to pay attention to something entails noticing and hence being able to say something about it. It must also, I think, be conceded that it involves being ready to encounter something, although one need not be prepared to encounter the sort of thing that is actually there. This, however, cannot be all that we are saying when we say that someone is attending to something, since we can be ready to behave in a manner appropriate to the presence of some object or event in our immediate environment without actually being conscious of it. Our disposition to act in this way may be a result of something we have been told, some inference we have drawn, or some observation made a few moments previously. In such cases we might be said to know, remember, or suspect that it was there, but we would not be observing, attending to, or conscious of it. In order for us to be conscious of something, our disposition to react to its presence must result from its impingement on our sense organs at the time.

With the qualification that the disposition must result from sensory stimulation, it becomes quite plausible to maintain that to be conscious of something is to be ready to react both verbally and otherwise to the presence of some object or event in one's immediate environment. On this theory the contribution of attending to skilled performance would be explained by pointing out that unless the individual is disposed to react in a manner appropriate to the presence of the relevant features of his own activity and the environmental situation in which it takes place, he is not likely to be very successful.

On this view 'consciousness', 'attention', and 'observation' refer to a temporary state of readiness for something. You would therefore expect them to exhibit the logical features of expressions referring to temporary states of affairs. Expressions like 'being conscious' or 'aware of' do exhibit these logical characteristics. The words like 'attending', 'observing', 'watching', 'looking', and 'listening', on the other hand, exhibit the logical behavior characteristic of expressions that refer to activities. This fact, as we have seen, appears to provide a formidable obstacle to any dispositional theory of the meaning of these words. Nevertheless, the difficulty can probably be overcome without appealing to any kind of internal process or activity by examining the notion of 'activity' itself. It is at least arguable that when we speak of an individual's activities, of the things he does, we refer to those changes in him that can be induced by such things as commands, entreaties, instructions, and deliberations. Any changes, whether muscular or nonmuscular, that he can decide or be asked to bring about in himself are things that he does. Paying attention and observing are not muscular movements, nor are they movements of a mysterious transcendental musculature; they are, so the theory might run, changes in the individual's short-term dispositions, readinesses, or sets (to use a term that has a wide currency in the psychological literature) that can be induced by appropriate commands, requests, or by decisions on the part of the individual himself.

In the light of these considerations we may restate the dispositional theory of attention, observation, and consciousness as follows: To observe or pay attention to something is to bring about a change in oneself such that the impingement of the object or phenomenon in question on one's receptor organs prepares one to respond both verbally and otherwise in a manner appropriate to the presence of something, while to be conscious of something is to be so disposed.

The Case for the Traditional View

Stated in this way my quarrel with the dispositional theory is less substantial than my agreement with it. My contention is not so much that it is wrong as that it is incomplete. It is incomplete because it makes no reference to the internal state of the individual that enables him to describe and respond appropriately to the presence of objects in his vicinity. On the view that I wish to defend, when we use what Ryle calls a 'heed concept', we are not merely referring to the disposition to respond in a manner appropriate to the presence of the thing in question and specifying how that disposition is brought into being, we are also referring to an internal state of the individual that is a necessary and sufficient condition of the presence of such a disposition. I shall now try to present arguments in support of this contention.

One of the major weaknesses of Ryle's account of mental concepts is, as he himself recognizes, his retention of the traditional extended use of the term 'sensation' (chapter 7). He is compelled to retain this use in order to provide something—having a sensation—that the observer of an object can be said to do heedfully. One of the advantages of the revised form of the dispositional theory that I have stated is that it dispenses with the necessity for this concession to the traditional misappropriation of mental concepts. But although it dispenses with the necessity of abusing the concept of sensation, it runs into serious difficulties when applied to those cases where we do speak of being conscious of or of attending to our sensations, i.e., in those cases where our state of consciousness results from interoceptive or proprioceptive stimulation or from the various twists and quirks of our sensory apparatus, rather than from the impingement on our sense organs of any specifiable state of affairs in our environment.

Suppose that having applied pressure to my eyeball, I am conscious of a sensation of light. According to the revised dispositional theory, this means that I am disposed to react to the presence of something. But what is it that I am disposed to react to? It cannot be the pressure on my eyeball, since to be conscious of light sensations is not the same thing as being conscious of pressure applied to the eyeball. But it cannot be the presence of the sensation either. Sensations, as we have seen, do not exist independently of our consciousness of them. There are not two things, my sensation and my consciousness of it, in the way that there are two things, a penny and my consciousness of the penny. The occurrence of a sensation entails someone's consciousness of that sensation.

To be disposed to react to a sensation therefore would be to be disposed to react to one's consciousness of that sensation. In other words, we now have an infinite regress of dispositions instead of the infinite regress of ghostly operations that appears so frequently in Ryle's criticisms of the traditional theories. We might be tempted to meet this objection by supposing that to say that someone is conscious of a sensation of light is to say that he is temporarily disposed to react as he would normally do if there had been a flash of light. But to be disposed to react as if there were a flash of light would be to believe or be tempted to believe that a flash had occurred; whereas it makes perfectly good sense to say that he was conscious of a vivid sensation of light, yet it never occurred to him for one moment to suppose that there had been any actual flash of light. In other words, an individual's state of consciousness is something over and above any dispositions that it arouses in him.

An objection that applies to any attempt to give a dispositional account of consciousness and attention is the objection that it always makes sense to ask the individual to describe what it is like to watch, listen, observe, or be conscious of something, whereas it does not make sense to ask him what it is like to have a certain capacity or tendency. We can only describe what something is like if it is an object, situation, or occurrence. We can describe, characterize, or define such things as relationships, capacities, and tendencies, but we cannot describe what they are like. We can describe what a car is like, but we cannot describe what its horsepower is like; we can describe what it is like for one billiard ball to strike another and propel it forward, but we cannot describe what the causal relationship is like; we can describe what it is like to swim, or what it is like to realize that one can swim, but not what it is like to be able to swim; we may be able to describe what it is like to be told or call to mind the fact that whales are mammals, but we cannot describe what it is like to know or believe that they are. If to be conscious of something were merely to be disposed to react in some way, it should be logically impossible for us to describe what it is like to be conscious of something. In fact there is no logical impossibility here. We are continually describing what it is like to watch, look at, listen to, or feel things.

It might be objected with some justification here that what we describe is not our consciousness but the things we are conscious of. As we have seen, part of what is meant by saying that someone is conscious of something is that he can say something about it. It is certainly true that when we describe some object in our environment of which we are conscious, our description is a description of the object itself, and not, as has sometimes been supposed, a description of our consciousness of that object. It is also true that we cannot describe the state of being conscious in abstraction from the things we are conscious of. But that does not mean that we do not on occasions describe our consciousness of things as distinct from describing the things themselves. When we say, to use a familiar example, that the penny looks elliptical when viewed at an angle, we are not describing the penny, nor are we describing the image that it projects on our retina; we are describing what it is like to look at a penny from that particular angle; we are saying that it is somehow like looking at an ellipse viewed full face. When we say this, moreover, we do not imply that we are disposed to act in a manner appropriate to its being an ellipse. The elliptical shape of the penny is not an optical or a psychological illusion (cf. Ryle's discussion of this problem, pp. 216–218).

When we describe a state of consciousness, we usually do so by comparing being conscious of one thing with being conscious of another. Nevertheless there are one or two expressions, such as 'pleasant', 'unpleasant', 'vivid', 'dim', 'acute', and 'vague,' that we apply to the states of consciousness themselves. These are somewhat unusual adjectives to apply to a state of readiness. Furthermore the difference between vividness and dimness, acuteness and vagueness is difficult to explain on a dispositional theory of consciousness. The only possible interpretation on such a theory is in terms of the appropriateness of the behavior, for which one is prepared, to the presence of whatever it is one is conscious of. Acute consciousness, however, does not guarantee the appropriateness of the resulting behavior. The statement, 'His consciousness of his own ineptitude was so acute that he was unable to do anything about it,' makes perfectly good sense. It also describes a situation with which some of us are only too painfully familiar. If we recognize that consciousness is some sort of internal state of the individual, these discrepancies between the intensity of the individual's consciousness and the adequacy of the behavior for which it prepares him no longer constitute a problem.

Finally, there are considerations of a more general nature. If there were no decisive arguments either way, we should probably prefer the dispositional to the internal process theory of consciousness and attention on the grounds of parsimony. As against this must be set the fact that in every other case where verbs having 'activity' characteristics are involved, it has been found impossible to apply a purely dispositional analysis, and in at least one group of cases the reference to internal processes within the individual cannot seriously be denied. The cases I have in mind here are thinking (in the sense of thinking about or thinking to oneself), pondering, calculating, imagining, dreaming, visualizing, and doing mental arithmetic. Ryle (p. 27) has made a strong case for the view that when we talk about someone thinking (in the relevant sense), pondering, calculating, or imagining we are not asserting the occurrence of any internal process or activity. He contends that the activity referred to, although sometimes covert, as when it consists of visualizing or performing mental arithmetic, need not be so. It may equally well consist in some entirely overt performance such as drawing, talking out loud to oneself, or playing a game of make-believe. To assert that someone is thinking or imagining does not discriminate between these two possibilities. This argument disposes, or at least appears to dispose, of the view that words like 'thinking' and 'imagining' necessarily assert the occurrence of covert activities, but there is no suggestion that these are dispositional concepts. Nor is there any attempt to deny that thinking sometimes consists in a purely covert process or that expressions like 'dreaming', 'visualizing', and 'mental arithmetic' refer to such processes. If this is conceded with respect to 'dreaming', 'visualizing', and 'mental arithmetic', it is difficult in view of the weight of traditional and common-sense opinion and the lack of any positive evidence against it, to see why a similar concession should not be made with respect to 'attending', 'observing', 'watching', 'looking', and 'listening'.

The concepts 'observing', 'watching', 'listening', and 'being conscious of' are, in fact, closely related to the concepts 'visualizing' and 'dreaming', in a way that is extremely difficult to explain if the former are regarded as dispositional concepts. For if we want to explain what sort of thing this business of visualizing or dreaming is, the answer that immediately suggests itself is to say that visualizing something is like watching it, except that there is nothing there really and you don't have to have your eyes open. Now if to watch something is merely to bring about a change in oneself such that the impingement of the thing in question on one's eyes prepares one to respond both verbally and otherwise in a manner appropriate to there being something there, this explanation becomes completely unintelligible. Apart from the fact that both visualizing and watching are things that the individual can be said to do, it is exceedingly difficult on this theory to find anything that the two cases have in common. We cannot say that to visualize is to be disposed to act and speak as if there were something impinging on one's eyes when in fact there is not. Any one who is so disposed would be suffering from a visual hallucination, and although having a visual hallucination may be said to involve visualizing, we can visualize things perfectly well without being hallucinated. The similarity between visualizing something and watching it lies in the internal state of the individual that is brought into being, not in the behavioral dispositions that state induces.

Conclusions

If the above arguments prove what I think they prove, are we back where we started at the beginning of Ryle's inquiry? Do these arguments merely put the Ghost back into the Machine? I do not think so. So far as I am aware, the criticisms I have made of the dispositional theory apply only to the dispositional analysis of consciousness and heed concepts generally. The dispositional analysis of intelligence, knowledge, belief, motives, and memory remains unaffected, except insofar as these concepts involve dispositions to pay attention to or become conscious of certain features of one's environment. Indeed, since Ryle himself appears to accept the view that words like 'watching', 'listening', and 'observing' entail a reference to a covert process of having sensations, it is only in the case of the heedful performance of muscular activities that the view that has been urged in this paper differs from the account that Ryle has given as far as recognizing a reference to covert states and processes is concerned. On Ryle's view, however, these processes are relatively unimportant; we learn to talk silently to ourselves in order not to disturb others; we could plan our course of action on paper, but it is often more convenient to do it in our heads. If, on the other hand, our very ability to describe and adapt our behavior to the objects and phenomena that impinge on our sense organs is dependent on a special state of affairs within ourselves, which can itself be described by the person in whom it occurs, the reference that is made to such a process in our use of expressions like 'attending', 'observing', and 'being conscious' can hardly be brushed aside as a matter of no great significance. If such a view is accepted, we can hardly avoid raising the question that Ryle has dodged persistently throughout his book, namely the question, "What are these curious occurrences within ourselves on which we can give a running commentary as they occur?" Lack of space unfortunately precludes any discussion of this fascinating problem here. It is my belief, however, that the logical objections to the statement, "Consciousness is a process in the brain," are no greater than the logical objections that might be raised to the statement, "Lightning is a motion of electric charges."

3

Is Consciousness a Brain Process?

Introduction

The view that there exists a separate class of events, mental events, that cannot be described in terms of the concepts employed by the physical sciences no longer commands the universal and unquestioning acceptance among philosophers and psychologists that it once did. Modern physicalism, however, unlike the materialism of the seventeenth and eighteenth centuries, is behavioristic. Consciousness on this view is either a special type of behavior, "sampling" or "running-back-and-forth" behavior, as Tolman (1932, p. 206) has it, or a disposition to behave in a certain way, an itch for example being a temporary propensity to scratch. In the case of cognitive concepts like 'knowing', 'believing', 'understanding', and 'remembering', and volitional concepts like 'wanting' and 'intending', there can be little doubt, I think, that an analysis in terms of dispositions to behave (Wittgenstein, 1953; Ryle, 1949) is fundamentally sound. On the other hand, there would seem to be an intractable residue of concepts clustering around the notions of consciousness, experience, sensation, and mental imagery, where some sort of inner process story is unavoidable (Place, 1954). It is possible, of course, that a satisfactory behavioristic account of this conceptual residuum will ultimately be found. For our present purposes, however, I shall assume that this cannot be done and that statements about pains and twinges, about how things look, sound, and feel, about things dreamed of or pictured in the mind's eye are statements referring to events and processes that are in some sense private or internal to the individual of whom they are predicated. The question I wish to raise is whether in making this assumption we are inevitably committed to a dualist position in which sensations and mental images form a separate category of processes over and above the physical and physiological processes with which they are known to be correlated. I shall argue that an acceptance of inner processes does not entail dualism and that the thesis that consciousness is a process in the brain cannot be dismissed on logical grounds.

The 'Is' of Definition and the 'Is' of Composition

I want to stress from the outset that, in defending the thesis that consciousness is a process in the brain, I am not trying to argue that when we describe our dreams, fantasies, and sensations we are talking about a process in our brains. That is, I am not claiming that statements about sensations and mental images are reducible to or analyzable into statements about brain processes, in the way that 'cognition statements' are analyzable into statements about behavior. To say that statements about consciousness are statements about brain processes is manifestly false. This is shown (a) by the fact that you can describe your sensations and mental imagery without knowing anything about your brain processes or even that such things exist, (b) by the fact that statements about one's consciousness and statements about one's brain processes are verified in entirely different ways, and (c) by the fact that there is nothing self-contradictory about the statement, "X has a pain but there is nothing going on in his brain." What I do want to assert, however, is that the statement "Consciousness is a process in the brain," although not necessarily true, is not necessarily false. "Consciousness is a process in the brain," on my view, is neither self-contradictory nor self-evident; it is a reasonable scientific hypothesis, in the way that the statement, "Lightning is a motion of electric charges," is a reasonable scientific hypothesis.

The all but universally accepted view that an assertion of identity between consciousness and brain processes can be ruled out on logical grounds alone derives, I suspect, from a failure to distinguish between what we may call the 'is' of definition and the 'is' of composition. The distinction I have in mind here is the difference between the function of the word 'is' in statements like, "A square is an equilateral rectangle," "Red is a color," or "To understand an instruction is to be able to act appropriately under the appropriate circumstances," and its function in statements like, "His table is an old packing case," "Her hat is a bundle of straw tied together with string," or "A cloud is a mass of water droplets of other particles in suspension." These two types of 'is' statement have one thing in common. In both cases it makes sense to add the qualification "and nothing else." In this they differ from those statements in which the 'is' is an 'is' of predication; the statements, "Toby is 80 years old and nothing else," "Her hat is red and nothing else," or "Giraffes are tall and nothing else," for example, are nonsense. This logical feature may be described by saying that in both cases the grammatical subject and the grammatical predicate are expressions that provide an adequate characterization of the state of affairs to which they both refer.

In another respect, however, the two groups of statements are strikingly different. Statements like, "A square is an equilateral rectangle," are necessary statements that are true by definition. Statements like, "His table is an old packing case," on the other hand, are contingent statements, which have to be verified by observation. In the case of statements like, "A square is an equilateral rectangle," or "Red is a color," there is a relationship between the meaning of the expression forming the grammatical predicate and the meaning of the expression forming the grammatical subject, such that whenever the subject expression is applicable the predicate must also be applicable. If you can describe something as red then you must also be able to describe it as colored. In the case of statements like, "His table is an old packing case," on the other hand, there is no such relationship between the meanings of the expression 'his table' and 'old packing case'; it merely so happens that in this case both expressions are applicable to and at the same time provide an adequate characterization of the same object. Those who contend that the statement, "Consciousness is a brain process," is logically untenable base their claim, I suspect, on the mistaken assumption that if the meanings of two statements or expressions are quite unconnected, they cannot both provide an adequate characterization of the same object or state of affairs: if something is a state of consciousness, it cannot be a brain process, since there is nothing self-contradictory in supposing that someone feels a pain when there is nothing happening inside his skull. By the same token we might be led to conclude that a table cannot be an old packing case, since there is nothing self-contradictory in supposing that someone has a table but is not in possession of an old packing case.

The Logical Independence of Expressions and the Ontological Independence of Entities

There is, of course, an important difference between the table/packing case example and the consciousness/brain process example in that the statement, "His table is an old packing case," is a particular proposition that refers only to one particular case, whereas the statement, "Consciousness is a process in the brain," is a general or universal proposition applying to all states of consciousness whatever. It is fairly clear, I think, that if we lived in a world in which all tables without exception were packing cases, the concepts of 'table' and 'packing case' in our language would not have their present logically independent status. In such a world a table would be a species of packing case in much the same way that red is a species of color. It seems to be a rule of language that whenever a given variety of object or state of affairs has two characteristics or sets of characteristics, one of which is unique to the variety of object or state of affairs in question, the expression used to refer to the characteristic or set of characteristics that defines the variety of object or state of affairs in question will always entail the expression used to refer to the other characteristic or set of characteristics. If this rule admitted of no exception, it would follow that any expression that is logically independent of another expression that uniquely characterizes a given variety of object or state of affairs must refer to a characteristic or set of characteristics that is not normally or necessarily associated with the object or state of affairs in question. It is because this rule applies almost universally, I suggest, that we are normally justified in arguing from the logical independence of two expressions to the ontological independence of the states of affairs to which they refer. This would explain both the undoubted force of the argument that consciousness and brain processes must be independent entities because the expressions used to refer to them are logically independent and, in general, the curious phenomenon whereby questions about the furniture of the universe are often fought and not infrequently decided merely on a point of logic.

The argument from the logical independence of two expressions to the ontological independence of the entities to which they refer breaks down in the case of brain processes and consciousness, I believe, because this is one of a relatively small number of cases where the rule stated above does not apply. These exceptions are to be found, I suggest, in those cases where the operations that have to be performed in order to verify the presence of the two sets of characteristics inhering in the object or state of affairs in question can seldom if ever be performed simultaneously. A good example here is the case of the cloud and the mass of droplets or other particles in suspension. A cloud is a large semitransparent mass with a fleecy texture suspended in the atmosphere whose shape is subject to continual and kaleidoscopic change. When observed at close quarters, however, it is found to consist of a mass of tiny particles, usually water droplets, in continuous motion. On the basis of this second observation we conclude that a cloud is a mass of tiny particles and nothing else. But there is no logical connection in our language between a cloud and a mass of tiny particles; there is nothing self-contradictory in talking about a cloud that is not composed of tiny particles in suspension. There is no contradiction involved in supposing that clouds consist of a dense mass of fibrous tissue; indeed, such a consistency seems to be implied by many of the functions performed by clouds in fairy stories and mythology. It is clear from this that the terms 'cloud' and 'mass of tiny particles in suspension' mean quite different things. Yet we do not conclude from this that there must be two things, the mass of particles in suspension and the cloud. The reason for this, I suggest, is that although the characteristics of being a cloud and being a mass of tiny particles in suspension are invariably associated, we never make the observations necessary to verify the statement, "That is a cloud," and those necessary to verify the statement, "This is a mass of tiny particles in suspension," at one and the same time. We can observe the microstructure of a cloud only when we are enveloped by it, a condition that effectively prevents us from observing those characteristics that from a distance lead us to describe it as a cloud. Indeed, so disparate are these two experiences that we use different words to describe them. That which is a cloud when we observe it from a distance becomes a fog or mist when we are enveloped by it.

When Are Two Sets of Observations Observations of the Same Event?

The example of the cloud and the mass of tiny particles in suspension was chosen because it is one of the few cases of a general proposition involving what I have called the 'is' of composition that does not involve us in scientific technicalities. It is useful because it brings out the connection between the ordinary everyday cases of the 'is' of composition, like the table/packing case example, and the more technical cases, like "lightning is a motion of electric charges," where the analogy with the consciousness/brain process case is most marked. The limitation of the cloud/tiny particles in suspension case is that it does not bring out sufficiently clearly the crucial problem of how the identity of the states of affairs referred to by the two expressions is established. In the cloud case, the fact that something is a cloud and the fact that something is a mass of tiny particles in suspension are both verified by the normal processes of visual observation. It is arguable, moreover, that the identity of the entities referred to by the two expressions is established by the continuity between the two sets of observations as the observer moves toward or away from the cloud. In the case of brain processes and consciousness there is no such continuity between the two sets of observations involved. A closer introspective scrutiny will never reveal the passage of nerve impulses over a thousand synapses in the way that a closer scrutiny of a cloud will reveal a mass of tiny particles in suspension. The operations required to verify statements about consciousness and statements about brain processes are fundamentally different.

To find a parallel for this feature we must examine other cases where an identity is asserted between something whose occurrence is verified by the ordinary processes of observation and something whose occurrence is established by special scientific procedures. For this purpose I have chosen the case where we say that lightning is a motion of electric charges. As in the case of consciousness, however closely we scrutinize the lightning we shall never be able to observe the electric charges; and just as the operations for determining the nature of one's state of consciousness are radically different from those involved in determining the nature of one's brain processes, so the operations for determining the occurrence of lightning are radically different from those involved in determining the occurrence of a motion of electric charges. What is it, therefore, that leads us to say that the two sets of observations are observations of the same event? It cannot be merely the fact that the two sets of observations are systematically correlated such that whenever there is lightning there is always a motion of electric charges. There are innumerable cases of such correlations where we have no temptation to say that the two sets of observations are observations of the same event. There is a systematic correlation, for example, between the movement of the tides and the stages of the moon, but this does not lead us to say that records of tidal levels are records of the moon's stages or vice versa. We speak rather of a causal connection between two independent events or processes.

The answer here seems to be that we treat the two sets of observations as observations of the same event, in those cases where the technical scientific observations set in the context of the appropriate body of scientific theory provide an immediate explanation of the observations made by the man in the street. Thus we conclude that lightning is nothing more than a motion of electric charges, because we know that a motion of electric charges through the atmosphere, such as occurs when lightning is reported, gives rise to the type of visual stimulation that would lead an observer to report a flash of lightning. In the moon/tide case, on the other hand, there is no such direct causal connection between the stages of the moon and the observations made by the person who measures the height of the tide. The causal connection is between the moon and the tides, not between the moon and the measurement of the tides.

The Physiological Explanation of Introspection
and the Phenomenological Fallacy

If this account is correct, it should follow that in order to establish the identity of consciousness and certain processes in the brain, it would be necessary to show that the introspective observations reported by the subject can be accounted for in terms of processes that are known to have occurred in his brain. In the light of this suggestion it is extremely interesting to find that when a physiologist as distinct from a philosopher finds it difficult to see how consciousness could be a process in the brain, what worries him is not any supposed self-contradiction involved in such an assumption, but the apparent impossibility of accounting for the reports given by the subject of his conscious processes in terms of the known properties of the central nervous system. Sir Charles Sherrington has posed the problem as follows:

> The chain of events stretching from the sun's radiation entering the eye to, on the one hand, the contraction of the pupillary muscles, and on the other, to the electrical disturbances in the brain-cortex are all straightforward steps in a sequence of physical 'causation', such as, thanks to science, are intelligible. But in the second serial chain there follows on, or attends, the stage of brain-cortex reaction an event or set of events quite inexplicable to us which both as to themselves and as to the causal tie between them and what preceded them science does not help us; a set of events seemingly incommensurable with any of the events leading up to it. The self 'sees' the sun; it senses a two-dimensional disc of brightness located in the 'sky', this last a field of lesser brightness, and overhead shaped as a rather flattened dome, coping the self and a hundred other visual things as well. Of hint that this is within the head there is none. Vision is saturated with this strange property called 'projection', the unargued inference that what it sees is at a 'distance' from the seeing 'self'. Enough has been said to stress that in the sequence of events a step is reached where a physical situation in the brain leads to a psychical, which however contains no hint of the brain or any other bodily part. . . . The supposition has to be, it would seem, two continuous series of events, one physicochemical, the other psychical, and at times interaction between them. (Sherrington, 1947, pp. xx–xxi)

Just as the physiologist is not likely to be impressed by the philosopher's contention that there is some self-contradiction involved in supposing consciousness to be a brain process, so the philosopher is unlikely to be impressed by the considerations that led Sherrington to conclude that there are two sets of events, one physicochemical, the other psychical. Sherrington's argument for all its emotional appeal depends on a fairly simple logical mistake, which is unfortunately all too frequently made by psychologists and physiologists and not infrequently in the past by the philosophers themselves. This logical mistake, which I shall refer to as the 'phenomenological fallacy', is the mistake of supposing that when the subject describes his experience, when he describes how things look, sound, smell, taste, or feel to him, he is describing the literal properties of objects and events on a peculiar sort of internal cinema or television screen, usually referred to in the modern psychological literature as the 'phenomenal field'. If we assume, for example, that when a subject reports a green afterimage he is asserting the occurrence inside himself of an object that is literally green, it is clear that we have on our hands an entity for which there is no place in the world of physics. In the case of the green afterimage there is no green object in the subject's environment corresponding to the description that he gives. Nor is there anything green in his brain; certainly there is nothing that could have emerged when he reported the appearance of the green afterimage. Brain processes are not the sort of things to which color concepts can be properly applied.

The phenomenological fallacy on which this argument is based depends on the mistaken assumption that because our ability to describe things in our environment depends on our consciousness of them, our descriptions of things are primarily descriptions of our conscious experience and only secondarily, indirectly, and inferentially descriptions of the objects and events in our environments. It is assumed that because we recognize things in our environment by their look, sound, smell, taste, and feel, we begin by describing their phenomenal properties, i.e., the properties of the looks, sounds, smells, tastes, and feels that they produce in us, and infer their real properties from their phenomenal properties. In fact, the reverse is the case. We begin by learning to recognize the real properties of things in our environment. We learn to recognize them, of course, by their look, sound, smell, taste, and feel; but this does not mean that we have to learn to describe the look, sound, smell, taste, and feel of things before we can describe the things themselves. Indeed, it is only after we have learned to describe the things in our environment that we can learn to describe our consciousness of them. We describe our conscious experience not in terms of the mythological 'phenomenal properties' that are supposed to inhere in the mythological "objects" in the mythological "phenomenal field," but by reference to the actual physical properties of the concrete physical objects, events, and processes that normally, though not perhaps in the present instance, give rise to the sort of conscious experience that we are trying to describe. In other words, when we describe the afterimage as green, we are not saying that there is something, the afterimage, that is green; we are saying that we are having the sort of experience that we normally have when, and that we have learned to describe as, looking at a green patch of light.

Once we rid ourselves of the phenomenological fallacy we realize that the problem of explaining introspective observations in terms of brain processes is far from insuperable. We realize that there is nothing that the introspecting subject says about his conscious experiences that is inconsistent with anything the physiologist might want to say about the brain processes that cause him to describe the environment and his consciousness of that environment in the way he does. When the subject describes his experience by saying that a light that is in fact stationary appears to move, all the physiologist or physiological psychologist has to do to explain the subject's introspective observations is to show that the brain process causing the subject to describe his experience in this way is the sort of process that normally occurs when he is observing an actual moving object and that therefore normally causes him to report the movement of an object in his environment. Once the mechanism whereby the individual describes what is going on in his environment has been worked out, all that is required to explain the individual's capacity to make introspective observations is an explanation of his ability to discriminate between those cases where his normal habits of verbal description are appropriate to the stimulus situation and those cases where they are not and an explanation of how and why, in those cases where the appropriateness of his normal descriptive habits is in doubt, he learns to issue his ordinary descriptive protocols preceded by a qualificatory phrase like "it appears," "seems," "looks," "feels," etc.[1]

Materialism as
a Scientific Hypothesis

In discussing the logical status of the thesis that sensations are processes in the brain, J. J. C. Smart (1959, pp. 155–156)[1] contends that I was partly right and partly wrong in maintaining that this thesis could and should be interpreted as a straightforward scientific hypothesis (Place, 1956). He argues that insofar as the issue is between a brain-process thesis and a heart, liver, or kidney thesis the issue is empirical and can be decided by experiment. But insofar as the issue is between materialism on the one hand and epiphenomenalism, psychophysical parallelism, interactionism, and so forth, on the other, the issue is nonempirical. I shall argue that Smart is partly right and partly wrong in maintaining that the issue between the kind of materialism that both he and I would wish to defend and the rival doctrines of epiphenomenalism, psychophysical parallelism, interactionism, and so forth, is a nonempirical issue.

In my own paper on this topic (Place, 1956, pp. 47–48) I argued that there are certain logical conditions that must be satisfied to enable us to say that a process or event observed in one way is the same process or event as that observed in (or inferred from) another set of observations made under quite different conditions.[2] In that paper I suggested only one logical criterion, namely, that the process or event observed in or inferred from the second set of observations should provide us with an explanation, not of the process or event observed in the first set of observations but of the very fact that such observations are made. I illustrated this point by comparing the case where the movements of the sun and the moon observed astronomically are used to explain the movement of the tides observed geophysically with the case where observations interpreted in terms of the motion of electric charges are used to explain not a separate event called 'lightning' but the fact that we see and hear the sort of things we do on a stormy night.[3] I would now want to add to this the rather obvious additional criterion that the two sets of observations must refer to the same point in space and time, allowing for such things as the time taken by the transmission of light and sound, distortions in the transmitting media, the personal equation of the observer, and differences in the precision with which location is specified in the two sets of observations.

For the purposes of the present argument it does not matter whether this account of the logical criteria used to establish the identity of an event described in terms of two different procedures of observation is correct or not. What is important is that there must be some logical criteria that we use in deciding whether two sets of correlated observations refer to the same event or to two separate but causally related events. The problem of deciding what these criteria are is a logical problem, which cannot be decided by experiment in any ordinary sense of the term; and since we cannot be certain that the criteria are satisfied in the case of sensations and brain processes unless we know what the criteria are, the issue is to that extent a philosophical issue. Moreover, even if we agree on the nature of these logical criteria, it is still open to the philosopher to question the logical propriety of applying them in the case of sensations and brain processes.

For the sake of argument, however, let us assume that these philosophical issues have been settled and that they have been settled in favor of the materialist hypothesis. We now find ourselves faced with a purely empirical issue, namely, whether there is in fact a physiological process, be it in the brain, the heart, the liver, the kidney, or the big toe, that satisfies the logical criteria required to establish its identity with the sensation process. As it happens, we already know enough to be quite sure that, if there is such a process, it must be situated in the brain, and even within the brain there are extensive areas that can be ruled out with virtual certainty as possible loci of consciousness—areas, for example, where brain lesions produce motor disturbances without any change in consciousness other than an awareness of the disability itself and emotional reactions to the problems it creates. But the empirical problem is not, as Smart seems to think, simply a matter of determining the precise anatomical location of this physiological process. It is still an open question whether there is, even in this relatively circumscribed area, a process that satisfies the logical criteria required to establish its identity with the sensation process.[4] Even assuming that we know what these criteria are and are satisfied that they are applicable in this case, we cannot regard the question as finally settled until a process satisfying the necessary criteria has been discovered or until we are sure that we know enough about the brain to be certain that no such process exists.

Until such time as this issue is settled by further psychophysiological research, materialism remains an empirical hypothesis—the hypothesis that there exists, presumably in the brain, a physiological process that satisfies the logical criteria required to establish its identity with the sensation process. If this hypothesis is confirmed, the need disappears for alternative theories designed to explain the relationship between sensation, considered as an independent nonphysiological process, and the physiological processes with which it is correlated. Theories like epiphenomenalism could then only be made tenable by refusing to accept the logical criteria put forward as establishing the identity of a process characterized by reference to two entirely different observation procedures or their application to the case of brain processes and sensation. Given a solution of the logical issues favorable to materialism, these theories can be ruled out on empirical grounds in a way that Gosse's theory of creation (Smart, 1959, pp. 155–156) cannot be ruled out.

In practice, of course, those who object to the materialist hypothesis are much more likely, and indeed would be much better advised, to make their stand among the logical issues I have mentioned than to accept the logical criteria put forward as establishing the identity of a physiological process with the sensation process and pin their hopes on the failure of scientific research to discover a process satisfying these criteria. It is among these philosophical issues that the real battle will be fought. To this extent Smart is right when he says that the issue between materialism on the one hand and epiphenomenalism, psychophysical parallelism, and so forth, on the other, will not be decided by a program of experimental research. But this does not affect my contention that materialism can and should be treated as a straightforward scientific hypothesis. It may be that the logical criteria for establishing the identity of the object of two types of observation are logically inapplicable to the case of sensations and brain processes. If so, I am just plain wrong in claiming that materialism can be treated as a scientific hypothesis; but if the criteria are applicable, I am right. I am not partly right and partly wrong.

5

Consciousness in Psychology

There can be no doubt, to my mind, that Watson is right when he argues that there is no place in contemporary scientific psychology for concepts that cannot readily be integrated into the fabric of scientific thinking as a whole (see Notes—Eds).

Where I do not agree with him is in supposing that there is any necessary incompatibility between the assumption that behavior is in part causally determined by conscious processes and the assumption "that there are no causal processes antecedent to behaviour which could not be described within the range of the concepts of physiology, chemistry, engineering and so on."

I have argued elsewhere (Place, 1956) that the view that consciousness, in the sense in which we are using it for the purposes of this symposium, is a process in the brain is a reasonable scientific hypothesis, which cannot be dismissed on logical grounds alone. It is not clear whether Watson thinks there is some logical contradiction in supposing consciousness to be a process in the brain. But if he does, the only argument he gives that can conceivably be construed as supporting this conclusion is the argument in which he maintains that consciousness is an intervening process quite different from those postulated by psychologists, because its occurrence is directly ascertained.

Treated as an argument against the mind-body identity thesis, this argument has consequences that I do not think Watson would want to accept. For if something that is directly ascertained cannot be the same thing as something whose existence is postulated on the basis of theoretical considerations, it follows that the planet Neptune, now observed by astronomers, cannot be the same planet as the planet whose magnitude, orbit, and position were independently calculated by Adams and Le Verrier before it was discovered in 1846. Nor will it ever be possible for a neurophysiologist to observe any of the brain processes currently postulated by the theoreticians, or any they may postulate in the future, since, if their occurrence were directly ascertained, they would not, on Watson's view, be the same processes.

I conclude that Watson has not provided any convincing reasons for holding that there is a logical contradiction involved in supposing consciousness to be a process in the brain. But if there is no logical contradiction involved, there is certainly no empirical evidence that is inconsistent with the hypothesis, and much that is difficult to account for on any other assumption. And if there are no logical or empirical considerations which make the hypothesis untenable, there need be no inconsistency involved in holding both that an individual's consciousness determines his behavior, and that "there are no processes causally antecedent to behaviour which could not be described within the range of the concepts of physiology."

It cannot be denied that the scientific investigation of consciousness presents serious methodological problems, but it is not at all clear that these problems are such as to put the phenomenon entirely beyond the reach of scientific investigation. If there is sufficient empirical evidence to warrant the conclusion that a phenomenon exists, there must be at least some acceptable empirical evidence concerning its properties, since we cannot have evidence of the existence of something unless we have evidence that there exists something having the properties in terms of which the thinking in question is defined. And if we have acceptable empirical evidence about at least some of the properties of consciousness, it is difficult to see how the phenomenon can be wholly insusceptible of scientific investigation.

Watson's argument seems to imply that there are some ways of investigating natural phenomena that are intrinsically acceptable from a scientific point of view, while other methods are intrinsically unacceptable. But this is surely misleading. The method of investigation that is scientifically acceptable depends on the nature of the phenomenon under investigation. A method that is quite unacceptable in investigating one phenomenon, because other methods less liable to yield erroneous conclusions are available, may be scientifically acceptable in investigating another phenomenon, because it is the only or best possible method available in the circumstances. Conclusions drawn on the basis of a method that has a large margin of error must necessarily be correspondingly tentative, but it is usually better to draw conclusions on the basis of unsatisfactory empirical evidence than none at all.

The methodological problems involved in the study of consciousness derive from the incurably "subjective" character of the reports on which we depend for our knowledge of the process. Introspective reports are almost invariably made some time, even if only a matter of seconds, after the events they report, and they are, therefore, almost certainly subject to the distortion that, as has been repeatedly demonstrated by psychological experiment, normally occurs when an individual attempts to reproduce from memory material of any complexity. But since, as things stand, we have no means of checking the accuracy of introspective reports against the reality they purport to describe, we have no basis for discriminating between what is distorted in the report and what is not, and can only assess the probable amount of distortion likely to be present by analogy with the amount of distortion present when the individual reports similar events where the accuracy of his report can be checked.

This is a serious methodological problem, but it is by no means unique to the study of consciousness. Similar problems arise in any situation where the scientist is dependent for his information on the retrospective reports of untrained human observers. Yet I do not think many psychologists or sociologists would argue that we ought to ignore such questions as the incidence and frequency of different types of sexual behavior over the past fifty years because we are completely dependent for our information on this topic on the retrospective reports of untrained human observers on matters about which they have strong motives for misrepresentation. Scientific prudence requires that any conclusions drawn on the basis of such evidence be treated with the utmost caution; but it is surely better, and more consistent with the aims and methods of empirical science, to base conclusions on the best empirical evidence available than to refuse to investigate a problem on the grounds that it cannot be studied in an acceptable scientific manner.

If conscious processes could not be investigated in an acceptable scientific manner, there would not exist, as there clearly does, a substantial body of information about them based on systematic empirical investigation. During the latter part of the nineteenth and the early years of the present century[1] a great deal of information was accumulated about the effects of various stimulus conditions on the resulting conscious processes as reported by introspective observers, which laid the foundation of our present knowledge of the physiology of the sense organs. In the medical field there exists a large, if relatively unsystematized, body of knowledge about the effects of various pathological conditions, physical as well as psychiatric, on conscious processes reported by the patient which, in spite of the development of more precise and objective methods, still plays an important part in diagnosis and in assessing the effects of treatment. The evidence collected, notably by Galton, on individual differences in mental imagery and other purely subjective aspects of thought processes represents a substantial, if neglected, contribution to empirical knowledge in psychology, and whatever we may think about the curious theoretical apparatus of psychoanalysis, Freud's contribution to our knowledge of dreams at a purely descriptive level can hardly be denied.

The reason why psychologists have virtually ceased to add to this body of knowledge is not that they have now discovered that all the conclusions drawn on the basis of introspection in the past can no longer be accepted. What was discovered at the beginning of this century[2] is that it is impossible to resolve theoretical issues by appeal to introspective evidence alone. For if one theoretical position predicts a given conscious phenomenon and another theory predicts the opposite, and if one set of introspective observations is consistent with one theory and another set of observations is consistent with the other theory, it is always possible to argue that the observations that are inconsistent with the theoretical position of one's choice are unreliable; and in the absence of an independent check on the reliability of the introspective reports, there is no way of resolving the issue.

As long as psychologists were content to assemble empirical information at a descriptive level, this problem did not arise. But when the stage was reached where further progress required the resolution of theoretical issues that could not be resolved on the basis of the only kind of evidence available, the scientific investigation of consciousness ground rapidly to a halt.

It follows that the only way to overcome this obstacle and revive the interest of psychologists in the scientific investigation of consciousness is to find some way of providing an independent check on the reliability of introspective reports. On a dualistic theory this is impossible, since, on this view, introspection is the only kind of evidence one can have of the nature of conscious processes. But if, as I have argued, consciousness is a process in the brain, it may eventually become possible to check the reliability of introspective reports against electrophysiological recordings of the processes they report, once these have been identified. Needless to say, the implications of such developments from the standpoint of the psychology of consciousness are as exciting as the social implications are alarming.

The philosophical problems that arise concerning the concept of consciousness would not worry the psychologist if he did not find himself inescapably involved in them whenever he tries to use the concept. If he could use the concept of consciousness as he uses concepts like time and cause, without feeling that he needs to consult what the philosophers have to say on the matter, there would be no problems.

That the psychologist should find this situation embarrassing is understandable. It is not just that he finds himself involved in matters that fall within the competence of specialists from another discipline. After all, psychologists are quite happy to defer to neurophysiologists in matters of brain function, and even to engineers in matters of psychological theory. But to have to defer to philosophers in matters of consciousness is a very different matter.

It is not only that the psychologist is trying very hard to secure and maintain the reputation of his discipline as a natural and empirical science and is therefore reluctant to become involved with a discipline that claims to handle its problems without recourse to empirical evidence at any point and that is not, like mathematics, recognized as an indispensable tool of scientific research. More important than this is the view, widely held by scientists, that there is no way of reaching a final and agreed conclusion in a philosophical argument. It is a consequence of this view that, if the psychologist is foolhardy enough to use the concept of consciousness, he becomes inescapably involved in problems to which he can never hope to obtain a final and agreed solution.

In order to meet this objection, we need to consider why the psychologist cannot use the concept of consciousness without becoming involved in philosophical problems. The reason for this is that you cannot say anything about consciousness from a scientific point of view without raising the question whether we have any scientifically acceptable evidence for the existence of such a process. Consciousness, as we have defined it, is a process intervening between input and output, the occurrence of which is directly ascertained by the individual in whom it occurs but which cannot, as things stand, be observed by anyone else. It follows from this definition that the only evidence we can have of the existence of such a process comes from the introspective reports that the individual gives about it. There is no doubt, of course, about the existence of these reports. It is a matter of empirical fact that people frequently make statements that, so they claim, are reports of events and processes inside them that others cannot observe. But are they really doing what they claim to be doing? Can we account for this verbal behavior without postulating some inner process to which the alleged introspective statements can be taken to refer?

These are questions that we can only answer by introducing considerations that are currently classified as philosophical. In order to decide whether an alleged introspective statement can be accounted for, without assuming that it refers to an inner process or event, we need to examine the logical implications of the words and expressions used in making the statement. In other words, we can only decide whether the introspective reports are what they purport to be by studying what Professor Ryle has called the "logical geography" of the words and expressions involved in giving, asking for, and talking about them, and seeing whether the assumption that they refer to inner processes is the only hypothesis that will fit the logical facts.

The facts of logical geography with which we are here concerned are logical facts about words and expressions in the natural language of the introspective observer, for our purposes, English. But because they are logical facts, it does not follow that they are not at the same time empirical facts about the English language.

It is true that the native English speaker requires no empirical evidence to tell him that if something is red all over, it cannot be green all over. The fact that something cannot be both red and green all over at the same time is not an empirical fact; it is a logically necessary truth. It is nevertheless an empirical fact used in such a way that the sentence, "Something cannot be red and green all over," expresses a logical necessary truth, and in such a way that a native speaker is justified in inferring that 'X is not green' from the statement, "X is red all over." It is with these empirical metalanguage statements about the logically necessary relations holding between the words and expressions of a given natural language that we are concerned when we study the logical geography of the words and expressions used by the subject in giving and talking about his introspective reports.

As I see it, it is an accident of the present stage in the evolution of human thinking that this particular branch of empirical inquiry happens to be the responsibility of the philosopher. In the past, philosophy has given birth to a number of empirical sciences, from physics in the seventeenth century to psychology in the nineteenth century, and there is no particular reason to suppose that its childbearing days in this respect are over. Indeed there is more than a little evidence that philosophy is at the present time heavily pregnant with an empirical scientific discipline concerned with the functional or meaning aspects of language.

If this development takes place and the notion of 'logical geography' becomes something more than a metaphor, the problem of deciding whether or not introspective reports refer to inner processes will cease to be a philosophical problem. It will be recognized as an empirical problem, falling within the competence of the empirical science of linguistics and, therefore, as a problem to which we can reasonably expect to find a definite solution and concerning which the experimental psychologist need have no inhibitions about consulting the relevant specialist.

The arguments I have presented are designed to undermine what I take to be the major premise of Watson's argument, namely that the use of the concept of consciousness is incompatible with the aims and methods of experimental psychology. I have tried to show that consciousness is a process for the existence of which we have considerable empirical evidence in the case of humans and strong circumstantial evidence in the case of the higher mammals, that in spite of the methodological problems involved, consciousness is a phenomenon susceptible to scientific investigation and one that does not require any supernatural or extra-physical explanation.

Watson, however, is not primarily concerned with the investigation and explanation of consciousness as a phenomenon in its own right. He is concerned with the use of this concept in explanations that are given by psychologists of the overt behavior of organisms. Now, although the arguments I have presented provide a case for retaining, or rather reviving consciousness as a proper subject of scientific research in psychology, they do not provide any very convincing support for the use of this concept in explaining behavior, whether human or animal, at the present time.

If consciousness exists and is causally related to behavior in the way it appears to be, it follows that an explanation of behavior that takes account of all the intervening processes on which the occurrence of behavior depends, must include consciousness among them. But this is true only of the final and complete explanation, which it is the object of scientific research to achieve but which is seldom achieved in practice and is certainly a very long way off as far as the behavior of organisms is concerned. But because we cannot yet fit all the pieces of the jigsaw together, it does not follow that we cannot at the present time provide perfectly satisfactory explanations of many aspects of behavior without mentioning consciousness (or any other kind of intervening process).

An explanation is what it is only insofar as the explicans is initially better understood than the explicandum. There can be no point in trying to explain behavior in terms of intervening processes if we already understand the behavior by itself better than we understand the intervening processes. And whatever may be true of the intervening processes postulated by the neurophysiologist and the cybernetician, it is surely the case that our knowledge and understanding of consciousness is very much less than the knowledge and understanding that we have of the overt behavior of the organism.

It would seem, therefore, that although Watson's contention that any reference to consciousness is incompatible with the aims of experimental psychology is unacceptable, we have to concede that our knowledge and understanding of this process is far too poorly developed at present to justify an attempt to make anything but the most tentative use of what we know about it in giving a scientific explanation of behavior.

6

The Infallibility of Our Knowledge of Our Own Beliefs

It would seem to be the case that if I assert a proposition of the form 'I believe that p', I cannot be mistaken. The proposition of the form, "I believe that p," may be false; but if it is, it must be the case that I am lying. Why should this be?

On what Ryle (1949) in *The Concept of Mind* called "the official doctrine," the infallibility of my knowledge of my own beliefs is explained on the assumption that a belief is a private inner state that I and only I can inspect. The objection to this theory is that if it were true, our knowledge of our own beliefs would be incorrigible in the sense that no one else is able to inspect my beliefs and thus correct any error I may have made in reporting them; but it would not be infallible, because there is no reason in principle why I should not make a mistake through careless introspection even though I am the only person who is in a position to correct it.

A more promising answer to the problem is suggested by Ryle's dispositional theory of mental concepts. It might be argued on this theory that to believe that p is to be disposed to assert p on occasions when the truth of p is a relevant consideration. Now since I cannot assert that I believe p without ipso facto asserting p, it would follow that in asserting that I believe p, I have ipso facto exercised and thus displayed my disposition to assert p. On this view, I cannot be mistaken in asserting that I believe p because the statement, "I believe p," is a self-verifying statement. It cannot be asserted without ipso facto demonstrating its own truth.

There is, however, a formidable objection to this explanation of the infallibility of our knowledge of our own beliefs in that it does not allow any room for the case where my assertion that I believe p is a lie. For if to believe that p is merely to be disposed to assert p, I cannot assert that I believe p without demonstrating that I believe p. The statement can never be false. Consequently, in order to allow for the case of lying, we have to amend the dispositional theory of belief by adding to the disposition to assert p the disposition to act on p in circumstances where p is or would be a relevant consideration. It may be objected that an account of belief in terms of the disposition to act on a proposition one is disposed to assert runs into difficulties in the case of beliefs that are related to matters far removed from the believer's immediate life situation, such as the nonhistorian's belief about the remote past or the nonastronomer's beliefs about the heavenly bodies.[1] However, since no one could conceivably have a motive for lying in claiming to believe something about a matter of no immediate concern to himself, the problem of distinguishing between lying about one's beliefs and sincerely asserting them does not arise with beliefs of this type. Hence there is no objection to supposing that where the belief concerns matters outside the believer's immediate life situation, his belief consists solely in a disposition to assert the proposition he believes and that it is only in the case of beliefs that relate to the individual's immediate life situation that believing p also involves a disposition to act on p.

On this amended form of the dispositional theory, the case where I sincerely assert that I believe p is a case where I am disposed both to assert and to act on p, whereas in the case where I am lying in asserting that I believe p, I am disposed to assert p but am not disposed to act on p. On this amended view, the statement, "I believe that p," is still partially self-verifying in that it demonstrates the existence of the disposition to assert p, which is part of what is meant by saying that I believe p. On the other hand it is not self-verifying with respect to the disposition to act on p, which, as we now construe it, is also implied by the statement that someone believes that p. But if I do not show that I am disposed to act on p when I claim to believe p in the way that I show that I am disposed to assert p, how does it come about that I can lie, but cannot be mistaken, when I falsely assert that I believe that p? Why should I not sincerely assert that I believe p and yet be honestly mistaken in supposing that I am disposed to act on p?

It is no use saying here that if I assert that I believe p in a case where I am not disposed to act on p, I must necessarily be telling a lie. This is merely to sweep that problem under the carpet. For to lie is to assert a proposition that one knows to be false. Hence a situation in which any false proposition must necessarily be a lie is merely a situation in which the speaker cannot avoid knowing that the proposition is false, if it is false. If, therefore, I am necessarily lying in asserting that I believe p when I am not in fact disposed to act on p, it follows that in asserting that I believe p, I cannot avoid knowing that I am not disposed to act on p if I am not so disposed. But why should I necessarily know that I am not disposed to act on p when I assert that I believe p but am not in fact disposed to act on p? What is the force of 'necessarily' here? Is this a matter of logical necessity? Or is it merely a contingent psychological necessity?

I suggest that in order to answer this question we need to consider what is involved in asserting a proposition. Clearly, if I assert a proposition p, I am performing a social act, an act that presupposes not only a speaker but also an audience. Moreover, my intention in asserting p must necessarily be to influence my audience in the direction of believing p. If I do not have this intention, I cannot properly be said to have asserted p. But if the account we have given of what is involved in believing p is correct, it follows that in trying to influence my audience to believe p, I am trying to influence them in the direction not only of asserting p themselves but also in the direction of acting on p. Thus, in asserting p, I am necessarily recommending p to my audience as a reliable basis for action.

However, from the fact that in asserting p I necessarily intend to influence my audience to adopt p as a basis for action, it does not follow that my audience cannot avoid being influenced in this way. Nevertheless, there is a substantial body of empirical evidence relating to the phenomena of suggestion and hypnosis that supports the view that the initial reaction of every human being who hears and understands a proposition asserted by another person is to accept that proposition at its face value as a reliable basis for action, and that the ability to question the propositions that are put to him by another person, rejecting some while accepting others, is a skill that is superimposed on this basic tendency to accept what one is told without question. Thus a study by Messerschmidt, quoted by Hull (1933), shows that the responsiveness of children to verbal suggestions of postural movement increases rapidly as the child's understanding of language increases up to an average age of eight years and then slowly declines. Hull comments as follows:

> As a plausible hypothesis to account for this reversal, it may be supposed that suggestion is based in a primitive habit tendency (of responding directly to verbal stimulation) that is useful in most situations but maladaptive in the special type of situation represented by this suggestion test. Presumably the maladaptivity is related largely to the fact that if a person responds positively and indiscriminately to all suggestions made by others, he is likely to be taken advantage of by his associates in that the energies needed for his own welfare will be diverted to that of those giving the suggestions. The rise of the curve accordingly represents the acquisition of a working knowledge of the language, which obviously must proceed a certain distance before its maladaptive possibilities may be encountered; and the gradual fall observed from about eight years on may be regarded as an indication of the progress in 'unlearning' those particular reactions to verbal stimuli which, having been established have proved maladaptive. (Hull, 1933, p. 85)

In the light of empirical evidence such as this, as well as in the light of a theoretical consideration of what is required for a child's acquisition of the ability to understand what is said to him, it seems not unreasonable to suppose that the child must necessarily begin by learning to accept a statement made by another person as equivalent in all respects to the actual existence of the environmental situation that the statement describes, and that unless he begins in this way he cannot learn to understand the meaning of what is said to him. In other words, unless a child begins by accepting whatever he is told and believes it implicitly, he cannot learn to understand what is said to him. If this is correct, it follows that anyone who listens to and understands an assertion made by someone else will necessarily believe that assertion and thus be disposed to act upon it, unless he has acquired an overriding disposition to reject assertions of that kind.

Now, in learning to reject certain assertions while admitting others, the individual must have available to him certain cues that enable him to differentiate between acceptable and unacceptable assertions made by others. It seems, moreover, that the cues to which he learns to respond in this way are of three kinds. In the first place he may learn to reject out of hand, or not to admit without serious question, propositions that are asserted by certain persons whom he has learned to identify as persistently unreliable informants or inveterate liars. Second, he may learn to reject or seriously question propositions asserted by persons whose propositions he would otherwise accept at their face value in a situation where the person concerned is judged to have a strong motive for lying or otherwise misrepresenting the true state of affairs. Finally, he will also learn to question and ultimately reject certain propositions purely on their merits, regardless of the source from which they come. When he does this, he will do so on the basis of some contradiction that he notices or suspects between the proposition that is being asserted and certain other propositions that he already believes and has successfully acted upon in the past. It would seem to be the case, moreover, that if he has no reason to question the veracity of his source and is not aware of and does not suspect any conflict between his existing beliefs and the proposition being urged upon him, there is nothing to prevent him from giving way to this underlying tendency to accept what he is told as a basis for subsequent action.

Now if, as I have argued, a human being has a built-in tendency to accept as a basis for action any proposition asserted by another person that he hears, or reads, and understands, unless there is something that restrains him from doing so, it seems not unreasonable to suppose that he will likewise have a built-in tendency to accept as a basis for action any proposition that he himself asserts. For no one can effectively assert a proposition without hearing and understanding what he is saying or without reading and understanding what he is writing. Hence on the principle whereby the inveterate liar eventually comes to believe his own propaganda,[2] an individual who asserts a proposition will not be able to resist the temptation to take the proposition he asserts as a reliable basis for action, unless there is something to prevent him from doing so. Now we have seen that the only conditions under which an individual can be restrained from accepting a proposition that he hears or reads and understands are (1) in a case where he has learned that the speaker is, or is likely to be, a systematically unreliable informant, (2) in a case where he has learned that the speaker is likely to have motives for mendacity or misrepresentation, and (3) in a case where he is aware of or suspects a conflict between the assertion and his existing beliefs. Applying this to the case where the individual understands the proposition he himself asserts, as he must do whenever he asserts it, it is evident that no rational being could learn to treat himself as a systematically unreliable informant without systematically undermining all rational connection between what he says—to himself or to others—and what he does. That way lies madness.

On the other hand, an individual can very profitably learn to question, though not systematically to reject, those propositions that he asserts or is inclined to assert where he himself has strong motives for mendacity or misrepresentation. This is a highly desirable habit of self-criticism that few people manage to acquire in the face of the strong impulse that we all have to believe, whenever possible, what it suits us to believe rather than what the evidence demands. So difficult is it to learn this discrimination and so directly does it conflict with the individual's natural inclinations as far as the beliefs he accepts and rejects are concerned, that it is inconceivable that a man who for this reason does not accept as a basis for action a proposition he has just asserted should be unaware that he does not in fact believe that proposition in question.

The only other case in which he could reject as a basis for action a proposition that he himself has just asserted is a case in which he is aware of or suspects a conflict between the proposition he has just asserted and other beliefs of his that he accepts as a basis for action. In this case, if, as I have argued, he is aware of or suspects a conflict between the proposition he has asserted and his other beliefs, it is again inconceivable that he should fail to be aware that he has been led by this apparent conflict to reject the proposition in question as a basis for action. But if, in the only two cases where a rational man can reject as a basis for action a proposition he has just asserted, it is inconceivable that he should be unaware that he has so rejected it, it follows that it is inconceivable that he should not know that he does not believe the proposition he has asserted, if he does not. And if he cannot avoid knowing that he does not believe a proposition he has asserted, if he does not, it follows that in such a case he must necessarily be lying if he claims to believe the proposition he asserts.

It will be noted that on this account not only is it inconceivable that an individual should not know that he does not believe a proposition he asserts, if he does not believe it; it is equally inconceivable that he should not know that he believes a proposition that he has considered, has accepted as a basis for action, but denies that he believes. For, as we have seen, someone who hears or reads and thereby understands a proposition, as he must have done if he has considered it, cannot fail to be influenced in the direction of accepting it as a basis for action, unless he consciously rejects it either on the grounds of the probable mendacity of its source or on the ground of a conflict with his existing beliefs. But since he cannot fail to know that he has consciously rejected it, if he has, it follows that he cannot fail to know that he believes it, if he has considered it and has not consciously rejected it. Hence in denying that he believes a proposition that he has not consciously rejected, he necessarily knows that he does in fact believe the proposition in question, in which case he is lying in denying that he believes it.

On the other hand, the account I have given does appear at first sight to allow that someone might either believe or not believe a proposition and yet not know that he believes it or does not believe it, provided that the proposition in question is one that he has not yet asserted or considered (since if he has not either asserted or considered it, he would not have any grounds for knowing whether or not he believed it). His situation would be like that of the woman who said she would not know what she thought about the question at issue until she heard what she had to say about it.

However, the implication in the case of the woman who did not know what she believed until she heard herself speak is that she has not yet made up her mind on the issue and only does so as she speaks. In other words, she does not yet either believe or not believe the propositions she will come to believe when she asserts them. But the case we are considering is one in which someone already believes something but does not know that he believes it because he has not yet asserted or considered it. The existence of such a case is in fact ruled out on the account of belief that I have suggested, since the only way in which an individual can acquire a disposition either to act or not to act on a proposition is as a result of hearing or reading and thereby understanding the proposition in question. If he has never asserted or considered it, he cannot have heard, read, or understood it and cannot, therefore, have a disposition to act on it; and if he does not have a disposition to act on it he cannot be said to believe it.

These considerations do not rule out the possibility that someone who has never in fact considered a given proposition or, if he has, has rejected it, might nevertheless be disposed to act *as if* he believed the proposition in question. For example, someone who suffers from an irrational phobia for cats is disposed to act as if he believes the proposition 'Cats are dangerous,' although he would quite properly deny believing this proposition. In such a case, his disposition to behave in this way does not proceed from his acceptance of the proposition he denies believing. It is an irrational impulse that exists independently of and despite his beliefs. Nevertheless, although the cat phobic can quite properly claim not to believe the proposition "Cats are dangerous," since he is not in fact disposed to assert this proposition, he cannot claim that he believes the contrary proposition "Cats are not dangerous." For on the view I am defending, to believe that cats are not dangerous entails being disposed not only to assert that they are not, as the cat phobic usually is, but also being disposed to act on this proposition, which the cat phobic is manifestly not disposed to do.

Thus we cannot say of the cat phobic either that he believes that cats are dangerous or that he believes that they are not. The trouble is that he does not behave like the man who cannot make up his mind whether to believe p or not-p and hence does not believe either. The phobic behaves like a man who *has* made up his mind and has made up his mind that cats are dangerous. Consequently, both the phobic himself and those who observe his behavior find themselves in some conceptual perplexity when they attempt to characterize his state of mind. Going on his behavior, we are inclined to say in spite of his protestation to the contrary that he shows quite unambiguously that he believes cats to be dangerous. But if he really believes that cats are dangerous, then his denial that he believes they are dangerous must be false and he must either be lying or be mistaken. Yet in such cases it is usually quite evident not only that the phobic is perfectly sincere in denying that he believes cats are dangerous but also that he is in no way deceived as to the character of his own mental and behavioral dispositions.

The truth is that in denying that he believes cats to be dangerous, he is not denying for one moment that he has an overpowering disposition to act as if they were. All he is denying is that this disposition proceeds from an acceptance of the proposition "Cats are dangerous." It is true that his acceptance of this proposition at some time in the past may have contributed to his present disposition to avoid cats. But if so, it is equally true that it is no longer sustained by any such acceptance. This is shown by the fact that however often he may rehearse to himself the contrary proposition "Cats are not dangerous," together with all the arguments and evidence that can be adduced for this proposition and against the proposition "Cats are dangerous," he cannot induce in himself a disposition to act on the proposition "Cats are not dangerous" in the face of the overwhelming irrational impulse to act as if they were.

Thus the case of the irrational phobia is not an example of someone who is mistaken in his assessment of his own beliefs; it is an example of someone in whom there is a disturbance of the normal and "rational" relationship between what a man asserts and the way he behaves, that is implied by the concept of belief.

If this account, or something like it, is correct, it is apparent that no definitive answer can be given in the present state of knowledge to the question, "Is the necessity that makes it impossible to avoid knowing that we believe a proposition, if we do, or that we do not believe it, if we do not, a logical necessity or a contingent psychological necessity?" If it turns out, as it may, that it is logically impossible to conceive of a language learning process that does not involve the initial acquisition of the tendency to accept at its face value as a basis for action any proposition that is understood, we should then, I suggest, be perfectly justified in regarding the necessity as logical. If, on the other hand, this turns out to be a purely accidental feature of the way human beings are constructed, we might accept it as a contingent psychological necessity. But in either case, the story that has to be told is too complicated for any short answer to have much value.

Thirty Years On—
Is Consciousness Still
a Brain Process?

Thirty years ago a paper of mine titled "Is consciousness a brain process?" was published in the *British Journal of Psychology* (Place, 1956). This paper together with Herbert Feigl's paper "The 'Mental' and the 'Physical,'" which appeared in volume 2 of the *Minnesota Studies in the Philosophy of Science* (Feigl, 1958), and Jack Smart's paper "Sensations and Brain Processes," which appeared in *Philosophical Review* (Smart, 1959), are generally held to be the three primary sources in recent philosophical literature for the materialist or identity view of the mind-brain relationship. There is therefore some justice in the claim that these three, and my own in particular as the first to be published, may be regarded as ancestral to the materialism that has become a widely accepted establishment view in contemporary philosophy, particularly in the United States. These days whenever the broadcasting media in the United Kingdom do a feature on the mind-body problem, it is a virtual certainty that it will be a philosopher, such as Dan Dennett or John Searle, who presents the materialist position. The only thoroughgoing dualist they seem to be able to find is the brain physiologist Sir John Eccles, with the psychologist, if there is one, sitting as usual on the fence. Truly a remarkable transformation from the situation that existed thirty years ago, when every philosopher you met was quite convinced that whatever answer to the mind-body problem, if there is one, is true, materialism must be false.

Contemporary philosophical materialism, however, is a horse of a very different color from the thesis I was arguing for in my 1956 paper. Two striking differences stand out. In the first place, the thesis I was arguing for was restricted in its application to mental events—to sensations, mental images, and thought occurrences and the associated activities of thinking, imagining, and paying attention in as far as they are covert or hidden from the view or hearing of another person. Mental states, I assumed following Ryle (1949), are dispositions—either capacities, analogous to a car's horsepower, or tendencies, like the car's tendency to understeer, that are causally dependent on features of the car's internal structure but are not the same thing as those internal features in the way that the explosion in the car's exhaust pipe is the same event as that which we hear when it backfires. Contemporary materialists by contrast have followed David Armstrong (1968) in his book *A Materialist Theory of the Mind* in holding that mental states in general and propositional attitudes in particular are identical with the unknown features of the brain microstructure on which, on my view, they are causally dependent. The only exception here is John Searle, who in both his 1983 book (Searle, 1983, pp. 264–271) and his 1984 Reith Lectures (Searle, 1984, pp. 20–23) claims to hold both of these, in my view, incompatible theories simultaneously. According to Searle, mental states are identical with and causally dependent upon the corresponding states of the brain. I say you can't have your cake and eat it. Either mental states are identical with brain states or one is causally dependent on the other. They can't be both.

One of the consequences of extending the identity theory from its original restriction to mental events so as to cover mental states is that whereas it is not too difficult to suggest what sort of a brain event something like a sensation or a mental image might be supposed to consist in, if you try to imagine what sort of a brain state something like my belief that it's going to rain tomorrow might be supposed to consist in, the mind quickly begins to boggle. We are confronted with the apparently insoluble philosophical problem of how the intentionality that is a prominent feature of mental states can possibly be construed as a property of the brain microstructure. As I see it, this problem is neatly sidestepped on the view that I hold by showing (1) that there are a number of mental event verbs, like 'paying attention to', 'watching', 'looking at', 'listening to', 'savoring', etc., that do not display this feature, and (2) that whenever the grammatical object of a mental event verb *is* intentional, it turns out that the intentionality is invariably attributable to a mental state or disposition that is involved in the mental event rather than to the mental event as such. Thus wherever a mental event is characterized by reference to an intentional object, the intentional object turns out to be one of the following: (a) a simile used to indicate the way the individual is inclined to characterize an experience, as in the case where a pain is characterized by reference to the part of the body from which it appears to emanate, (b) the objective of a disposition with which a mental activity is performed, as in the case of 'looking for something', or (c) an embedded sentence that characterizes the belief, intention, or other disposition brought into being by a mental event, as when a decision is characterized by reference to the intention to do something in which it results.

If to this is added the demonstration by John Burnheim[1] and more recently by C. B. Martin and Karl Pfeifer (1986) that physical dispositions and their descriptions bear all the marks of intentionality mentioned by such philosophers as Elizabeth Anscombe (1965),[2] Roderick Chisholm (1957) and Bill Lycan (1969),[3] we reach the conclusion that intentionality is the mark, not, as Brentano thought, of the mental but of the dispositional.[4] Combine this with Ryle's thesis that dispositional statements are concealed hypotheticals—which I still think, despite the criticisms of Peter Geach (1957) in *Mental Acts* and Armstrong in his 1968 book, is a tenable view—and the vexed problem of intentionality becomes a problem about the role of dispositional statements in causal judgments, not in any way specific to the mind-body problem.

I do not expect this way of sidestepping the problem of intentionality to recommend itself to philosophers any more than my contention that the thesis that consciousness is a brain process is an empirical scientific hypothesis recommended itself to philosophers in the 1950s and 1960s, even those like Smart who were in general well disposed toward the materialist position. The reason for this is that my objective in putting forward the thesis in the first place was and is diametrically opposed to the interests of philosophers in this matter. For what I was trying to do was to clear away the tangle of philosophical objections which, as I saw it, were impeding empirical research in neurophysiology and physiological psychology aimed at discovering the physical nature of consciousness and its location within the brain. This objective requires the effective liquidation of the mind-body problem as a philosophical issue so that it can be handed over as an empirical issue to be resolved by the neuroscientist. Needless to say, philosophers have a vested interest in precisely the opposite objective of keeping the mind-body problem as a live philosophical issue.

It is this need to retain the mind-body problem as a live philosophical issue and to preserve the status of the philosopher as the relevant expert in such matters that, in my view, explains the remarkable turnaround in philosophical attitudes to materialism, which can be dated rather precisely to the publication of Armstrong's book in 1968. Before 1968, virtually all the philosophical literature on the identity theory was hostile; after 1968 more and more philosophers began to climb onto the materialist bandwagon. For once the identity thesis is extended from the identity of mental events with brain events to the identity of mental states with brain states, the insoluble philosophical problem of explaining how a propositional attitude could possibly be construed as a state of the brain allows the philosopher to adopt the materialist position without losing his status as the relevant expert in matters of intentionality and its representation in the brain. It is in this light that I read such bizarre theories as Davidson's Anomalous Monism (Davidson, 1970), Dennett's account of brain functioning in terms of the combined effects of the decisions of a committee of homunculi (Dennett, 1978), and Fodor's innately preprogrammed language of thought (Fodor, 1975).

But the aspect of this revolution in philosophical attitudes that I want to focus upon relates to the other major respect in which contemporary philosophical materialism differs from the materialism I was advocating in 1956. As I have already mentioned, in the 1956 paper and my reply to Jack Smart's paper (Place, 1960) my contention was that materialism as applied to mental events is a reasonable scientific hypothesis, which cannot be ruled out of court by a priori philosophical argument. Not only was that the only part of the thesis of my 1956 paper that Smart criticized in his 1959 paper; it is also one of the features of the original thesis that is conspicuously missing from contemporary philosophical versions of materialism. Contemporary philosophical materialists are inclined to treat the empirical evidence of mental-cerebral correlation as irrelevant to the issues with which they are concerned and seek to demonstrate the truth of materialism by means of a purely a priori argument of which Davidson's argument for his principle of anomalous monism is a prime example.

Although its a priori character and the effect of its conclusion (that there are no psychophysical bridge laws), in nullifying any empirical evidence of psychophysical correlation is clear enough, the argument itself is notoriously difficult to state. As I read it, it divides into two parts of which only the second is at all explicitly stated. Part 1 goes roughly as follows:

1. Every human action has one or more propositional attitudes as its immediate cause.
2. Every human action has a brain state as its immediate cause.
3. Events cannot have more than one immediate cause.

ERGO

4. The set of propositional attitudes that constitute the immediate cause of a particular human action is identical with the brain state that constitutes the immediate cause of that action.

Part 2 then proceeds as follows:

5. All causation presupposes a universally quantified causal law relating events or states of the cause type to states or events of the effect type.
6. No such universally quantified causal law can be stated relating propositional attitudes to the action types they cause.
7. Universally quantified causal laws can, however, be stated relating brain states and events to the action types they cause.

ERGO

8. No universally quantified law statement can be true that relates particular brain states with which they are (by 4 above) identical. In other words, there are no psychophysical bridge laws.

I accept that both these arguments are valid. I am also myself committed, as I shall explain later, to a version of the argument in part 1, though with mental events rather than propositional attitudes or mental states as its subject matter. However I reject both conclusions, in each case because I reject one of the premises from which it is deduced. In the case of part 1, I reject conclusion 4 because I reject premise 3; and I reject premise 3 because, on my view, the brain state that causes an action is an indirect rather than an immediate cause of the action it leads to. The immediate cause is the propositional attitude or mental state, and that state is causally dependent on, not identical with, the state of the brain, the microstructure.

In the case of part 2, I reject conclusion 8 partly because I reject the prior conclusion 4 which asserts the identity of the propositional attitude and the brain state on which, in my view, it depends, but partly also because I reject proposition 6. The reason for this is that I hold that a propositional attitude statement or indeed *any* dispositional statement is itself a universally quantified causal law in the sense that is required for the truth of proposition 5. All that a causal judgment requires, in my view, is a statement that is universally quantified over events or states of the types to which the causal judgment relates. It matters not if the events in question are restricted to the behavior of a particular individual or to the limited window of the time constituted by the duration of the particular disposition in question.

In other words, dispositional statements of which propositional attitude statements are a subvariety are statements of the form, "If at any time between $t1$ and tn causal condition $c1$ combines with causal conditions $c2$ . . . cn, an event of the e type will occur." A statement of this form is all that is required to deduce the counterfactual "if at any time between $t1$ and tn the causal conditions $c1$ . . . cn had been fulfilled, an event of the e type would have occurred" which following John Mackie (1962), I take to be what is meant by saying that the conditions $c1$ . . . cn are causally effective relative to events of the e type.

I want to emphasize this analysis of causal judgments not only because of its relevance for my rejection of Davidson's a priori argument for anomalous monism, but also because, as we shall see, it plays a crucial role in the argument to which I propose to devote the remainder of this paper. This argument is in effect my third and I hope finally successful attempt to rebut the objection that Jack Smart (1959) raised to my contention that materialism is an empirical scientific hypothesis whose truth or falsity will ultimately be demonstrated one way or the other by the empirical evidence of neurological and psychophysiological research.

As those who have read Smart's paper will remember, the argument (Smart, 1959, pp. 155–156) runs roughly as follows. Smart begins by conceding that the issue as to whether consciousness is to be located in the heart, the liver, the brain, or in some other organ of the body is an empirical issue. That issue he takes to have already been conclusively decided in favor of the brain. But the real issue is not the issue between the liver thesis, the heart thesis, and the brain thesis; it is the issue between the view that mental events are identical with some as yet unspecified physical events whether in the brain, heart, liver, or elsewhere and the view that they are mere epiphenomena or causally ineffective byproducts of the physical events with which they are correlated. With respect to *that* issue, he maintains, any evidence that is consistent with the identity thesis will also be consistent with epiphenomenalism. No crucial experiment is conceivable that would enable us to decide the issue between the two theories. The situation is compared with the issue between the explanation of the fossil record in terms of the theory of evolution and the explanation of the fossil record in terms of Gosse's theory according to which the fossil record was laid down by the Creator at the creation of the universe in 4004 BC in order to test the faith of nineteenth-century Christians. In such cases, Smart maintains, there is and can be no decisive empirical evidence either way. The only thing we can do is appeal to the principle of Ockham's razor to eliminate the more complex and ontologically less economical hypothesis in favor of the simpler and ontologically more economical one.

When I replied to this objection in my 1960 paper, I conceded that the crucial issue with respect to the truth of the mind-brain identity thesis is whether or not the thesis makes sense, not whether or not it will be supported by the empirical evidence. To concede this, I now think, was to concede the substance of Smart's objection and thus allow the focus of discussion to be steered away from the empirical evidence and toward the purely philosophical issues. Over the years, as the debate has developed, I have come increasingly to think that this was a false move; and it was in this spirit that I returned to the issue in a paper titled "Twenty years on—Is consciousness still a brain process?" which I read at University College, London, and at the University of Glasgow during the course of 1976 and which was eventually published (Place, 1977) in a journal now, I believe, defunct, called *Open Mind*, published by the Open University.

Perhaps the best way to give you the flavor of this second attempt to reply to Smart's objection is to quote the opening paragraphs of the paper as it was published in 1977:

Since the discovery of the electroencephalogram by Hans Berger in 1929 we now know beyond all reasonable doubt what had long been suspected, namely: that whenever a human being engages in some kind of mental activity such as performing an arithmetical calculation in his head, or simply paying attention to sensory stimulation in one or other of the sensory modalities, there is a corresponding change in the pattern of neural activity in his brain. And although we are still a long way from the stage of being able to read a man's private thoughts from a study of the electrical activity in his brain, the complexity and variety of the patterns of electrical activity revealed by the electroencephalogram are more than sufficient to justify the belief that all the complexity and variety of the thought processes and conscious experiences of an individual human being are exactly and completely reflected in the complexity and variety of the concurrent brain activity. More recently, the development of computer technology and the theory of artificial intelligence has made it possible to explain how the brain might be supposed to carry out virtually all those operations traditionally attributed to the mind. At the same time neurological evidence of the way in which behaviour and intellectual performance depend on the integrity and proper functioning of the brain as a whole and its constituent parts has shown beyond all reasonable doubt that intellectual performance and behaviour are generated and controlled by the brain not merely, as Descartes supposed, at the level of tactical execution, but at the level of strategic decision also.

Faced with evidence such as this, it is no longer possible to hold with Descartes that when a man thinks, there are two quite distinct processes taking place, namely, a mental process which strictly speaking has no extension or position in physical space and which constitutes the thought process as it appears in the consciousness of the individual in question, and a concomitant physical process located in his brain whose function is merely to provide the separate mental process with information from the sense organs about the current state of the environment and organise the execution of the appropriate movements of the body when the mental process has reached the point of deciding what to do. (Place, 1977, p. 3)

Considered as a reply to Smart's objection this argument is suggesting that while the issue between the identity theory and epiphenomenalism may be empirically undecidable, as Smart claims, there is another issue—namely, the issue between the identity theory and Cartesian dualist interactionism—that *is* empirically decidable and is in process of being decided in favor of the identity view. What the evidence shows is that whenever a mental process occurs, there occurs a corresponding brain process that has the same degree of complexity as the mental process reported by the subject, has all the causal properties required to generate the behavior that the mental process is supposed to generate, and whose occurrence is a causally necessary condition for the occurrence of that behavior.

However, this evidence can be used to demonstrate the falsity of dualist interactionism only if there is an a priori principle that can be invoked in order to exclude the possibility of two simultaneous parallel processes, one a mental process and the other a brain process, both contributing to the causation of the ultimate behavioral output. Intuitively this seems right; and certainly the adoption of psychophysical parallelism and epiphenomenalism, both of which seek to protect dualism by denying the existence of a causal connection between mental events and their apparent behavioral outcome, seems to suggest that this intuition is widely shared by philosophers who have thought about this matter since the days of Descartes. Nevertheless, intuition, however widely shared, is no substitute for solid argument. In my 1977 paper I tried to deal with the problem by invoking Davidson's (1969) principle whereby an event is individuated by the unique position it occupies relative to its causes on the one hand and its effects on the other. As I pointed out in that paper,

It follows from this principle that you cannot have two events or processes with the same causal antecedents and the same consequences or effects. Now as we have seen, the empirical evidence shows that whenever a mental process occurs there also occurs a brain process which has exactly the same causal antecedents and the same consequences or effects as the mental process appears to have. But since by Davidson's principle only one process can have *that* particular set of causal antecedents and consequences, we are compelled to conclude either that the mental process and the brain process are one and the same process or if, as most philosophers have held, they are two different processes, then one of these processes cannot in fact have the causal antecedents and consequences that it appears to have. (Place, 1977, p. 3)

Unfortunately, as my colleague Roger White (personal communication) has since convinced me, this principle of Davidson's cannot be sustained. White's objection is essentially Hume's (1978) point[5] that the causal relation is a relation between two discrete events or states such that whatever happens in practice it must always be conceivable that the cause event or state might occur or be the case without the effects event or state being the case. It follows that events or states that are causally related must be individuated by something other than the causal relation into which they enter.

There is, however, another argument that can, I believe, be used to show that the causes of an event cannot include more than one event. Every event comes about, and every state of affairs is maintained, by a number of causal factors. The set of causal factors that contribute to the coming about of an event or to the maintenance of a state of affairs in a particular case is said to be *sufficient* for the occurrence of that event or the maintenance of that state of affairs. This means that whenever all the causal factors in question are present, an event of the same type will occur or a state of affairs of the same type will persist; whereas if any one of those factors is missing, the event will not occur and the state of affairs, will not be maintained. In a case where the effect is a state of affairs, all the causal factors that maintain that state of affairs will themselves be states of affairs. Moreover, in a case where the effect is an event, all the causal factors except one will likewise be states of affairs that are in position, as it were, for a longer or shorter period of time prior to the coming about of the effect. There will be one and only one triggering event that completes the set of causal factors jointly sufficient for the coming about of the effect that will begin *immediately* after the triggering event occurs.

Now if this is correct, it follows in the case we are considering that when a human agent does something or says something as an apparent end result of a mental process, if, as we have good empirical evidence for thinking it is, every mental process is invariably accompanied by a causally effective brain process, it cannot be the case that the conclusion of *both* of the two distinct processes assumed to be operating here acts as a triggering event with respect to the initiation of the agent's action or utterance. And given the empirical evidence for the causal efficacy of the brain process in such case, we have to conclude, I suggest, that either the two processes are one and the same or that the mental process is causally impotent and, hence, epiphenomenal with respect to the agent's action or utterance.

It is true that there are two counterexamples that have been suggested to me in which two events can be said to jointly trigger a single effect, though neither of them, it seems to me, offers a viable way out of the dilemma I have just described. The first is the case where two events that act in opposite directions on the same object or substance occur simultaneously. For example,[6] suppose you have a balance with the weight equally distributed between the two arms, and two weights, which may be equal or different, fall simultaneously onto the two arms. The net effect will clearly be different from what it would have been if only one of the two weights had fallen onto one of the two arms. Here, it may be argued, we have an example of an event that is brought about by two separate triggering events.

Now you might say that since the two events have to be simultaneous, this is not really two discrete triggering events but rather a single triggering event clearly different from the triggering events constituted by the two weights falling separately. But, be that as it may, this example is evidently not going to provide a useful analogy for the case of mental processes and brain processes, since in the case of the balance the simultaneity of the falling of the two weights is purely fortuitous; whereas it could hardly be maintained that the coincidence of the conclusion of the mental process with that of the corresponding brain process is a matter of coincidence. A much better analogy for what is envisaged by the dualist interactionist is provided by the backup computer or computers that are installed in spacecraft (and, I believe, now in some aircraft), which perform the same calculations as the main computer and are used both as a check on the calculations of the main computer and as a substitute in the event of the main computer breaking down. The case in which the ultimate output of the system is determined on the basis of the outputs of both computers in the case where there are only two would then be the analogy for the version of dualist interactionism in which both the mental process and the correlated brain process contribute to the ultimate effect.

This conception of the mental process as a kind of backup computer providing a check on the calculations made by the main computer in the brain is not a view that is likely to satisfy either the dualist or the biologist. For the dualist it fails to give the mental process its unique and indispensable role in the control of behavior; for the biologist it is difficult to see why we should be required to postulate an extraphysical mental process simply to act as a backup to the brain activity, especially when we know that there is ample spare capacity in the human brain, if such backup computational facilities were needed.

But on this model, even if we grant that the mental process makes a causal contribution to the final outcome that is distinguishable from the one made by a parallel brain process, in the case where the two calculations disagree, the final decision as to which of the two is to determine what the individual finally says or does has to be made by the brain. For, as we have seen, the empirical evidence rehearsed above shows that the brain process is both sufficient and necessary for the production of the verbal or behavioral output. Consequently, in a case where there can be only one event occupying a particular position in a causal chain, the empirical evidence points fairly decisively to that position being occupied by an event in the brain. But if the final decision as to what to say or do is taken in the brain, it must be the case that if dualism is true the sense we have that our thoughts and feelings determine what we say and do has to be an illusion. Even if we interpret our thought processes as playing an essential backup role in relation to the main computer in the brain, qua mental process, the final decision on what to say and do has to be ephiphenomenal; and this, it may be thought, brings us right back to Smart's contention in his 1959 paper to the effect that, whatever may be true of the issue between interactionism and the identity theory, the issue between the identity theory and epiphenomenalism is not empirically decidable.

In my 1977 paper I tried to dismiss both epiphenomenalism and psychophysical parallelism by means of the following argument:

> Not only do both these theories conflict with the intuitions of commonsense, in that they both deny that our thought processes and sensations have any effect on the way we behave; they also have the character of those gratuitous *ad hoc* assumptions calculated to protect a theory from any possible falsification by the empirical evidence which, as Karl Popper has repeatedly argued, are unacceptable in a genuine scientific theory. (Place, 1977, p. 4)

While I would not want to retract any part of that argument now, there is, it seems to me, another and more decisive argument against psychophysical parallelism and epiphenomenalism as tenable versions of dualism. This is the argument that if either of these theories were true, there can be no causal connection between a mental event and the description that is purportedly given of that mental event in the subject's introspective report. But if the occurrence of an event is not a causal factor in the giving of the description that purports to be given of that event, it cannot be a genuine description of the event in question. Consequently there is no way, consistent with either epiphenomenalism or psychophysical parallelism, whereby we can use the introspective reports of other people as evidence of the nature of their mental processes or have any reason for believing in the existence of such processes in the case of others. While there are some, no doubt, who think that solipsism is the only consistent form of mentalism, it is hardly a strong position from which to argue for any thesis with the object of convincing another mind of its truth. I conclude, therefore, as I concluded in the 1977 paper

> that the hypothesis that mental processes are the same processes as the brain processes concurrent with them is the only hypothesis which is consistent with the empirical evidence, with our commonsense belief that how and what we think and feel affects what we say and do and with the proprieties of scientific method. (Place, 1977, p. 4)

It will be noted that, insofar as these arguments depend on the principle that there can only be one triggering event relative to another event as effect, they only have application to a mind-brain identity thesis that is restricted to the relation between mental events and brain events. But, since that is precisely the version of the thesis to which I have consistently subscribed for the past thirty-two years, this is no skin off my nose. I suspect, however that there is an alternative replacement for the Davidsonian principle whereby events are individuated by the unique position they occupy in a causal nexus that would enable an Armstrongian to benefit from this line of argument. For it appears to be a plausible metaphysical principle that the only properties that are predicable of events and states of affairs are properties of a causal and temporal kind. The suggestion would be that any spatial properties are predicable only of the substances involved in the event or state of affairs, as illustrated by the example of the telephone conversation between the UK and Australia that cannot be plausibly located in either place or anywhere in between.[7] If this is correct, we could then go on to argue that if two states or events involve the same individual substances, have the same onset and duration in time and have the same causes and effects, since there are no other respects in which they can differ, they must, by Leibniz's principle of the identity of indiscernibles, be one and the same state or event, as the case may be.

If I am not mistaken, what this line of argument shows is that the doctrine of the impotence of consciousness to which both epiphenomenalism and psychophysical parallelism are committed is not just contrary to the intuitions of common sense and to the requirement that a scientific theory be in principle susceptible to falsification; it renders both theories totally incoherent by depriving them of any explanation of how there could be such a thing as an individual's self-report of his or her own mental processes or mental states. But if psychophysical parallelism and epiphenomenalism are incoherent, and if, as I am inclined to think, the dual-aspect theory collapses into the identity theory, we are left, assuming that idealism is not a viable option for scientific purposes, with the choice between dualist interactionism and the identity theory. And *that*, if I am right, is an empirical issue that is in process of being decided by an increasingly formidable body of empirical evidence in favor of the identity theory.

Token- versus Type-Identity
Physicalism

In order to think clearly in philosophy one must constantly bear in mind the distinction between talking *de re* about the things themselves and talking *de dicto* about the language we use to talk about them. Thinking in terms of the symbolism of formal logic can often lead us astray in this respect. An example where formal logic leads us to treat what is really *de re* as *de dicto* is the widespread assumption that all conditionals including causal counterfactuals are to be analyzed according to the formula 'If *p* then *q*.' The effect of this is to convert what is in fact a specification of the *de re* conditions governing the occurrence of an event or the existence of a state of affairs into what Ryle (1949) calls an "inference licence" or "inference ticket" that talks *de dicto* about the conditions under which one statement or proposition *q* can be inferred, namely, if another statement or proposition *p* is true.[1]

Another case where formal symbolism leads us astray but in the opposite direction is to be found in Lynne Rudder Baker's (1997) paper "Why constitution is not identity." Baker takes it as axiomatic that an identity relation is one that conforms to the formula '$a = a$' and concludes quite rightly that by this criterion the relation between an entity and its constitution, of which the proposed identity relation between consciousness and the brain process or complex of brain processes in which it consists, is a prime example.

Identity Statements Are Metalinguistic

The reason for this is that a statement that conforms to the formula '$a = a$' is a *de re* statement about the number of items in two groups, whereas a statement asserting the identity of an object or process with its constitution or makeup is a *de dicto* statement that asserts that two descriptions differing in sense (Frege, 1892, *Sinn*) nevertheless refer to (Frege's *bedeuten*) the same object. Suppose I have four and only four coins in my left-hand trouser pocket and four and only four coins in my right-hand trouser pocket. In this case the number of coins in both pockets is the same. The formula '$a = a$' is satisfied. But that equality is not identity. It is numerical equality.

"His Table Is an Old Packing Case" as a de dicto Identity Statement

Though I didn't call it that (I spoke, having at that time read no Frege, of "the 'is' of composition"), I gave as an example of what I have since come to recognize as a true identity relation, the case where a man's table is in fact nothing more than an old packing case (Place, 1956, pp. 45–46). It should be evident that in this case what we have are two descriptions that differ in sense but which refer to one and the same object. Describing an object as a table describes its function, as something that one can write on and eat off. Describing something as a packing case mentions its former and intended function; but in the present context it indicates that the object is one that, if the case is large enough and strong enough, allows it to be used as a table when inverted. Here there is nothing that satisfies the formula '$a = a$.' On the other hand the example exactly parallels the example of the Morning Star and the Evening Star, which Frege (1892) uses to introduce the sense (*Sinn*) and reference (*Bedeutung*) distinction.

The Token- /Type-Identity Distinction

This brings us to the main topic of this paper, the distinction between token- and type identity. For both "His table is an old packing case" and "The Morning Star is the same object as the Evening Star" are cases of token identity, cases where two descriptions with different senses *just happen* to apply to one and the same particular object. Such cases are extremely common. Indeed any nonanalytic proposition that asserts the coapplication of two conceptually unconnected predicates of the same object is of this kind. But so are all those that apply in the case of an aggregated collection of objects, such as the coins in my pocket which all happen to be copper. But the target case, in my paper the claim that consciousness is a process in the brain, is not like this. Hence we have two *types* of thing, consciousness and a certain as yet unspecified *type* of brain activity, which *don't just happen* to satisfy two descriptions but are such that the features that lead us to apply the one description also leads us to apply the other, and where the absence of the same features would in all cases lead us to withdraw both. This, in other words, is a typical case of type- rather than token identity. But whereas the typical token-identity statement, "His table is an old packing case," if true, is contingent and synthetic, the typical type-identity statement of which "Water is H_2O" is a paradigm case is necessary and analytic. Why should this be?

Explaining Why Type Identities Are Typically Analytic

Though I didn't then speak of the 'is' in "Is consciousness a brain process?" as an 'is' of identity, while the terms 'token-' and 'type identity' had not then been introduced, I did attempt to answer this question in the passage in my 1956 paper with the introduction of the "His table is an old packing case" example. However, in its original form this passage is not at all clearly expressed. I had an opportunity recently to correct this deficiency in an as yet unpublished paper I presented at a one-day conference celebrating forty years of Australian Materialism, held at the University of Leeds in June 1997. Fortunately the revisions I proposed in that paper have since been incorporated in the version of the 1956 paper that appears in the second and in other respects, much revised edition of W. G. Lycan's *Mind and Cognition* (1999). In its revised form the passage in question now reads as follows:

> There is . . . an important difference between the table/packing case and the consciousness/brain process case in that the statement "his table is an old packing case" is a particular proposition which refers only to one particular case, whereas the statement "consciousness is a process in the brain" is a general or universal proposition applying to all states of consciousness whatever. It is fairly clear, I think, that if we lived in a world in which all tables without exception were packing cases, the concepts of "table" and "packing case" in our language would not have their present logically independent status. In such a world a table would be a species of packing case in much the same way that red is a species of color. It seems to be a rule of language that *whenever it becomes generally accepted that every member of a class of objects or states of affairs which is identified by its possessing one characteristic also possesses another characteristic which is identified in a way that is logically independent from the way the first characteristic is identified, a statement asserting the inherence in an object or state of affairs of the first characteristic will come to entail a statement asserting the inherence in that object or state of affairs of the second characteristic.* If this rule admitted of no exception it would follow *from the fact that it is not self-contradictory to imagine the existence of an object or state of affairs which possesses the one characteristic without possessing the other that it is empirically possible for the two characteristics to occur independently.* It is because this rule applies almost universally, I suggest, that we are normally justified in arguing from the logical independence of two expressions to the ontological independence of the states of affairs to which they refer. This would explain both the undoubted force of the argument that consciousness and brain processes must be independent entities because the expressions used to refer to them are logically independent and, in general, the curious phenomenon whereby questions about the furniture of the universe are often fought and not infrequently decided merely on a point of logic. (Place 1956, p. 46; Lycan 1999, pp. 15–16—changed wording in italics)

Stated in terms of the token- /type-identity distinction, what I am claiming in this passage is that, whereas token-identity statements are typically synthetic and, if true, contingently so, type-identity statements are typically analytic and, in so far as their denial is self-contradictory, necessarily true. The reason for this is that in the case of predicates that are coextensive, or where the extension of the one in-cludes the extension of the other, a conceptual connection develops between the two. The only exceptions to this rule are cases where the extensional equivalence or overlap is not a matter of common observation, where the observations on the basis of which the predicates are assigned are widely separated in time and space.

One such case is the case where the predicates water and H_2O are found to be coextensive. Here the observations on the basis of which we describe a sample as a case of water and the observations on the basis of which we describe it as H_2O are widely separated. Nevertheless, the fact that the predicates have the same ex-tension (given one or two qualifications such as the inclusion of ice and steam in the concept of water) is so well established and so widely known that "Water is H_2O" has become an analytic statement and, by the criterion of what it is self-contradictory to deny, a necessary truth. That this conceptual connection has de-veloped is shown by the observation that in cases of doubt a chemical test show-ing that a sample has the chemical composition H_2O takes precedence over all other criteria in showing that it is in fact water.

A similar outcome is to be expected in the case of consciousness and the par-ticular pattern of brain activity, yet to be identified, in which presumably it con-sists. As things stand, the existence of such a pattern of brain activity is, as I ar-gued in 1956, a hypothesis that will be confirmed or disconfirmed by future neuropsychological research. If, as seems increasingly probable, such research establishes both the existence and the nature of the pattern of brain activity in which consciousness consists, and these results become widely known, the de-velopment of a similar analytic and necessary connection between the two is to be expected.

The Token-Type Distinction in Anomalous Monism

It goes almost without saying that this is a very different account of the semantic relation involved in type-identity statements such as "Water is H_2O" from the ac-count in terms of the concept of rigid designation given by Kripke (1972) and Putnam (1987). It also implies a very different approach to the issue between token- and type-identity physicalism from that represented by Donald Davidson's (1970) "anomalous monism." Anomalous monism or token-identity physicalism has two features in common with what, if you will forgive me, I shall refer to henceforth as the "classical theory," the theory I presented in my 1956 paper. They both in their different ways emphasize the token- /type-identity distinction, and they are both reductionist theories, in the sense that they both collapse all mental states and processes into either brain states or brain processes, or in the case of the classical theory into dispositions to talk and behave in a variety of overt and covert ways. There, however, the similarity ends.

Perhaps the most fundamental difference between anomalous monism and the classical theory concerns the assumption Davidson takes for granted "that there is a categorical difference between the mental and the physical" (Davidson, 1980,

p. 223). This the classical theory denies. On this view the mental is what Wittgenstein (1953) calls a "family resemblance concept." There is no one feature that marks off all mental things from all nonmental or, if you insist, 'physical' things. All the important categorical distinctions—those between processes, instantaneous events and dispositional states, between properties and relations—are found on both sides of the mental/physical divide.[2] This is not stated in so many words. But it is implicit (a) in the endorsement of the analysis of "cognitive concepts like 'knowing', 'believing', 'understanding', 'remembering', and volitional concepts like 'wanting' and 'intending' . . . in terms of dispositions to behave" (Place, 1956, p. 44), (b) in the consequent restriction of the identity theory to the "intractable residue of concepts clustering around the notions of consciousness, experience, sensation and mental imagery, where some sort of inner process story is unavoidable" (Place, 1956, p. 44), and (c) in the use of a series of nonmental examples, from "His table is an old packing case" through "The cloud [is] a mass of droplets or other particles in suspension" to "Lightning is a motion of electric charges" (Place, 1956, pp. 46–47), to illustrate the kind of relation postulated between consciousness and the brain process with which it will be found to correlate.

Propositional Attitudes and the Oratio Obliqua

It is ironic that in characterizing mental verbs—the nearest Davidson comes to giving an account of what he thinks distinguishes the mental from the physical—he claims that "we may call those verbs mental that express propositional attitudes" (Davidson, 1980, p. 210) and then proceeds to give a list of examples that coincides almost exactly with those that the classical theory excludes from the scope of the identity theory on the grounds that in these cases "an analysis in terms of dispositions to behave (Wittgenstein, 1953; Ryle, 1949) is fundamentally sound" (Place, 1956, p. 44). Davidson, not surprisingly, rejects this behaviorist account of propositional attitudes; but he does so in a manner that shows that he has failed to grasp what a propositional attitude is and what, in his own words, "the vocabulary of propositional attitudes" amounts to.

A propositional attitude, properly so-called, is a dispositional mental state whose potential manifestations are characterized by means of an embedded declarative sentence in oratio obliqua or indirect reported speech in the position of the direct grammatical object of a mental/psychological verb. In formal notation a propositional attitude is a dispositional state characterized by means of a sentence of the form 'X Ψs *that p*,' where X is a person, Ψ is a psychological verb, and *p* is a declarative sentence in oratio obliqua.

As Peter Geach (1957, p. 9) points out in the only discussion of it that I know of in the philosophical literature, this is "the same construction as is used with 'verbs of saying' to report the gist or upshot of somebody's remark rather than the actual words he used." As used to characterize a propositional attitude it allows for the fact that someone who is disposed to make an assertion or statement of a particular kind and act accordingly will express the proposition in question in a variety of different ways on different occasions. Consequently, to use oratio recta to quote a particular sentence the individual might have used on a particular occasion would be to misrepresent the essentially open-ended character of this as of other dispositions. It is a striking fact that of the eight verbs mentioned by Davidson the verb 'to hope' is the only one whose grammatical object is restricted to embedded declarative sentences in oratio obliqua. All the other verbs on Davidson's list take at least one other construction as well. There is 'believe in O', 'intend to A', 'desire O', 'know O' and 'know' + an interrogative sentence introduced by an interrogative pronoun, 'notice O', 'perceive O' and 'perceive' + interrogative, 'remember O' and 'remember' + interrogative, where O is any object or person and A is any verb of action.

Although these alternative constructions do not involve an embedded *declarative* sentence and do not therefore describe a propositional attitude in the strict sense of that word, those that take an interrogative are using an embedded sentence as a way of quoting the "gist or upshot" not of a type of statement the individual is disposed to make but of a type of question he or she is in a position to answer and answer correctly. Hence the restriction of this construction to what Ryle (1949) calls "got it" verbs such as 'know', 'perceive', and 'remember'.

Furthermore, even in the cases where the grammatical object stands for an object or action, there is reason to think that the name or description by which it is identified is still a quotation of the name or description the individual in question is disposed to use when characterizing the goal toward which the disposition in question is oriented. The evidence for this is that, as in the case of the names and definite descriptions that occur within embedded oratio obliqua sentences, whether declarative or interrogative, names and descriptions that occur by themselves as the grammatical objects of such verbs are subject to the phenomenon Frege (1892) calls "indirect reference," Quine (1980) calls "referential opacity," and Geach (1968, p. 165) calls "non-Shakespearianity" (a reference to "A rose by any other name would smell as sweet"), and within these "opaque contexts," as Quine calls them, is a suspension of the principle whereby any name or description that picks out the same object can be substituted for a name or description without altering the truth value of a statement, or what we may call the 'thrust' of an imperative or interrogative in which it occurs. The suspension of this principle within an opaque context is readily explained by the fact that such contexts are quotations of what someone has said or might be expected to say. For, if the alternative name or description was not available to the individual in question, to substitute it would be to misrepresent that individual's linguistic dispositions.

It is ironic that the best evidence we have that this is the correct interpretation of the phenomenon of referential opacity comes from Davidson's (1982) own paper "Rational animals" in which he shows that what would be opaque contexts, if the subject of the sentence were a linguistically competent human being, become transparent when the subject of the sentence is a linguistically incompetent animal.[3]

What this shows is that Davidson's "vocabulary of propositional attitudes" is not a vocabulary but a grammatical construction. It is the use of oratio obliqua or indirect reported speech to characterize the orientation of a disposition to talk in a particular way and act accordingly, a construction which, though extended to cover the behavioral dispositions of animals, has literal application only to those of linguistically competent humans. This can be seen as a vindication of the classical theory, which maintains that verbs taking this construction serve to characterize behavioral dispositions and do not, therefore, *require* a reduction to states of the brain, whether as types or as tokens, in order to render them consistent with a physicalist standpoint. At the same time Davidson's contention that locutions of this kind can never enter into strict psychophysical laws is also vindicated. For, if by a strict law is meant a law that asserts an invariable coincidence between the extensions of two concepts, it is evident that dispositional concepts with their necessarily open-ended intensional character, and not just those that are characterized by means of the oratio obliqua construction, have no place in such laws. This might be an embarrassment if the classical theory were committed, as are Medlin (1967)[4] and Armstrong's (1968) "central state materialism," to the view that dispositional states are type-identical with the states of the brain with which they are correlated. But since more recent versions of the classical theory (Place, 1967, p. 61; Armstrong et al., 1996, pp. 30, 109–110, 115–122) identify this as a causal relation between "distinct existences," and since, on my view, causal relations require no such strict laws,[5] this is no embarrassment for that theory.

Mind-Brain Identity—Empirical Hypothesis or A Priori Dogma?

We have seen that from the standpoint of the classical theory the importance of the token- /type-identity distinction lies in the fact that whereas token identities are typically synthetic, contingently true, if they are true and verified empirically, type identities are typically analytic, necessarily true in the sense that their denial is self-contradictory and true a priori. The focus of interest is on the conditions under which type-identity statements are synthetic, contingent, and subject to empirical verification, namely, the conditions that obtain in the case of the proposed type identity between consciousness and some as yet unspecified brain process. In such cases the fact that the two predicates invariably have the same extension remains to be demonstrated. Only when it is, and the ensuing identity statement becomes a matter of common knowledge, will it become an analytic, necessary, and a priori truth.

To this discussion anomalous monism has nothing to contribute. The analytic-synthetic distinction is not mentioned in this connection, though the Quinean character of Davidson's position suggests that he endorses Quine's (1951) repudiation of that distinction. What is clear is that he rejects on a priori grounds the possibility of formulating a true type-identity statement equating a mentally characterized entity on the one hand with a physically (neurophysiologically) characterized entity on the other. But since there is no way that a psychophysical token-identity statement could be verified by simple inspection in the way the statement that someone's table is an old packing case is verified, this effectively rules out the possibility of establishing the truth of any putative psychophysical token-identity statement by empirical means.

Davidson, nevertheless, maintains in the light of a purely a priori argument that every particular event characterized in mental language is one and the same as an event characterized in the language of neuroscience. But since no such token-identity statement can be verified empirically, we shall never know which events these are.

Davidson's A Priori Argument for Token-Identity Physicalism

It may be argued that the token-identity physicalist need not be concerned by the fact that there is no conceivable prospect of the truth of any psychophysical token-identity statement being established in the future that does not depend on the prior establishment of the truth of a psychophysical type-identity statement. For, unlike type-identity physicalism, token-identity physicalism is not committed to any prediction as to what future empirical research will reveal. It is one of those doctrines, beloved of philosophers, theologians, and the peddlers of superstition, that are rightly despised by empirical scientists in that they are so crafted as to render them immune to empirical disconfirmation (cf. Popper, 1963).

As originally formulated by Davidson (1970), the case for token-identity physicalism rests not on the outcome of future psychophysiological research but on an a priori argument.

The argument appears to take the form of the Hegelian Dialectic:[6]

1. *Thesis*
   Mental events, their causes, and their effects are not subject to the kind of law (strict and universally quantified over individuals) that physical theory aims to formulate.
2. *Antithesis*
2a. Mental events cause human actions.
2b. All causation involves the kind of law (strict and universally quantified over individuals as well as occasions) that physical theory aims to formulate.[7]

ERGO

2c. The relation between a mental event and the human action it causes is subject to the kind of law (strict and universally quantified over individuals) that physical theory aims to formulate.

BUT 1 and 2c are contradictory. They can be reconciled, however, by

3. *Synthesis*
3a. Every mental event is token-identical with some physical event.

3b. There are and never will be any true strict law statements universally quantified over individuals covering the causal relation between mental events so formulated and the actions they cause (= 1 above).

3c. There either is or ultimately will be a true strict law statement universally quantified over individuals covering the causal relation between the various physical events with which particular mental events are token-identical and the actions they cause (= 2c above).

3b and 3c are consistent. Hence, if we can accept that 3b = 1 and that 3c = 2c, then the apparent conflict between 1 and 2c is reconciled.

While this argument undoubtedly provides those who see a problem in reconciling the doctrine of the freedom of the human will with scientific determinism with a *motive* for subscribing to token-identity physicalism, it falls, like all arguments of this form, a long way short of providing a watertight a priori argument for the truth of the doctrine, even if the truth of all the argument's premises is accepted.

Conclusion: "Perfect Correlation Is Identity"

I conclude that, apart from the dubious advantage that it is less susceptible than is the type-identity variety to empirical disconfirmation, token-identity physicalism has nothing to recommend it over its more robust type-identity rival. Moreover, so far from protecting physicalism from empirical disconfirmation, the token-identity version is itself in serious danger of being sidelined, if not actually falsified, by the emergence in the light of current and future research of the kind of "perfect correlation" between psychological and physiological measures that according to the originator of the identity theory, psychologist E. G. Boring (1933, p. 16), constitutes identity. What Boring perhaps should have said is that if two measures correlate perfectly and spontaneously without requiring any experimental controls to induce them to do so, we have cast iron evidence that they measure one and the same thing.[8] If, as seems more than likely, future research using the recently discovered techniques of brain imaging will allow us to identify such perfect correlations between mentally and physically specified variables, we shall be in a position to assert with confidence that at least *some* specifiable type-identity statements involving mentally and physically characterized processes are known to be true. In that case, who will give a fig for token-identity physicalism?

The Two-Factor Theory
of the Mind-Brain Relation

The Incoherence of the Mental/Physical Distinction

In a recent article (1999b) I criticized Ryle's failure, acknowledged in his *Dilemmas* (Ryle 1954), to develop an adequate account of the notion of a "category" in the following paragraph:

> Ryle's failure to sharpen up the notion of "a category" is unfortunate for two reasons. Firstly, because he needs to rebut the claim made by Descartes and his followers that the distinction between the mental and the physical, between the *res cogitans* and the *res extensa*, is a distinction of category, using the term "category" in its Aristotelian sense in which a category is the kind of thing you end up with if you go on asking the question "And what kind of a thing is that?" and of which the category of substance (οὐσία) is the prime example. Secondly, because the distinction he himself draws between "disposition verbs," "activity verbs" and "achievement verbs" corresponds to the distinction between *states of affairs* of which dispositions are an instance and which persist unchanged over a period of time, *processes* which are extended over time with continuous change and *instantaneous events* (stops and starts) whereby one state or process ends and another begins, which occur at moments of time, but are not extended over time. Not only do these groupings have a much better claim to be described as "categories" than do the mental and the physical, it is evident that the distinction between these three basic categories can be drawn on either side of the mental/physical divide. That means, if I am not mistaken, that if *they* are categories, "the mental" and "the physical" are not.

In this passage I argue:

1. that the distinction between the mental and the physical is *not* a distinction between two fundamentally different categories of thing;
2. that the distinction between states of affairs, processes and instantaneous events *is* a distinction between three fundamentally different categories of thing; and

3. that the distinction between states of affairs, processes and instantaneous events cuts across that between the mental and the physical.

If these three propositions are true, it would be surprising if the relation that holds between mental processes and brain processes were the same as that which holds in the case of mental states and brain states or between instantaneous mental events and instantaneous brain events. I shall argue, as I have been arguing for more than forty years, that that is indeed how things are.

I still think, as I put it in "Is consciousness a brain process?" that "In the case of cognitive concepts like 'knowing', 'believing', 'understanding', 'remembering', and volitional concepts like 'wanting' and 'intending', . . . an analysis in terms of dispositions to behave (Wittgenstein, 1953; Ryle 1949) is fundamentally sound" (Place, 1956, p. 44). I also think that a different account of the mind-brain relation is to be given in the case of these dispositional mental states from that which is called for in the case of the mental processes, which I referred to collectively by the term "consciousness." Mental processes, I maintain, just *are* processes in the brain. Dispositional mental states, on the other hand, are not, in my view, states of the brain. Unfortunately, apart from indicating my adherence to the Wittgenstein-Ryle dispositional analysis of such concepts, thereby excluding them from the scope of what became known as the mind-brain identity theory, I said nothing at that time about the relation between dispositional mental states and the brain states with which they are undoubtedly correlated.

The Critique of Ryle's Hypothetical Analysis of Dispositions

This proved to be a serious omission. The year after my paper appeared, Peter Geach (1957) published, in his book *Mental Acts*, a critique of the hypothetical analysis of dispositional concepts in general (chapter 3) and the dispositional analysis of mental state concepts (chapter 4). In making these criticisms, Geach was advocating a return to something like traditional mind-body dualism. It was left to Brian Medlin (1967) and David Armstrong (1968) to combine the criticism of Ryle's dispositional theory with the proposal to extend the identity theory from the case of mental processes to dispositional mental states, now construed as categorical internal states of the person rather than as a matter of the truth of certain hypotheticals about his or her possible future behavior. Because of the prejudice among philosophers in favor of a unitary solution to the mind-body problem and my own failure to argue the case for the alternative view, it is the Medlin-Armstrong version of the identity theory that has prevailed.

Obstacles in the Path of the Two-Factor Theory
of the Mind-Brain Relation

In arguing for what I eventually (Place, 1967, p. 60) came to see as the correct account of the relation between dispositional mental states and the states of the brain with which they are correlated, the view that the dispositional state is causally dependent on, and cannot therefore be identical with, the underlying state of the structure of the entity whose dispositional property it is, I have been hampered by two other factors besides the prejudice I have already mentioned on the part of philosophers in favor of a unitary solution to the problem. The first is the problem that arises concerning the categorical, here-and-now-existing status of dispositions. If you say that dispositions are distinct existences from their structural underpinnings, dispositions become very peculiar entities indeed. They seem to consist in nothing over and above what would happen in the future if certain conditions were to be fulfilled. Yet dispositions exist now, not just in some indefinite and possibly never to be realized future. How can that be? How much more comfortable to suppose, not just in the case of mental dispositions but in the case of dispositions in general, that the disposition just *is* what undoubtedly exists here and now, its structural underpinning.[1]

The other factor that has made my view difficult to defend is that the style of philosophizing on which it relies, the conceptual analysis of ordinary language using simple nontechnical and commonplace examples, has gone out of fashion in philosophical circles in recent years. Why that should be I shall not attempt to explain, except to say that its fall from favor appears to have coincided with the cognitive revolution, which undermined behaviorism as a standpoint in psychology and linguistics, another outmoded intellectual position to which I still subscribe.

Conceptual Analysis and the Problem
of Mental Self-Knowledge

Nor is there much that I can say by way of introducing what for many will be an unfamiliar way of doing philosophy. Suffice it to say that, as I construe it, conceptual analysis is a branch of empirical sociolinguistics that studies the semantic and pragmatic conventions governing the construction of intelligible sentences in natural language. Its contribution to issues such as the mind-body problem is to unravel the complex interplay of such factors in our ordinary "folk psychological" talk.

The conceptual-analytic evidence that persuades me that a different account has to be given of the mind-brain relation in the case of mental dispositions from that which applies in the case of mental processes comes from Ryle's (1949) book *The Concept of Mind*. In his chapter on "Self-knowledge" (chapter 6) he says

> Even if you claimed that you had experienced a flash or click of comprehension and had actually done so, you would still withdraw your other claim to have understood the argument, if you found that you could not paraphrase it, illustrate, expand or recast it; and you would allow someone else to have understood it who could meet all examination-questions about it, but reported no click of comprehension. (Ryle 1949, pp. 170–171)

The point I take Ryle to be making in this crucial passage is that whereas we have what he elsewhere describes as "privileged access" to private experiences, such as the occurrence of "a flash or click of comprehension," we have no such privileged access to our mental dispositions. This is shown by the absurdity of the following:

(a) "James is very intelligent."
     "How do you know?"
     "He told me he was."
(b) "James knows what time it is."
     "How do you know?"
     "He told me he did."
     "But did he tell you what time it is?"
     "No."

Ryle's explanation of the absurdity of these interchanges is that 'being intelligent' and 'knowing what time it is' are not introspectible inner states of the person concerned; they are dispositions, something like the brittleness of a glass which only manifests itself under certain broadly specifiable conditions. In the case of the glass, the brittleness manifests itself only when the glass is dropped onto a hard surface, is struck by a hard object, or is otherwise subjected to severe mechanical stress. In the case of "being intelligent," the disposition manifests itself only when the individual is confronted by a difficult intellectual or practical problem. In the case of "knowing the time," it manifests itself only when the individual is asked or asks himself or herself that question. In both these mental cases, asking the individual questions is a good way of finding out whether the predicate in question applies; but these questions are not like the questions a doctor asks when he or she wants to know whether the patient feels pain and what sort of pain it is. They are questions designed to *test* the individual's ability to solve the problem posed by it in the case of intelligence or to answer the question correctly in the case of knowing the time. Whether the answer given solves the problem in the one case or is correct in the other is a matter that is decided by objective criteria, not by the individual concerned, as in the pain case.

Privileged Access to Mental Propensities

It is sometimes argued that mental propensities, such as believing a certain proposition to be true, wanting something to come about, or intending to do something, are in a different category from mental capacities, in that the individual *does* have privileged access to his own dispositional mental state from which others are excluded. But this is only because in these cases stating what you believe, asking for what you want, and stating your intentions are in themselves manifestations of the dispositions in which believing, wanting, and intending consist.[2] The same is true of statements in which the individual sets out what he or she knows. But in this case, in order to qualify as knowledge, what the individual says must be true and, with the doubtful exception of statements describing one's own private experiences, no one has privileged access to the truth of one's own propositions. In the case of beliefs, desires, and intentions no such correctness qualifications apply. Except in cases where the individual is deliberately lying so as to conceal their true propensities, *any* expression of belief, desire, or intention will count as a manifestation of the disposition in question.

The Dispositional and Categorical Aspects of Pain

There is, of course, an argument that comes down to us from Wittgenstein's observation that "the expressions of pain replace crying" (Wittgenstein, 1953, 2, section 244) to the effect that the same analysis can be given of our knowledge of our own pains. The reason for this is not far to seek. It is part of the concept of pain that pains are unpleasant things we want to alleviate, get rid of, and wherever possible avoid; and wanting, as we have seen, is an archetypical dispositional notion. But this kind of wanting differs from, say, wanting an apple; to say that someone wants an apple does not imply that there exists an apple that they want, but to say that someone is in pain *does* imply that there exists a sensation that they want to be rid of. That sensation, moreover, is an ongoing process, which, unlike for example the infernal blare of the neighbor's radio, is sensed only by its owner.

Sharpening the Distinction between Two Forms
of Mental Self-Knowledge

Even in those cases, such as believing, wanting, and intending, where we have some kind of privileged access to our own mental state, we do not sense our own beliefs, desires, or intentions. We just know intuitively what they are. Moreover, whereas the privileged access we have to private events such as the sensation of pain or Ryle's "click of comprehension" can only be explained by the fact that they are events occurring inside their owner's sensory apparatus, the privileged access we have to our own beliefs, desires, and intentions does not come from the fact that they themselves are internal states of our sensory apparatus. It comes partly from the fact that the act of reporting them is itself a manifestation of the disposition in which they consist and partly from the fact that these dispositions are manifested in occurrent thoughts and feelings to which we do indeed have privileged access in the same way that we have privileged access to our sensations. But even then, our access to our own beliefs, desires, and intentions ceases to be privileged, once those dispositions have been manifested in behavior, in a way that no private experience loses its privileged status. If it is in fact raining, once I have put up my umbrella or run for shelter, it no longer makes sense to doubt the existence of my belief that it is raining, in the way that, despite my groaning, you can still doubt the existence of my pain. For although the groaning is as much a manifestation of a disposition as is putting up the umbrella or running for shelter, the cause of that disposition, the pain sensation, is inaccessible to others in a way that the cause of the belief that it is raining, the rain itself, is not.

From Epistemology to Ontology

What these epistemological differences show is that mental processes and events are things of a very different kind or category from mental dispositions. They also show that whereas our inability to detect the private thoughts and feelings of another person is to be explained by the fact that these events are taking place inside their owner's skin, our inability to detect another's mental capacities and propensities simply by inspection is due to the fact they have not yet been put to the test. It is not due to the fact that these states are located inside their owner's skin. It may be true that they are so located. I don't think it is. But that is not why we can't detect their presence. The existence of a disposition, whether 'mental' or 'physical', can never be demonstrated unless and until it is manifested in some shape or form. Showing that an entity has the internal structure that is normally associated with its having a certain capacity or propensity counts for nothing if, when subjected to the appropriate test, no such manifestation appears.

The Categorical/Structural Basis of Dispositions

The notion that dispositions, particularly physical dispositions such as the brittleness of glass, have what was referred to as a "categorical basis" in the microstructure of the dispositional property bearer has been commonplace ever since Gilbert Ryle's *The Concept of Mind* first brought the topic of dispositions to the attention of philosophers. Thus in his *Thinking and Experience* published in 1953 Ryle's contemporary and colleague at Oxford, Henry Price, wrote:

"There is no *a priori* necessity for supposing that *all* dispositional properties must have a 'categorical basis.' In particular, there may be mental dispositions which are ultimate . . . " (Price, 1953, p. 322). This passage has a number of interesting implications:

1. It implies that most, if not all, *physical* dispositions have a "categorical basis."
2. Since the adjective "categorical" as applied to the basis is evidently intended to contrast with the *hypothetical* character of the dispositions themselves, as claimed by Ryle, and since Leibniz's Law rules out the possibility that *one* and the same thing should be categorical under one description and hypothetical under another, it implies that the disposition and its categorical basis are two distinct and *separate* things, which are presumably related in such a way that the categorical basis stands as cause to the disposition as effect.
3. If, as Ryle claims, the relationship between a disposition and its manifestations or "exercises," as he calls them, is not a causal relation, the effect of Price's supposition that there are some mental dispositions that have no "categorical basis" would be to put such dispositions wholly outside the causal nexus, in agreement with much traditional thinking about such matters.

In his *Mental Acts* published in 1957 Peter Geach concludes a withering attack on Ryle's hypothetical analysis of dispositions with these words:

> A physicist would be merely impatient if someone said to him: "Why look for, or postulate, any actual difference between a magnetized and an unmagnetized bit of iron? Why not say that if certain things are done to a bit of iron certain hypotheticals become true of it?" He would be still more impatient at being told that his enquiries were vitiated by the logical mistake of treating "X is magnetized" as categorical, whereas it is really hypothetical or semi-hypothetical. (Geach, 1957, p. 6)

The implication of what Geach is saying in this passage is that when the physicist looks inside the iron bar for an explanation of its magnetic properties he is studying the very nature of the dispositional property itself. In other words Geach is rejecting the idea implicit in Price's contrast between the hypothetical character of the disposition and the categorical nature of its basis in the microstructure of the property bearer that this is a causal relation between "distinct existences," to use Hume's phrase, in favor of the view that the disposition and its categorical basis are one and the same thing.

This view that was later to become the cornerstone of Medlin's (1967) and Armstrong's (1968) "central state materialism" has at first sight a number of conspicuous advantages over its never very clearly expounded predecessor:

1. It appears to offer the advantage of ontological economy. Instead of two things, the dispositional property and its categorical basis, we now have only one thing described in two different ways: (a) in terms of its potential manifestations, and (b) in terms of its microstructural constitution.
2. When applied to the mind-body relation it has the additional advantage of allowing the conclusion that all mental things, and not just mental processes as I had argued in 1956, are brain things. Mental dispositions are states of the brain.
3. It readily explains our commonsense understanding of such matters according to which the brittleness of the glass exists long before it actually breaks.
4. The existence of the categorical basis thus provides a convenient truth maker for the otherwise problematic subjunctive conditional to the effect that if the appropriate conditions *were to be* fulfilled, a manifestation of the disposition *would* exist or occur.

On the other hand, if the disposition and its basis are one and the same thing, it no longer makes sense, as C. B. Martin has pointed out (Armstrong et al., 1996, pp. 81–86), to contrast the hypothetical character of the disposition with the categorical character of its basis in the microstructure of the property bearer. Both are equally categorical. It was for this reason that in *Dispositions: A Debate* (Armstrong et al., 1996) I gave up talking about the categorical basis of a disposition and spoke instead about its basis in the microstructure of the property bearer. Finally, under the influence of the sharpness example where the knife's ability to cut and the needle's ability to pierce depend on features of its *macrostructure*, the fineness of the edge or point, rather than on its *microstructure*, I began to speak of the "structural basis" of the disposition. In so doing, I was conceding that dispositions exist categorically before and in the absence of their manifestations. What I was not conceding was that the structural basis and the disposition are one and the same thing.

Dispositions and Their Structural Bases Are Two Distinct and Causally Related Things

Those, such as Geach (1957), Medlin (1967), Armstrong (1968), and Martin (Armstrong et al., 1996), who hold that dispositions and their structural basis are either one and the same thing or two aspects of the same thing typically do so on purely a priori grounds, on grounds of ontological economy (Ockham's razor). My view, the view that, with one notable group of exceptions to be considered in a moment, the structural basis of a disposition stands as cause to the disposition as effect, though inspired in the first place by Ryle's hypothetical analysis of dispositional statements to which I still subscribe, is based on an examination of a number of examples where the structural basis of the disposition is a matter of common knowledge. Following Hume, I take it as axiomatic that if two things are causally related, they must be, to use his phrase, "distinct existences." They cannot be two descriptions of one and the same thing.

I first came to this conclusion from an examination (Place 1967; Armstrong, et al., 1996, p. 30) of the relation between the horsepower of an internal combustion engine and such features of the internal structure as the cubic capacity of its cylinders. More recently (Armstrong et al., 1996, pp. 114–115), I reached the same conclusion in the light of the relation between the propensity of a knife to cut or a needle to pierce and the fineness of its edge or point. Another example that makes the same point is the following:

Suppose we have an electrical circuit linking
a live battery,
an ON/OFF switch,
a changeover switch, and
two lamps: one red, one green.

Suppose further that these are wired up in such a way that when the ON/OFF switch is closed and the changeover switch is in the left position, a circuit is made via the red lamp but not via the green lamp whereas when the changeover switch is in the right position, a circuit is made via the green lamp but not via the red.

In this setup, so long as the ON/OFF switch is closed and the changeover switch is to the left, only the red lamp will be illuminated. When the changeover switch is moved to the right, the red lamp will go out and the green lamp will come on. But consider what happens when the ON/OFF switch is in the open (OFF) position. In this case, whatever the position of the changeover switch, neither lamp will be illuminated. But suppose we *now* move the changeover switch from left to right. Neither lamp will come on. Nevertheless something has changed. What has changed is the dispositional property of the system. Before, if the ON/OFF switch had been closed, the red light *would have* come on. Now, if it were to close, the green light *would* come on.

In such a case, I submit, there is no temptation to say that the change in the position of the changeover switch is *the same thing as* the change in the dispositional property of the system. They are two different things, one of which, the position of the changeover switch, stands as cause to the other, the change in dispositional property, as effect.

Stuffs, Processes, and Compositional Type Identity

This is in sharp contrast to what we are inclined to say about the *process* whereby the changeover switch moves from one position to the other. Here we *do* want to say that it is the *very same* process as that which results in the change in the dispositional property of the system from one in which closing the ON/OFF switch brings on the red lamp to one where it brings on the green. The same principle applies in all cases where the kind of entity that is at issue is a stuff like water or common salt or a process like convected heat or a flash of lightning. In these cases it would be absurd to suggest that being H_2O is the cause of something's being water, that being NaCl is the cause of something's being common salt, that being in molecular motion is the cause of convected heat, that being an electrical discharge through the atmosphere is the cause of something's being a flash of lightning. In all these cases we are dealing, not with a causal relation between distinct existences but with two descriptions of the very same thing.

Compositional Type Identity in the Case of Dispositions: Solidity, Fluidity, and Volatility

In the final chapter of *Dispositions: A Debate* (Armstrong et al., 1996, pp. 168–169) C. B. Martin cites an example of a compositional type identity involving a disposition. This is the case of the fluidity of liquid, which is the same thing as the propensity of its constituent molecules to roll over one another. By the same token, the solidity of a solid is the propensity of its constituent molecules to preserve their relation and proximity to one another, while the volatility of a gas consists in the propensity of its constituent molecules to fly apart unless constrained by an airtight vessel from doing so.

The first thing to be said about this series of examples is that although this identification of a dispositional property with its molecular counterpart provides an essential prolegomenon to an explanation of the phenomenon, it does not by itself provide us with an explanation of why the molecules composing some substances under some conditions tend to roll over one another, why others remain stationary, and why yet others fly apart. That explanation, when it is given, will be a causal explanation, and the cause will be something over and above its effect, the existence of the disposition.

Second, since this is an identity relation, Leibniz's Law requires that both sides of the equation be dispositional properties, the only difference being that one is a dispositional property of the whole while the other is a dispositional property of the parts that make up the whole.

Third, it is tolerably certain that every dispositional property, provided that, unlike the Aristotelian entelechies, it has been properly specified, has a causal explanation in terms of the structure of the property bearer. A possible exception here is the "charm" of the quark, a dispositional property whose bearer, the quark, is on our present understanding too small and featureless to have any kind of structure that would explain the dispositional property, without which we would have no reason to postulate its existence.

Fourth and by contrast, the cases such as solidity, fluidity, and volatility where a compositional type identity is specifiable between a molar and molecular description of a disposition are rare, if not very rare. Such identities would seem to apply only in cases where the manifestation of the disposition is a state or process that exists or takes place entirely within the substance of the property bearer. It seems that where a dispositional property manifests itself in its effect on things external to the property bearer, no such compositional type identity is specifiable. The reason for this is that identities are subject to Leibniz's Law, which holds that every predicate that is true of something under one description must also be true of it under any other description that applies to the same thing. Now dispositions are characterized by their manifestations. This means that they are located where those manifestations exist or occur. If the manifestations take place outside or at the point of interaction between the property bearer and the external world, as in the case of the horsepower of an engine that is manifested at the drive shaft, the iron bar whose magnetic properties are manifested in the magnetic field surrounding it, or the circuit described above whose dispositional properties are manifested in the two lamps, the dispositional property is located somewhere quite different from the microstructural features on which the existence of the dispositional property depends. Consequently, the possibility that they might be one and the same thing is ruled out by Leibniz's Law. Only where the manifestations are located within the substance of the property bearer can the disposition and its counterpart at the molecular level have the same location. Only then, as in the solidity, fluidity, and volatility cases, can the two descriptions be descriptions of one and the same thing.

If that is correct, since mental dispositions such as beliefs, desires, and intentions evidently affect the way the property bearer interacts with his or her environment, we can be tolerably certain that this is a case where no compositional type identity will be specifiable between the mental disposition and the brain state with which it is found to be correlated when that is discovered. As in other cases where the disposition manifests itself in the interactions between the property bearer and things external to it, the relation between a mental disposition and the brain state with which it is correlated will prove to be a causal relation between "distinct existences" in which the brain state stands as cause to the mental disposition as effect.

Unmanifested Dispositions as Laws of the Nature of the Property Bearer

We have seen that one of the principal advantages that accrue from the supposition that dispositions and their structural basis are one and the same thing is that it enables us to make sense of the claim that a disposition exists as a matter of categorical fact, even though it has not yet been manifested and may never be so. According to Ryle, when we ascribe an unmanifested dispositional property to something, *all* we are saying is that if, sometime in the future, certain conditions were to be fulfilled, certain manifestation events would occur. This cannot be right. There must be some here-and-now-existing state of the disposition owner that makes that prediction true. But if as now appears, it is only in exceptional cases that we can identify the unmanifested disposition with a state of the underlying structure of the property bearer, and given that even in these cases the underlying structure turns out to be just *another* unmanifested disposition, in what does an unmanifested disposition consist?

In order to explain how I came to the answer to this question that I now give, I need to go back to the origins of the debate between David Armstrong and me, which was later broadened to include contributions from C. B. (Charlie) Martin and published in 1996 as *Dispositions: A Debate* (Armstrong et al., 1996). The starting point of this debate was a paper titled "Causal laws, dispositional properties and causal explanations," which I published in 1987 in *Synthesis Philosophica,* the international version of the Serbo-Croat philosophy journal *Filozofska Istrazivanja.* In this paper I argued for the following theses:

1. The difference between an accidental generalization and a causal judgment lies in the fact that the latter entails a counterfactual to the effect that if the one event or state of affairs (the cause) had not occurred or existed, the other event or state of affairs (the effect) would not have occurred or existed.
2. Since no such events or states of affairs actually existed, the truth of a causal counterfactual can never be established by observation.
3. The only way to establish the truth of a causal counterfactual is by deducing it from a universal law statement which, to use Goodman's (1965) term, is said to "sustain" it.
4. But as Goodman also points out, the law statement that "sustains" a counterfactual need not be universally quantified over a class of individuals to which a predicate applies. A dispositional statement restricted to the behavior of a particular individual will do just as well, provided the occasion referred to in the counterfactual falls within the period over which the disposition obtains.

In *Dispositions: A Debate*, in common with both my fellow participants, I endorsed C. B. Martin's truth maker principle. The principle, however, is subject to a variety of interpretations. As I interpret it, it holds that a contingent assertion is true and a contingent negation is false if and only if the event or state of affairs whose existence the assertion asserts or the negation denies actually exists. Since the event or state of affairs they depict never existed, the claim that a causal counterfactual is true presents a particular difficulty for such a view. Goodman's observation that the truth of a causal counterfactual is deduced from a law statement allows us to recognize that causal counterfactuals share a truth maker with the law statements that "sustain" them; while his further observation that dispositional statements function as law statements in sustaining causal counterfactuals shows us that in such cases, and perhaps in all cases, it is the existence of the disposition that acts as the truth maker.

When this observation is combined with the evidence reviewed above showing that dispositions depend causally on and are thus "distinct existences" from the underlying structure of the property bearer, it is a short step to the view to which I now subscribe, namely that the dispositional properties of particular things are substantive laws of the nature of the property bearer. This view only occurred to me after *Dispositions: A Debate* had gone to press. I suddenly realized that the dispositional properties of particular entities were playing the same role in my theory that Armstrong's (1997) substantive Laws of Nature were playing in his: the role of acting as truth maker for the law statements formulated by scientists insofar as they are true. From this it was but a short step to the idea that the dispositional properties of particular things are the substantive laws, not, as for Armstrong, of nature in general but of the nature of the individual entities whose dispositional properties they are. This is essentially the same view as that argued for by Nancy Cartwright (1989) in her *Nature's Capacities and their Measurement*. She too rejects Laws of Nature in general as constituents of the universe. She sees the laws formulated by scientists as rough and ready generalizations describing the typical "capacities," as she calls them, of individual entities.

You may say that this makes dispositions very queer entities indeed, and I would agree that it does. But one has only to think of black holes to realize that substantive laws of the nature of the individual property bearer are no queerer than many of the entities postulated by contemporary physics and a deal less queer than Armstrong's substantive laws of nature in general. What is shocking, perhaps, is to find such entities in our own backyard, as it were, in familiar things like the brittleness of the unbroken glass, the flexibility of the rubber that has never been stretched, and the desire that has never been evinced, let alone acted on.

Toward a Neuropsychological Theory of the Mind-Brain Relation

I contend that the two-factor theory of the mind-brain relation I have outlined is much better placed than is its rival, central state materialism, to point us in the right direction when searching in the brain for the neural correlates of the mental processes, mental events, and dispositional mental states whose existence we acknowledge at the level of commonsense observation. So long as the identity theory was restricted to the mental process/brain process relation, the only conceptual problem confronting the neuroscientist who is looking for the brain processes in which, on this view, conscious experiences and other mental processes consist, is the problem of showing how the properties we attribute to those experiences could be the properties of a brain process as Leibniz's Law requires. That problem, as I showed in "Is consciousness a brain process?" disappears once we recognize that all we ever say about a conscious experience, when we describe what it was like to have it, is how it resembles some other experience or type of experience that we identify by reference either to its publicly observable causal antecedents and/or to its publicly observable behavioral effects (what it makes us say or do). Once that is appreciated, we realize, as I put it then, that " . . . there is nothing that the introspecting subject says about his conscious experiences which is inconsistent with anything the physiologist might want to say about the brain processes which cause him to describe the environment and his consciousness of that environment in the way he does" (Place, 1956, p. 49).

Once the identity theory is extended from the case of mental processes to include dispositional mental states, a viper's nest of new problems confronts us. How do we explain the causal role of propositions in the control of behavior (or 'action', as it is now called)? How could something as abstract as a proposition have a causal role, let alone be a state of the brain? What neural counterparts could there possibly be for the grammatical objects of psychological verbs such as 'believing', 'wanting', and 'intending'? What could intentional inexistence or referential opacity possibly amount to in neural terms?

These problems, if not entirely resolved, are at least made much more tractable, once it is accepted that mental dispositions and their neural basis are two causally related things rather than one and the same thing. It becomes apparent that these problems arise partly from the peculiar nature of dispositions in general, physical as well as mental, and partly from the peculiar way in which mental dispositions are characterized in ordinary language. Viewed in this light, the task of looking for a state of the brain that gives *the system as a whole* these dispositional properties without actually having them itself appears much more manageable.

One set of problems that disappears once the matter is viewed in this way is that of Donald Davidson's (1970) worries about the causal role of propositional attitudes, the apparent impossibility of constructing a nonvacuous covering law universally quantified over agents that would provide a logically acceptable foundation for our commonsense belief in the causal potency of the agent's beliefs and desires with respect to the way she talks and behaves, together with the possibility, not to say probability, that the brain state that correlates with my belief that today is Monday is quite different from that which correlates with your belief that it is. As is well known, these worries led Davidson to his espousal of what has become known as "token-identity physicalism," the doctrine that every particular (token) mental state is identical with a particular brain state, but there are no "psycho-physical bridge laws" connecting mental state types to brain state types.

It should be apparent that the alleged absence of "psycho-physical bridge laws" is no problem, once you accept Goodman's observation that a dispositional statement restricted to the behavior of a single individual is all that is needed to "sustain" a causal counterfactual as much in the physical as in the mental domain, that dispositional statements are the only covering laws needed to underpin causal judgments, and that the existence of dispositions, qua substantive laws of the nature of the property bearer are all that is needed to account for the lawfulness of nature. Add to this the suggestion that dispositions are the "invisible glue" that binds a cause to its effects and there is no longer any reason to be puzzled about the causal role of mental states, and, perhaps more important, no a priori reason to deny the possibility of formulating generalizations on the basis of empirical research about the relations between mental states and their neurological underpinning.

10

The Causal Potency of Qualia
Its Nature and Its Source

Epiphenomenalism Is False

Qualia are the properties of an experience, such as a sensation, mental image, or emotional response, that we describe when we state what it is like or was like to have that experience. It has frequently been argued in recent years that qualia in this sense are causally impotent. That this cannot be so is shown by an argument I first deployed in my "Thirty years on—Is consciousness still a brain process?" (Place, 1988, p. 218)[1], though I subsequently discovered that the same argument against epiphenomenalism had been used some twenty years earlier by Brian Medlin (1967, pp. 110–111). The argument takes as its premise the principle that for a report of an event to be a first-hand report of that event, there has to be a direct causal relation between the perception of the event by the observer and the report that the observer makes. Since such reports are our only evidence for believing in the existence of phenomenal experiences in the case of others, it follows that if epiphenomenalism were true, we would have no grounds whatever for believing in the existence of phenomenal experiences and their qualia. It may be argued that this does not affect *my* assurance that the qualia of my experiences correspond to the description I give of them. However, if epiphenomenalism were true, no one else would have grounds to believe me; and what use is a private conviction if no one else is convinced by it.

Neuropsychological Evidence for the Biological Function of Qualia

If qualia are causally potent with respect to the reports that are given of them, it is difficult to believe that something so rich and omnipresent should not have other functions besides triggering those reports. What those other functions are we can assert with some confidence in the light of recent and not so recent neuropsychological evidence.

In his book *Perception and Communication* Donald Broadbent (1958) drew the conclusion, on the basis of dichotic listening experiments in which two different auditory messages are simultaneously fed into the two ears, that the function of selective attention is to protect the central processing unit in the brain from overload. As he puts it, this unit is a "limited capacity channel." In his book *Decision and Stress* (Broadbent, 1971) he suggests that the function of the selective attention mechanism is to generate what he calls the "evidence" on the basis of which the limited capacity channel "categorizes" the current sensory input. I have since suggested that we can equate this "evidence" with conscious experience and its qualia. This equation is supported by a number of pieces of neuropsychological evidence.

The first of these in order of publication is Nick Humphrey's (1974) study of the rhesus monkey Helen, who had virtually the whole of her striate cortex (V1) surgically removed. The effect of this operation was that, although she was still able to use her eyes "to move deftly through a room full of obstacles and could reach out and catch a passing fly" (Humphrey, 1974, p. 241), "after years of experience she never showed any signs of recognising even those objects most familiar to her, whether the object was a carrot, another monkey or myself" (Humphrey, 1974, p. 252).

What was missing in this case was not the ability to categorize as such, since the ability to categorize objects by sound, smell, taste, or feel was unaffected. What was missing from the visual modality was the "evidence" on which such categorization is based. What was not clear at that stage, but became clear later, was that the "evidence" which was no longer available as a result of the destruction of the striate cortex is in fact the process of phenomenal/conscious experience and, above all, its properties, its qualia.

The evidence for this comes from two sources. One source is Larry Weiskrantz's (1986) study, in his book *Blindsight,* of the effect of striate cortical lesions in humans. This shows that in humans lesions of the striate cortex (V1) result in the abolition of visual sensory experience and its qualia in an area of the visual field that corresponds precisely to the area of the lesion. Although visual sensory experience and its qualia are abolished in the affected part of the visual field by the lesions of V1, and although the ability to identify and categorize objects in the "blind" field is lost,[2] just as it was in the case of Humphrey's Helen, many visual discriminative abilities remain intact. As in Helen's case the most striking of these is the ability to reach out for and grasp objects presented to the blind part of the field. Helen's other remarkable retained ability, that of using vision to avoid obstacles in her path, is not reported in the human blindsight data that has been published to date, presumably because in all cases studied thus far, the lesion has only affected a part of one half of the visual field with the result that the need to avoid obstacles relying on "information" derived from the blind part of the field does not arise. However, I am reliably informed (personal communication from Dr. A. J. Marcel) that informal studies of patients with bilateral lesions of the striate cortex have shown that they too can avoid obstacles that they cannot "see."

Nevertheless, despite these striking similarities with the monkey data and the obvious anatomical similarity between the layout of the human and monkey brains, because until recently our only evidence of the presence and absence of sensory experiences and their qualia came from the verbal reports of human subjects, it was still possible to argue that such phenomena occur only in human beings. But with the publication in *Nature* of Alan Cowey and Petra Stoerig's (1995) paper "Blindsight in monkeys" and their follow-up papers (Cowey & Stoerig, 1997; Stoerig & Cowey, 1997) we now have incontrovertible empirical evidence that lesions of the striate cortex in monkeys abolish visual sensory experience and its qualia in exactly the same way that they do in human subjects. Moreover, provided we can find some other discriminative response that is mediated by the alternative midbrain pathway comparable to the reaching for an object response in primates, we now have a methodology that should enable us to test for the presence and absence of visual sensory experiences and their qualia in other species.

Consciousness and the Zombie-Within

The conclusion that sensory experiences and their qualia are present in animals, and the probability that their evolution extends back many millions of years reveals the claim that qualia are causally impotent and functionally irrelevant as the absurdity that it demonstrably is. What the blindsight evidence shows is that there are two parallel input-output processing systems in the brains of all the "higher" mammals, probably all mammals and possibly all vertebrates. One, concentrated in the mammalian cerebral cortex, appears to coincide with the traditional concept of consciousness. It has the function of dealing with inputs that are problematic and thus in need of extensive "processing," either because they are unexpected or because they are significant relative to the organism's current or perennial motivational concerns.

In contrast to consciousness so conceived there is a wholly unconscious input-output system, mediated by structures in the midbrain that I refer to (Place, 2000c) as the "zombie-within." Its functions are (a) to separate the problematic inputs, which it passes on for processing by consciousness, from the unproblematic and (b) to deal with those that are unproblematic in that similar inputs have been frequently encountered and dealt with by consciousness in the past and raise no emotional/motivational concerns. These unproblematic inputs are either ignored or routed to output as an automatic reflex.

In consciousness, as we have seen, the first step in the process of dealing with problematic inputs is to generate a sensory experience whose qualia will provide the "evidence" on the basis of which the organism can classify or categorize them into things of a kind for which a range of possible response strategies are available in its repertoire. The second step is to react emotionally both before and after categorization, so that in the third step a response may be selected that is appropriate both to the nature of the situation confronting the organism and to its emotional/motivational concerns with respect to it. Finally there is the process of response execution.

In all these later stages conscious experience and its qualia play a role. What this role is in relation to emotional reaction is not altogether clear to me; but I suggest that it has to do with preserving a record of motivationally significant events as they occur in the organism's experience so that they can be readily recollected in the form of mental imagery when contingencies with similar motivational significance are encountered in the future. It is, needless to say, the occurrence of such mental imagery that constitutes, before the evolution of language and linguistic thinking, the major contribution of conscious experience and its qualia to the process of conscious response selection. Finally, experiences and their qualia generated by the sensory feedback from the response and its environmental consequences play a vital role in the control of deliberate voluntary action as it develops.

The Causal Relation: Spatiotemporal Conjunction

For our present purposes I shall mean by a causal relation a relation between a set of causal factors that are immediate in the sense that all are still present when or so long as the other term of the relation, the effect, exists or occurs. Causal factors and their effects are of two kinds: states of affairs that are extended over time and instantaneous events that occur at moments of time but are not extended over time. For the purpose of this analysis, a process in which continuous change persists over time counts as a state of affairs, though its onset and offset are instantaneous events. All causally potent instantaneous events would appear either to initiate such a process of change or to mark its termination or completion.

Causal relations are of two kinds: static and dynamic. In a static causal relation a spatial relation between two or more spatially extended physical objects persists over time. In this case both the effect and its causes are all states of affairs. In a dynamic causal relation, the effect and one, but only one, of the causal factors (the "triggering event") is an instantaneous event. The other causal factors are states of affairs.

Both what we may call the "primary cause," in the case of a static causal relation, and the triggering event, in the case of a dynamic causal relation, consist in a spatiotemporal conjunction between two or more spatially extended "physical" objects. This conjunction may consist in actual physical contact between the objects involved but may consist, as in the cases of magnetic and gravitational attraction, in a degree of proximity sufficient to ensure a manifestation of the effect. There is also a similar spatiotemporal conjunction in both cases between the effect and its causes.

The Problem of Necessary Connection

However, as Hume first pointed out, these spatiotemporal conjunctions, though necessary, are not a sufficient condition for the existence of a causal relation between one event or state of affairs and another in which it stands in such a relation of conjunction. The spatiotemporal concomitance may, as we say, be purely accidental. Besides the spatiotemporal conjunction of objects and the spatiotemporal conjunction of events and/or states of affairs, there must also be what Hume calls "a necessary connection" between a cause and its effect.

This necessary connection is not a matter of logical necessity. Cause and effect are "distinct existences." It is always possible to describe them in some other way than as the cause of this or the effect of that. So described, there is no self-contradiction involved in asserting that one exists and the other does not, or vice versa. In *A Treatise of Human Nature,* Hume (1978) notoriously gave up the attempt to locate the necessary connection in the causal relation itself, and concluded that there is nothing to it but a disposition of the mind to expect the effect given the cause, due to repeated experience of the conjunction of the two in the past. In the *Enquiry Concerning the Human Understanding* (Hume, 1902), he began to move in the direction of the right answer when he defined a cause as "an object, followed by another . . . where if the first object had not been the second had never existed" (p. 76).

More recently this so-called "counterfactual theory of causal necessitation" has been elaborated by such philosophers as Nelson Goodman (1965), John Mackie (1962; 1974), and David Lewis (1973). To Goodman in particular we owe the observation that, since we can never observe what would have happened if things had been different from the way they actually were or are, the truth of a counterfactual can only be established or "sustained," to use Goodman's verb, insofar as it is deduced from a universal law statement.

The difficulty with this view is that it tells us only what it *means* to say that an observed conjunction between cause and effect *had to be* as it was. It tells us nothing, as it stands, about what it is that is present in a causal relation that is absent in an otherwise indistinguishable accidental concomitance. The clue to answering that question begins to emerge when Goodman draws our attention to the fact that the universal statement that is needed to sustain a causal counterfactual does not need to be universally quantified over the individual concerned. A statement ascribing a dispositional property to a particular individual will do just as well, provided the occasion to which a causal counterfactual relates falls within the period over which the dispositional property exists. If a dispositional property exists, its existence makes true a universally quantified statement of the form, "*If at any time* there exists an event or state of affairs of the cause type (the manifestation conditions of the disposition) and all the other causal factors are in place, an event or state of affairs of the effect type (a manifestation of the disposition) will exist." Given a statement of this form, the required causal counterfactual can be deduced.

The Two Aspects of Causation: Spatiotemporal
Conjunction and Dispositional Properties

It follows from this that it is the existence of the dispositional properties of the objects involved in a spatiotemporal conjunction that makes the difference between a genuine causal relation of which the causal counterfactual is true and a mere accidental concomitance of which it is not. From this a number of consequences follow.

In the first place it becomes clear that in every causal relation the existence of the effect depends on two factors (1) the spatiotemporal conjunction of two or more objects, and (2), as C. B. Martin has argued (Armstrong et al., 1996, pp. 135–136), the reciprocal dispositional properties of the objects involved. Thus the event whereby a portion of salt dissolves in a body of water and the state of affairs whereby it remains so dissolved both depend on (a) the immersion of the salt in the water, (b) the propensity of the salt to dissolve in water, and (c) its "reciprocal dispositional partner," the propensity of the water to dissolve the salt.

Second, it explains another observation of Martin's (Armstrong et al., 1996, pp. 135–136) that every effect is a manifestation of those dispositions.

Third, it supports my own claim (Armstrong et al., 1996, p. 22) that since a spatiotemporal conjunction is a relation rather than a property, the only causally potent properties involved in causal relations are dispositional properties.

The Application of This Analysis to Experiences, Qualia,
and the Categorization of Sensory Input

What happens if we apply this analysis of causation to the case of conscious experience and its qualia? Here, as we have seen, we have a causal relation in which the experience stands as cause to the response of categorizing the current input in a particular way as effect. On this analysis, the cause, the conscious experience and its qualia, must consist of two elements, a spatiotemporal conjunction and the reciprocal dispositional properties of the components of that conjunction that determine the nature of the effect it produces.

In view of the aura of mysticism that surrounds much of the discussion of conscious experience, the suggestion that it involves some kind of spatiotemporal conjunction, comparable with the stone's striking the pane of glass or the earth's proximity to the sun, may seem strange. Yet the idea that the "evidence" on which the brain bases its interpretation of current sensory input is organized into temporally and, in the case of vision at least, spatially extended chunks or patterns has been familiar to psychologists since the early years of the century. I refer to the phenomenon of figure-ground organization, as illustrated by figure 10.1. Here we have a stimulus that generates two different qualia, each of which generates a different interpretation or categorization of the stimulus. With the white as figure and the black as ground it is interpreted as a vase. With the black as figure and the white as ground, it is interpreted as two faces looking at one an-

Figure 10.1   Figure-ground reversal (after Rubin, 1915).

other. What makes the difference is a shift in the spatiotemporal relations—not indeed between two spatially extended physical objects but between two spatially extended patterns of neural activity in the brain.

However, if the pattern of figure-ground organization is the spatiotemporal conjunction that invariably precedes the response of categorizing the current input in a particular way, what is the disposition that ensures that, given the first, the second must follow? Can we say anything more about it than that it is the disposition that is manifested in the way the input—that is, generating the experience/pattern-of-figure-ground-organization—is interpreted or construed?

Qualia Cannot be Dispositional Properties

Since qualia are defined as properties of experiences, since by our initial argument they must be causally potent, and since by the subsequent argument dispositional properties are the only causally potent properties (as distinct from spatiotemporal relations) that there are, I was led to conclude in an earlier version of this paper that *they* are the dispositional properties that link experiences/patterns-of-figure-ground-organization to the interpretations they invite or suggest. What seemed to support this suggestion was the observation to which I and my old friend and former colleague J. J. C. Smart have repeatedly drawn attention,[3] whereby the only way we have of characterizing a conscious experience is by citing the various possible interpretations of the current input that it suggests. That,

I take it, is what we are doing when we describe an experience by means of a simile—"It's as if so-and-so were the case."

Against this supposition is the undoubted fact that dispositional properties, though in some sense they exist prior to and in the absence of their manifestation, produce no effect and leave no trace of their existence until such time as the conditions for their manifestation are fulfilled. Qualia are not like this. They make themselves felt from the moment that the experience whose qualia they are begins to exist. In the earlier version of this paper I tried to circumvent this objection by pointing out that the disposition to interpret an experience in some way seldom remains unmanifested for more than a moment. Nature, I argued, abhors an uninterpreted experience as much as it abhors a vacuum. But this will not do. It is the qualia whose nature invites the interpretation. They are the *bearers* of the disposition to interpret the current input that way, not the disposition itself.

But if that is correct, there is no longer any room for the distinction between a conscious experience and its qualia considered as properties of that experience. The qualia just *are* the experience, the pattern of figure-ground organization whose dispositional properties manifest themselves in the way the current input is interpreted and, in the case of a linguistically competent human subject, in the way the subject describes it.

Qualia and the Brain

Had it turned out that qualia are dispositional properties of experiences rather than the experiences themselves, it would have been possible to argue, in line with a great deal of traditional thinking, that they are not in fact one and the same thing as the brain states that underlie them and with which they are correlated. I have developed the argument for this view in a paper titled "The two factor theory of the mind-brain relation" (Place, 2000a).[4] The argument rests on the observation that, in all cases where the manifestation of a disposition is a matter of the interaction of the property bearer with things external to it, the only features of the underlying structure of the property bearer that are correlated with the existence of the disposition stand as cause to the existence of the disposition as effect. But, as Hume has taught us, if two things are causally related, they must be "distinct existences." They cannot be one and the same thing under different descriptions.

If this view is correct, as I am convinced it is, we are left with the problem of explaining what it is that exists here and now so long as a disposition remains unmanifested, if, as now appears, what exists here and now in such a case is not one and the same thing as its structural underpinning. But since qualia are not dispositional properties of experiences, that is not a problem that arises in this case. If, as I have argued, qualia are causally potent, they must *have* dispositional properties that determine what interpretation of the current input is selected by the pattern of figure-ground organization in which, on this view, the quale consists; but they are not themselves those dispositional properties. There is, therefore, in my view, no escaping the conclusion that I reached forty-five years ago (Place, 1956) that conscious experiences, phenomenal experiences, "raw feels," qualia—call them what you will—just *are* one and the same thing as the brain processes with which they are correlated. There is no "hard problem" (Chalmers, 1996). As I put it all those years ago: " . . . there is nothing that the introspecting subject says about his conscious experiences which is inconsistent with anything the physiologist might want to say about the brain processes which cause him to describe the environment and his consciousness of that environment in the way he does" (Place, 1956, p. 49).

11

Consciousness and the "Zombie-Within"
A Functional Analysis of the Blindsight Evidence

The Evolution of a Theory

In this chapter I develop a theory of consciousness and its unconscious counter-part that I call the "zombie-within." It has its source in two lines of research, both of which originated in the 1950s, now more than forty years ago. One of these was an attempt made by the present author in two papers published in the *British Journal of Psychology*, "The concept of heed" (Place, 1954) and "Is consciousness a brain process?" (Place, 1956), to examine the implications for the science of psychology of the work of Wittgenstein (1953; 1958) and Ryle (1949) on the linguistic analysis of what Ryle calls the "logical geography of our ordinary mental concepts." The other was the late Donald Broadbent's (1958) experimental and theoretical analysis of the phenomenon of selective attention in his book *Perception and Communication*.

Place's "The Concept of Heed" and "Is Consciousness Brain Process?"

In *The Concept of Mind* Ryle (1949) shows that many of our most common psychological verbs, such as 'know', 'believe', 'understand', 'remember', 'expect', 'want', and 'intend', do not, as had been traditionally supposed, refer to processes within the individual of whom they are predicated, to which he or she has "privileged access" through the process known as "introspection." These verbs refer to dispositions or performance characteristics of the individual that are manifested as much in what he or she publicly says and does as in his or her private mental processes. However, the application of these same techniques of linguistic analysis also shows "an intractable residue of concepts clustering around the notions of consciousness, experience, sensation and mental imagery, where some sort of inner process story is unavoidable" (Place, 1956, p. 44). It was this "intractable residue" to which I was referring when I argued in the same paper that "the thesis that consciousness is a process in the brain is . . . a reasonable scientific hypothesis, not to be dismissed on logical grounds alone" (Place, 1956, p. 44). Central to this concept of consciousness was the idea that the verb phrase "paying attention to————" refers to an internal nonmuscular activity whereby the individual "exercises a measure of control over the vividness or acuteness of his consciousness of (a) the sensations to which he is susceptible at that moment, or (b) such features of the environment as are impinging on his receptors, without necessarily adjusting his receptor organs or their position in any way" (Place, 1954, p. 244). In contrast to Ryle who had argued that to pay attention was to perform whatever task one was engaged in at the time with a disposition to succeed in it, I pointed out that

> Close attention to his own activity will be of no avail to the unskilled person because he has not learnt to discriminate between the relevant and irrelevant features. On the other hand an acute consciousness of the details of his own activity in relation to the environment may actually detract from the efficiency of performance in the case of an individual who has learnt to make many of the adjustments involved automatically. (Place, 1954, p. 247)

Here we have the germ of two ideas that are fundamental to the theory expounded below: (1) the idea that conscious experience is not, as it has been too often portrayed by philosophers, a mere passive spectator of what is going on inside and outside the organism, but, when properly focussed, is an integral part of the process whereby the behavior of the organism is brought into an adaptive relation to the environmental contingencies, and (2) the idea that in order to perform that function successfully, the implementation of the tactical details of a skilled performance must be handed over, as it were, to what I am here calling the "automatic pilot" or "zombie-within" in order to free consciousness to concentrate on those features of the task where important strategic decisions are called for.

Although I did not emphasize this point at the time, it will be apparent that the role assigned in this account to consciousness in general and conscious experience in particular is one that has as much application to the control of animal behavior as it has to that of human beings. What I did not then appreciate is that the other function of consciousness, which I emphasized both in "The concept of heed" and in "Is consciousness a brain process?"—that of enabling the individual to give a verbal description of those aspects of the current situation on which attention is focused—also has its roots in a mechanism that plays a key role in animal problem solving. For, as is shown by research on the effects of lesions of the striate cortex in man and monkey (blindsight), without conscious experience of the stimuli involved a monkey is unable to categorize and thus recognize either individuals or things of a kind (Humphrey, 1974). What I did emphasize, particularly in "Is consciousness a brain process?" was the idea that the remarkable ability of human subjects to give a running commentary on their private experiences, either at the time or shortly thereafter, is a by-product of the ability to give a description of and running commentary on that individual's current stimulus environment insofar as attention and consciousness are focused upon it.

Broadbent's *Perception and Communication* (1958) and *Decision and Stress* (1971)

This theory of the functions of attention and consciousness, as I was later to discover (Place, 1969), bears a remarkable resemblance to the theory of selective attention expounded by the late Donald Broadbent (1958) in his book *Perception and Communication*. Basing his conclusions on results obtained from dichotic listening experiments in which conflicting auditory messages are fed by earphones into the two ears, Broadbent introduced the idea that in the brain there is a central information-processing unit that is a limited-capacity channel, in the sense that it can process only a limited amount of information coming in from the sense organs at any one time. Such a limited-capacity channel or LCC requires a selective attention mechanism that protects it from overload, partly by excluding aspects of the current total input that are unproblematic and thus do not need to be processed, and partly by holding other inputs that need to be processed in a short-term memory store or buffer until the LCC-entry bottleneck clears.

In *Decision and Stress,* Broadbent (1971) introduced a number of modifications to the model he had outlined in the 1958 book. Three are particularly important for our present purpose: First, he introduced the term 'state of evidence' (i.e., evidence about the current state of the environment) to refer to the output of the selective attention mechanism and the input into the limited-capacity channel, a notion which corresponds to that of "raw" or uninterpreted experience in traditional psychology. Second, he proposed that the function of the limited-capacity channel is to pigeonhole and categorize the evidence passed through from the selective attention mechanism, where "to pigeonhole" is to routinely assign an unproblematic input to its classification and 'to categorize' is either to create a new classification or to extend or otherwise modify an existing classification so as to accommodate an otherwise unclassifiable input. However, as is shown by the blindsight evidence described below, the kind of routine automatic behavior that on the present hypothesis is assigned to the zombie-within requires no conscious experience to supply the evidence and no categorization of objects in the affected part of the visual field. Nevertheless, the individual is able to perform routine visually guided tasks, such as reaching for objects and, in the case of the monkey at least, avoiding obstacles. I infer from this that no classification of the input is necessary for the automatic routine control of behavior by visual stimuli or those in the other sensory modalities that, on this hypothesis, is mediated by the automatic pilot or zombie-within and that, therefore, Broadbent's routine pigeonholing of nonproblematic inputs does not exist. The only classification of sensory inputs that occurs is the categorization in consciousness of problematic inputs. (3) He proposed that the parts of the input that are not in the current focus of attention are not filtered out completely, as proposed in 1958, but rather contribute, to a lesser extent than the part that is in the focus, to what Broadbent calls the "category state," the final outcome of the categorization process. Although Broadbent himself does not use that terminology, another way of putting the point would be to say that the input in the focus of attention stands as "figure" to the inputs outside the focus as "ground."

Humphrey's "Vision in a Monkey without Striate Cortex" (1974)

In his 1974 paper, Nicholas Humphrey writes:

> In 1965 Weiskrantz removed the visual striate cortex from an adolescent rhesus monkey, Helen. In the 8 years between the operation and her death in 1973 this monkey slowly recovered the use of her eyes, emerging from virtual sightlessness to a state of visual competence where she was able to move deftly through a room full of obstacles and could reach out and catch a passing fly. (Humphrey, 1974, p. 241)

Nevertheless, "After years of experience she never showed any signs of recognizing even those objects most familiar to her, whether the object was a carrot, another monkey or myself" (Humphrey, 1974, p. 252). The full significance of this observation for the theory of consciousness has only become apparent in the light of two subsequent discoveries. The first of these was Weiskrantz's (1986) demonstration that, in addition to retaining the same visual abilities (apart possibly from the ability to avoid obstacles which is not demonstrable in a subject with only a partial lesion of the striate cortex), lesions of the striate cortex in man have the effect of completely abolishing visual conscious experience in the affected part of the visual field. The second discovery was Cowey and Stoerig's (1995; 1997; Stoerig & Cowey, 1997) demonstration that lesions of the striate cortex in the monkey have the same effect in abolishing visual conscious experience of stimuli in the blind field as they do in human subjects, despite the fact that the animal can reach for objects in that part of the visual field with almost the same accuracy as for objects in the intact field.

When combined with these subsequent discoveries and interpreted in the light of Broadbent's model, Humphrey's observations show (1) that the function of conscious experience is to provide the evidence on which categorization of current inputs is based and without which no categorization of those inputs is possible, (2) that, relying only on the subcortical visual inputs available to it, the unconscious automatic pilot or zombie-within can learn by the process of trial and error to make many very accurate visual discriminations, including the ability to reach for objects and avoid obstacles by sight, and (3) that the behavior controlled by the unconscious automatic pilot or zombie-within (e.g., reaching for "unseen" objects and avoiding "unseen" obstacles in the visual field) does not require any categorization of the inputs to which the system is responding (human subjects describe such responses as "pure guesswork").

Weiskrantz's *Blindsight* (1986)

As already mentioned, Weiskrantz has shown that the effect of lesions of the striate cortex in man is to abolish conscious experience in the affected part of the visual field. It does so, presumably, by depriving the cortex of the raw material on which the evidence for categorization of inputs is based. Nevertheless, as we have also seen, patients such as Weiskrantz's subject DB show some remarkable visual discrimination abilities, such as the ability to reach for objects in the blind field with considerable accuracy, the phenomenon to which Weiskrantz has given the name "blindsight." For our present purposes, the two most important additional points to emerge from Weiskrantz's study are (1) that the visual discrimination abilities displayed by the blindsight patient always fall short of the ability to judge spontaneously what kind of a stimulus has been presented to the blind field (thereby confirming Humphrey's observation that without striate cortex categorization of a visual input is impossible), and (2) that human subjects with striate cortical lesions can be induced to display the considerable discrimination abilities they retain in the blind part of the visual field only by persuading them to guess the location of something, or which of two specified alternatives was present, in a case where they insist that they saw nothing, showing thereby that without conscious experience of the input the subject has no way of checking his judgment against evidence on which such judgments are normally based.

Cowey and Stoerig's "Blindsight in Monkeys" (1995)

In addition to showing that we can use Humphrey's (1974) study as evidence of the effect of completely depriving an organism of its visual conscious experience, Cowey and Stoerig's (1995) paper also provides us with the first conclusive evidence that Descartes was mistaken in thinking that because only humans have language, because only they can describe what their conscious experiences are like, conscious experience is an exclusively human phenomenon. It also provides us with a methodology that when suitably adapted to the species in question should allow us to demonstrate the blindsight phenomenon in other species of mammal, in birds, in other vertebrates, and perhaps even in some invertebrates. If this latter prediction is fulfilled, it will show beyond serious doubt that conscious experience has been present in the brains of free-moving, living organisms for a very long time indeed. Even with only the monkey evidence available, the idea, supported by many contemporary philosophers, that conscious experience is a functionless epiphenomenon that appears only with the emergence of homo sapiens can no longer be sustained.

The Ventral and Dorsal Visual Pathways

Neuropsychological research on visual agnosias (Farah, 1990; Milner & Goodale, 1995) has drawn attention to the functional significance of an anatomically identified bifurcation within the visual areas of the brain between two streams or pathways, the ventral stream and the dorsal stream. As originally defined by Ungerleider and Mishkin (1982), these two pathways bifurcate downstream of the striate or primary visual cortex (V1). The ventral stream travels via the extrastriate visual areas (V2–V5) to the inferotemporal cortex. The dorsal stream travels upward to terminate in the posterior parietal cortex. In other words, the bifurcation between the two pathways lies entirely within the cerebral cortex.

Studies of the behavior of patients with lesions restricted to one or the other of these two pathways show that lesions of the ventral stream result, depending on the site and extent of the lesion, in a variety of functional disorders involving the loss or disturbance of visual conscious experience associated with a loss or disturbance of the ability to recognize objects and the situations in which they occur, conditions such as prosopagnosia (loss of the ability to recognize faces) and simultanagnosia (loss of the ability to recognize the relations between multiple objects in a visually presented scene). Lesions of the dorsal stream, on the other hand, result in disturbances of the visual control of voluntary movement.

Since the two pathways bifurcate downstream of the striate cortex (V1), they cannot be invoked to explain the phenomena of blindsight, i.e., the visual functions that survive lesions of V1. However, as is shown on figure 11.1, there is another pathway converging on the posterior parietal cortex, most of which consists of structures lying outside the cortex in the midbrain (superior colliculus and pulvinar). I call this the "subcortical (S-C) to dorsal[1] pathway." For although it is shown for convenience on figure 11.1 above both the dorsal and ventral streams properly so called, in fact, until it reaches its destination in the posterior parietal cortex, it is composed of structures (the superior colliculus and pulvinar) which lie below the cortex in the midbrain and thus below both dorsal and ventral streams.

As is apparent from figure 11.1, identifying the S-C to dorsal pathway gives us a second pair of visual pathways with the same destinations as the dorsal and ventral streams (the posterior parietal and inferotemporal cortices respectively) but bifurcating at the retina rather than downstream of the primary visual cortex (V1). Balancing the S-C to dorsal pathway is what we may call the "ventral pathway" (to distinguish it from the ventral stream that forms part of it), consisting of the lateral geniculate nucleus, the primary visual cortex (V1), the ventral stream (V2–V5), and the inferotemporal cortex. The two pathways so defined differ in two respects:

(1) Apart from the lateral geniculate nucleus, all the structures composing the ventral pathway are in the cortex, whereas all the structures composing the S-C to dorsal pathway, apart from its final destination, the posterior parietal cortex, are subcortical. (2) Unlike the ventral pathway, all of whose component struc-

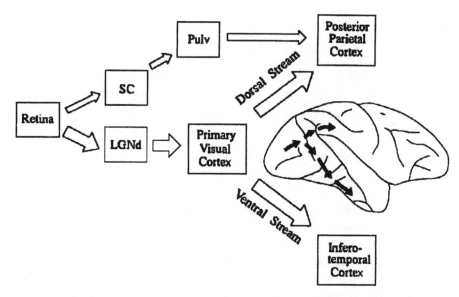

Figure 11.1   The ventral and dorsal streams (after Milner & Goodale, 1995, figure 3.1, page 68). Reprinted by permission of Oxford University Press.

tures apart from its destination, the infero-temporal cortex, are concerned only with the processing of visual information, all the structures composing the S-C to dorsal pathway without exception process information from all sensory modalities.

<h2 style="text-align:center">Recent Work on Attention</h2>

Recent work on the phenomenon of selective attention within conceptual analytic philosophy, experimental cognitive psychology, and neuroscience has shown that Broadbent's conclusions are in need of considerable modification and elaboration. A recent development that supports the notion that one of the functions of selective attention is to protect consciousness, considered as a limited-capacity channel, from overload by alerting it only to those inputs that are problematic for one reason or another comes from conceptual analysis as practiced by philosophers in the ordinary language tradition. At a one-day conference on attention and consciousness held in the Department of Philosophy, University College London, on May 26 1995, the Oxford philosopher Paul Snowdon presented an analysis of the concept of attention in ordinary language in which he drew a distinction between what he calls "Attention-N" ('N' for 'noticing') represented by passive voice expressions such as "Her attention was caught by an unusual—" and what he calls "Attention-A" ('A' for 'active') represented by active voice expressions such as "She paid close attention to the color and shape of the object or to what she was doing." It looks as though Attention-N is an unconscious involuntary mechanism for ensuring that problematic inputs and only such inputs are processed by consciousness, while Attention-A is a mechanism for ensuring that the focus of consciousness is maintained on a problematic input until it has been adequately categorized. There is evidence to suggest that the involuntary catching of attention by problematic inputs is a midbrain function mediated primarily by the superior colliculus and pulvinar,[2] while the conscious voluntary active holding of the focus onto an input until adequate categorization is achieved is mediated by the posterior parietal cortex.[3]

From a neuroscientific perspective, Michael Posner (Posner & Petersen, 1990; Posner & Dehaene, 1994) has adduced evidence that in addition to the function that it shares with the intracortical dorsal pathway of mediating the visual control of voluntary movement, the S-C to dorsal pathway (posterior parietal cortex, pulvinar, and superior colliculus) also has an important role in the control of selective attention, constituting, as it does, what he calls the "posterior attention system" (Posner & Dehaene, 1994, p. 76).

The posterior system would seem to have two functions: (1) that of bringing problematic inputs into the focus of attention in the first place (Snowdon's Attention-N), and (2) that of maintaining such inputs in the focus of attention until an adequate categorization is achieved (Snowdon's Attention-A). Of these two functions the first involves a mechanism that is necessarily unconscious and involuntary in the sense that the individual cannot decide or, in the true sense of that word, be instructed to notice things. We often say "Notice this" or "Notice that"; but such instructions only work if they are accompanied either by pointing at or otherwise highlighting the feature in question or by a verbal description of what is to be noticed, thereby creating an expectation of what is to be noticed. In either case the effect of the instruction is to facilitate rather than directly induce the noticing, which remains essentially involuntary. By contrast, the function of maintaining the focus of attention on a problematic input, once it has been noticed, until an adequate categorization has been achieved is an activity that is subject to conscious and voluntary control. If, as the evidence seems to suggest, tasks involving conscious and voluntary control are mediated by the cerebral cortex while those that are unconscious and involuntary are mediated by the midbrain and hindbrain, it looks as though Snowdon's Attention-A is mediated by the posterior parietal cortex and his Attention-N by the superior colliculus and pulvinar, with the superior colliculus controlling the peripheral aspects (the orientation of the receptor organs) and the pulvinar the ingate into consciousness.

The other attentional system that Posner distinguishes, the 'anterior attention system' (anterior cingulate and basal ganglia), would seem, in light of the evidence adduced by Pashler discussed below, to have the function of initiating and maintaining concentration on the processes of response selection and response execution. This type of selective attention, like that which maintains the focus of attention on a problematic input until adequate categorization of it is achieved, is under conscious and voluntary control and is to that extent also part of Snowdon's Attention-A.

Finally there is the recognition for which I am personally indebted to Harold Pashler (1991; 1998) that Broadbent's threefold system of limited-capacity channel with a bottleneck or filter which protects the LCC from overloading by restricting input access to it, and a buffer which holds prospective inputs until the bottleneck clears, has more than one embodiment in the brain. Pashler has shown in his experimental dual task studies that the response selection system is also a limited-capacity channel protected by a filter or bottleneck restricting access into it from what Broadbent calls the "category states" generated by his limited-capacity channel, the input categorization system. A similar bottleneck is to be expected restricting access into the response execution system. Similar bottlenecks may also exist in the human cerebral cortex to control access to the name-concept selection system (Wernicke's area) and the sentence articulation system (Broca's area). As we have seen, controlling access into the response selection and response execution systems and maintaining the focus of attention on these tasks until an appropriate response has been selected and its execution is complete would seem to be functions performed by Posner's anterior attentional system.

The Complementary Functions of Consciousness and the Unconscious Zombie-Within

The picture that emerges from the various strands of evidence described above is of two parallel but complementary and continuously interacting input-to-output transformation systems in the brain which I shall refer to respectively as 'consciousness' and the unconscious 'automatic pilot,' or 'zombie-within.'

Consciousness as an Input-Output Transformation System

On this hypothesis, consciousness is a limited-capacity channel (LCC), or rather a sequence of three such channels, which, together with what I call the 'emotion servo,' have four sequentially ordered functions: (1) the function of categorizing on the basis of what Broadbent (1971) calls the "evidence," [and which I equate with conscious experience, any input that is identified by the zombie-within as problematic, in that it is either unexpected or motivationally significant, i.e., significant relative to the individual's current or perennial motivational concerns (LCC 1),] (2) the function of reacting emotionally to inputs that have been identified as problematic, both before they have been categorized ('physical' pleasure/pain) and after they have been categorized ('mental' pleasure/pain), thereby ensuring that the subsequent processes of response selection and response execution are brought into an adaptive relation to the individual's current and perennial motivational concerns (the emotion servo), (3) the function of selecting a response appropriate both to the presence of a thing of that kind and to the individual's motivational concerns with respect to it (LCC 2), and (4) the function of initiating and monitoring the execution of the response selected (LCC 3).[4]

The evidence suggests that although much of what goes on is unconscious (in the sense that the details are not available to be described or reported by the human subject), the whole of the cerebral cortex in mammals is devoted to the implementation of consciousness in this functional sense. In general it would seem that what the human subject reports are the outcomes of the processes of selective attention, categorization, emotional reaction, response selection, and response execution, rather than the processes themselves. The exceptions to this rule are (1) the process of sensory conscious experience that can, to some extent, be described independently of the way it is finally (as opposed to tentatively) categorized, and (2) the thoughts (images and subvocal speech) that contribute to, but do not exhaust, the process of response selection, just as conscious experience of the feedback from the output as it develops contributes to but does not exhaust the process of response execution.

The Unconscious Automatic Pilot or Zombie-Within

The functions of the unconscious automatic pilot or zombie-within are (a) that of continuously scanning the total current input so as to alert consciousness to any input it identifies as problematic, and (b) that of protecting consciousness from overload either by ignoring those nonproblematic inputs that require no response or by responding appropriately but automatically and without categorization to those for which there already exists a well-practiced skill or other "instinctive" response pattern.

Like its namesake in popular mythology, the zombie-within is a creature of habit, routine, and unquestioning conformity to the instructions it receives from consciousness. Anything out of the ordinary is immediately passed on for processing by consciousness. The one respect in which it differs from the traditional picture of its mythical namesake is in its capacity to learn from experience, limited though that is to the progressive shaping of minor variations in behavior by their immediate consequences.

The evidence suggests that, with one possible exception, all the functions of the zombie-within are mediated by structures in the midbrain and brain stem. The one possible exception is in the case of the visual functions of reaching for objects and avoiding obstacles that are retained when visual conscious experience is abolished by lesions of the striate cortex (V1), thus occluding the ventral visual pathway and yielding the phenomenon of blindsight. The dorsal visual pathway, which is known to mediate these functions although it is composed in the main of midbrain structures such as the superior colliculus and pulvinar, also includes the posterior parietal cortex. It may be, however, that although the functions of reaching for objects and avoiding obstacles do not require visual conscious experience and are, to that extent, to be regarded on the present hypothesis as functions of the zombie-within, they do require the integration of visual information supplied by the zombie along the S-C to dorsal pathway with conscious experience of the somesthetic feedback from the movements involved as they develop, and that this integration is the contribution to these functions made by the posterior parietal cortex.

Interactions between the Two Systems

Although, as the blindsight phenomenon shows, there are other forms of interaction between the two systems, the three most important interactions between consciousness and the zombie-within are (1) the action of the zombie in alerting consciousness in general and conscious experience in particular to problematic inputs, (2) the gradual transfer to the zombie-within of stimulus-stimulus expectations and stimulus-response connections formed within consciousness as they become habitual (for PET scan evidence of this process, see Raichle et al., 1994), and (3) the integration of the two systems in a well-developed motor skill where, as the syntactic organization of movement becomes increasingly automatized, i.e., gets taken over by the zombie, the easier it becomes for the mechanisms of selective attention to ensure that consciousness is focussed on those aspects of the task that are crucial from the point of view of effective strategic decision making and the timely initiation of the selected response.

Modules within Consciousness and the Zombie-Within

The multiple functions identified within both consciousness and the zombie-within imply a multiplicity of modules within both systems. Figure 11.2 shows the arrangement of these modules as I currently construe it. As you will see, the diagram shows the output from the sense organs splitting into two streams, consciousness on the left, the zombie on the right.

Modules within the Zombie

The zombie is shown as consisting of four functionally defined modules: (1) the problematic input detector (PID), which separates inputs into problematic and nonproblematic on the basis of relatively coarse criteria of unexpected/expected and motivationally significant/insignificant, and transmits the former via (2) the involuntary attention focuser (peripheral), which mobilizes and directs movements of the head, eyes, and body so as to bring the source of the problematic input within the range of all relevant sense organs, (3) the involuntary attention focuser (central), which attracts the focus of conscious experience to that part of the sensorium where the problematic input is located, while either ignoring or routing nonproblematic inputs to output via (4) the automatic pilot.

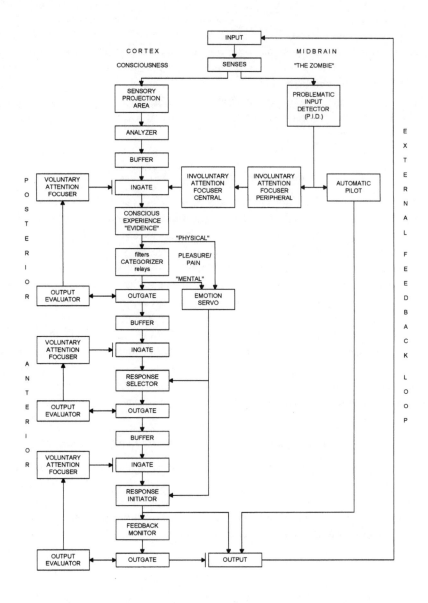

Figure 11.2 Consciousness and the "zombie-within"—suggested layout of modules.

Modules within Consciousness

Consciousness, as shown here, consists of three sequentially ordered limited-capacity channels (LCCs) concerned respectively with input categorization (perception), response selection, and response execution. The concept of the limited-capacity channel comes from Broadbent (1958) whose 1971 book *Decision and Stress* restricts its application to the process of input categorization. The evidence that there is more than one such channel in the brain comes from Pashler (1991; 1998). In order to protect it from overloading, Broadbent's model requires that each LCC be provided with a system of subordinate modules, including (a) an ingate, which controls access to the LCC, (b) a buffer or short-term memory store, in which inputs waiting to obtain access to the LCC are held until the ingate clears, (c) an attention focuser, which maintains the focus of attention on the task in hand until it is satisfactorily completed, and (d) an output evaluator, which checks the candidate outputs of the LCC and allows the attention focuser to open the ingate to a new input once the previous information-processing task has been satisfactorily completed, while at the same time opening (e) an outgate, which allows the approved output schema to proceed either directly to the initiation of a response or into the buffer of the next LCC in line.

In the case of the input-categorizing LCC, the limited-capacity channel is shown as divided into two separate modules, conscious experience which, to use Broadbent's (1971) term, provides the 'evidence' on which categorization is based and without which the blindsighted subject's judgments become 'pure guesswork,' and the categorization response itself. A similar division is shown within the response executor LCC between response initiation and feedback control.

Lying outside this system of three limited-capacity channels are two modules, the analyzer and the emotion servo. The existence of the analyzer is suggested by the known functions of the visual cortical areas V1–V5. Recordings from individual cells in these areas have revealed what are known as 'feature detectors', cells that fire in response to the presence within the current retinal input of various features and patterns that are relevant for the identification of objects and situations in the organism's visual environment. The features that are detected in this way become more and more abstract and involve responding to activity spread over a wider and wider area of the visual field the further they are from V1. Recent research by Steve Luck and Nancy Beach (1998) confirming the Feature Integration Theory (FIT) of Anne Treisman and her colleagues (Treisman, 1988; Treisman & Gelade, 1980; Treisman & Gormican 1988) suggests that the effect of the module here identified as conscious experience is to bind the information provided by these individual feature detectors into a single Gestalt, thereby generating the evidence on which categorization or interpretation of the input is subsequently based.

Whereas the analyzer is construed as a module that precedes and prepares the ground for the process of input categorization, the emotion servo is brought into play by the action of the input categorization LCC. This activation occurs both before categorization in response to 'raw', uninterpreted conscious experience, as in the case of 'physical' pleasure and pain, and after categorization, as in the case of 'mental' pleasure and pain. Its function is to provide motivation both for response selection and for response execution.

The Problematic Input Detector (PID)

Fundamental to the system whereby behavior is controlled by the brain as set out on figure 11. 2 is the problematic input detector (PID). The PID is that part of the zombie-within which determines whether a current input is or is not problematic, alerting consciousness to it if it is, either ignoring it or allowing it to proceed automatically to the selection and execution of a response if it is not.

In order to understand how the PID works, two questions need to be answered: (1) What sorts of input qualify as problematic? (2) How, given that input categorization does not occur before consciousness has been brought into play, are such inputs detected by the zombie?

Varieties of Problematic Input

An input is problematic if (a) it is unexpected, or, (b) if expected, it is motivationally significant, i.e., significant relative to the individual's current or perennial motivational concerns. An input is motivationally significant if it is (c) something the individual is searching or on the look out for, (d) a stimulus that is intrinsically pleasant or unpleasant (i.e., one whose pleasantness or unpleasantness does not depend on how it is categorized or interpreted), e.g., the pleasantness of the sensation of being stroked or the unpleasantness of the sensations of pain and nausea, and (e) a stimulus that has been associated with a motivationally significant past event, such as Plato's lyre which reminds the lover of his beloved.

How Different Varieties of Problematic Input Are Detected

Given the principle of association by contiguity, it can be predicted that an organism will build up a vast number of stimulus-stimulus expectations based on observed regularities in the way an input of one type is invariably succeeded by an input of another type. Given a background of such expectations, a second input that differs from that expected on the basis of past experience, given the first input, is going to stand out like a sore thumb.

We may suppose that the PID is sensitized to respond to the objects of search by the active disposition that initiates the search and guides it until either the object is found or the search is abandoned.

Although any such effect, if it exists, is concealed by the fact that intrinsically pleasant and unpleasant stimuli immediately attract conscious attention, there is some evidence to suggest that emotional reactions elicited by conscious experience of the stimuli before categorization may also be elicited by the alternative input system that serves the zombie-within. A study by Zihl, Tretter and Singer (1980), cited by Weiskrantz (1986, pp. 125–126), reports "an autonomic electro-dermal response . . . to [moving] visual stimuli in the absence of 'seeing'" in a case of blindsight; while Tranel and Damasio (1985), also cited by Weiskrantz (1986, pp. 137–138), "showed that two prosopagnosic patients who failed to rec-ognize familiar faces verbally nevertheless displayed a clear and strong skin con-ductance response to photographs of familiar faces relative to control faces." This evidence raises the possibility that emotional reactions to intrinsically pleasant and unpleasant stimuli may not be, as it subjectively appears, a response to con-scious experience of the stimuli in question. It may rather be a response to a pre-conscious input reaching the zombie-within that in turn attracts the focus of con-scious attention to the stimulus and emotional reaction as a unitary Gestalt. It suggests that these emotional reactions are triggered by a direct connection be-tween the problematic input detector (PID) and the emotion servo. But since its only function would appear to be to ensure a more rapid mobilization of motiva-tional resources than if it were routed through consciousness, this connection has been omitted from figure 11.2 in favor of the phenomenologically more signifi-cant contrast between emotional reactions that do and do not depend on the way the experience is conceptualized.

It is suggested that the function of the dream imagery characteristic of REM sleep is to 'stamp in' associations between events that have occurred during a previous waking period and motivationally significant past events at the expense of motivationally neutral associations formed during the same period. In REM sleep conscious experience is, as it were, being allowed to "freewheel" when de-coupled from sensory input, thus leaving it free to generate images, particularly visual ones, whose form is determined only by the new associative links formed as a result of the attention focusing and categorizing of problematic inputs that have taken place during the preceding period of waking and by the individual's current emotional preoccupations.

Conscious/Phenomenal Experience

Conscious/phenomenal experience, on this view, is the first stage in the process whereby problematic inputs are processed by consciousness. Its function is to provide the evidence on which the categorization of problematic inputs is based, by modifying the figure-ground relations (see figure 10.1, p. 110) within the cen-tral representation of the input until an adequate categorization is selected.

Intrinsic Figure-Ground Differentiation
versus Imposed Figure-Ground Organization

Two kinds of figure-ground relation need to be distinguished. On the one hand there is the intrinsic figure-ground differentiation whereby one part of the current input (the figure) stands out, is more salient, and thus catches the attention more readily than the rest (the ground), simply by virtue of the sharpness and magnitude of the contrast between the two. The other is the figure-ground organization, properly so called, that is imposed on the input from the sensory projection areas of the cortex by the process whereby conscious/phenomenal experience is generated.

The two forms of figure-ground differentiation are connected in that the sharper the intrinsic figure-ground contrast, the more strongly structured and therefore less malleable is the input that is available for molding by conscious experience. In other words, the larger and simpler the intrinsic contrast between figure and ground (salience), the less room there is for conscious experience to impose a different pattern of figure-ground organization.

Conscious/Phenomenal Experience
as Imposed Figure-Ground Organization

We have seen that on the present hypothesis it is the output, or "evidence," as Broadbent (1971) calls it, generated by the process of selective attention that constitutes the conscious/phenomenal experience to which the introspecting subject is responding when she describes what it is like either to receive sensory input from a particular input source in the environment or to imagine being exposed to it. The luminosity, or "phosphorescence," which is the most striking feature of conscious/phenomenal experience from the standpoint of the introspective observer, enables a linguistically competent human to give a running commentary both on the sequence of events in her stimulus environment and her conscious/phenomenal experience of those events at the time and to provide a first-hand report on some of them subsequently. It also enables the organism to check its categorization of a problematic input against the evidence on which the categorization is based. Without this check the blindsighted subject loses all confidence in the sometimes remarkably accurate discriminations he is able to make relying solely on the subconscious system. Such discriminations, he insists, are "pure guesswork." This lack of confidence may also explain the inability of blindsighted patients to initiate voluntary action based upon their blind field discriminations to which Marcel (1988) has drawn attention.

Mental Imagery

Mental imagery is a form of conscious experience that occurs in a variety of different contexts—in dreams, in daydreaming, in the recollection of past events, and in planning the future. Phenomenologically it resembles and can sometimes be confused with the kind of sensory conscious experience that provides the evidence for the categorization of an input. Moreover, there is evidence from a study using positron emission tomography (PET) (Kosslyn et al., 1995) that when a subject forms a visual image of a picture he or she has just been shown, the same pattern of activity develops in all the principal visual areas of the cortex, including V1, as that which occurs when the subject is looking at the actual picture. This reinstatement of the cortical activity involved in sense perception in the absence of the input otherwise required for its occurrence is undoubtedly the substance behind Hume's much criticized claim "that all our simple ideas in their first appearance are deriv'd from simple impressions, which are correspondent to them, and which they exactly represent" (Hume, 1978, p. 4). Aside from the fact that its form is not determined by current sensory input, the principal difference between a mental image and a perceptual experience is its relation to the process of categorization. We have seen that in sense perception conscious experience precedes and provides the evidence on which categorization is subsequently based. In the case of a mental image, as Kant (1929, pp. 182–183) demonstrates in developing his concept of the "schema," the construction of a mental image presupposes a prior categorization or conceptualization of what the image is to be an image of.

In order to account for this kind of control over the process of conscious experience on the present model as laid out on figure 11.2, we would have to include a number of "re-entrant" (Edelman, 1987) or "recurrent" (Jordan, 1986) circuits feeding back from the categorization and response selection modules.[5] Such circuits are well attested anatomically: Jordan (1986) has shown that, along with the reverberatory circuits (Hebb, 1949) required to bridge the gap between the offset of the first stimulus and the onset of the second, such circuits are an essential feature of any neural network that can learn to "expect" or "anticipate" the second of two sequentially ordered stimuli on presentation of the first. As we have already seen, an extensive repertoire of such expectations is required as a background against which an unexpected input will stand out as figure and thus be referred to consciousness by the zombie-within.

It seems that the recurrent circuits required to account for the generation of mental imagery would need to feed back from the categorization and response selection modules to the sensory projection areas (such as V1 in the case of a visual image) to ensure that conscious experience is supplied with the necessary "raw material," to the analyzer to ensure that it is given the necessary structure, to the relevant ingate to ensure access into conscious experience, and to the voluntary attention focuser to ensure the maintenance of the image until it has served whatever purpose it was intended to fulfil. However, in order to avoid too much complication these circuits are not shown on figure 11.2. The only recurrent circuits shown are those connecting the outgate of each of the three LCCs to its respective ingate and the external feedback loop connecting the motor output to sensory input.

It is suggested that in the case of a mental image these recurrent circuits impose a pattern of figure-ground organization on a field that is intrinsically weakly structured (figure 11.3) and does not, therefore, restrict the pattern of organization that can be imposed on it in the way a more salient and strongly structured input would do. This results in a pattern of figure-ground organization that in the ex-

Figure 11.3   A weakly structured field.

treme case bears no relation to any objective structure in the input source. In the case of vision, the Rorschach (1932) ink blots provide a classic example of a series of such weakly structured fields, which permit and thus promote the formation of a wide variety of such images.[6]

We know from the introspective reports of human subjects that such images occur both in waking consciousness as part of the thought process whereby solutions to problems are generated and as the predominant feature of the dreams that occur during the rapid-eye-movement (REM) phase of sleep. In the latter case there is strong circumstantial evidence for the occurrence of such imagery in the sleep of those mammals in which it occurs.[7] Although there is at present no corresponding evidence for the occurrence of mental imagery as an aid to animal problem-solving, it would be surprising if an ability that is almost certainly present during sleep were not exploited for more obviously practical purposes during waking.[8]

Categorization

Categorization is the process whereby problematic inputs are classified according to the kind of object or situation of whose presence in the organism's stimulus environment the input is a reliable indicator. It is the function of categorization to ensure that the universal, kind, or category under which an input is subsumed lines up with what Skinner (1969) calls the "contingencies" operating in the organism's environment. A contingency for Skinner is a sequence of events whereby, under certain antecedent conditions, behaving in a certain way will have certain predictable consequences. By classifying its problematic inputs in a way that enables it to anticipate the consequences of selecting one form of behavior rather than another, the organism puts itself in a state of readiness to select a successful behavioral strategy appropriate both to the presence of an object or situation of that kind and to whatever may be the organism's current behavioral objectives as and when the occasion for action arises.

Two Components of Categorization: The Input Filter and the Output Relay

We have seen that Broadbent (1971) distinguishes two processes within what we are here calling 'categorization', namely, pigeonholing and categorization proper. On his view, 'pigeonholing' is simply a matter of slotting an input into a preexisting category, whereas 'categorization' in his sense involves either creating a new category altogether or modifying the boundaries of an existing category so as to fit a new instance. This way of construing the matter is mistaken insofar as it assumes that the organism cannot respond adaptively to an input without specifically classifying it as an encounter with an object or situation of a particular kind. On the present hypothesis, only problematic inputs require classification in this way. Once a behavior pattern has become habitual, direct input-to-output transformations replace responses mediated by categorization and motivational choice. Evidence that such replacement of one pattern of brain activity by another as behavior becomes habitual comes from the study by Raichle et al. (1994) mentioned above.

The categories that make up an individual's conceptual scheme, to one of which every problematic input must be assigned in order for the process of categorization to succeed, have two components. One component is the filter, which selects those inputs that satisfy the entry criteria for the concept in question and rejects those otherwise similar inputs that do not satisfy them. The other component is what we may think of as a relay, which preselects all those behavioral strategies that can be relied on to yield a predictable consequence, when emitted in the presence of an object or situation of that kind. Once this set of behavioral strategies has been preselected, a choice is made between them in the light of subsequent environmental conditions and the organism's motivational attitude to the expected consequences of adopting one course of action rather than another. In the case of a linguistically competent human being, an important group of behavioral strategies that are preselected in this way are strategies for selecting appropriate words and sentence frames for describing objects and situations of the kind in question.

The Emotion Servo

Skinner's concept of the "three-term contingency" (antecedent conditions, behavior called for under those conditions, and the consequences of so behaving) not only provides a clue to the nature of the concepts or categories the organism uses in classifying its problematic inputs; it is also the key to understanding the operation of what we are calling the 'emotion servo'. As we have seen, the function of this module is to modulate behavior in such a way as to bring it into conformity with the organism's motivational objectives. As the contingency unfolds and as its conformity or lack of conformity to those objectives becomes apparent, so the organism's emotional reaction changes. The same sequence of events will evoke a different sequence of emotional reactions depending on the organism's motivational attitude to the anticipated or actual consequences of its behavior. If the consequence is attractive, anticipating its appearance produces excitement; its actual occurrence, pleasure; its failure to appear when expected, first anger then misery or depression. If the consequence is repulsive or, as Skinner would say, "aversive," anticipating its appearance produces fear or anxiety; its actual occurrence, first anger then misery or depression; its failure to appear when expected, relief.

Each different variety of emotional response is characterized (a) by the type of situation that evokes it: i.e., whether it is prospective, as in excitement and fear; retrospective, as in anger, relief, and depression; or focused on the moment, as in pleasure and disgust, (b) by its position on the pleasant–unpleasant dimension: i.e., pleasant, in the case of excitement, pleasure, and relief; unpleasant, in fear, disgust, and depression; mixed, in the case of anger and apathy, (c) by its position on the arousal dimension: i.e., high, in the case of excitement, anger, and fear; moderate, in pleasure and disgust; low, in relief, apathy, and depression, and (d) by a characteristic impulse: i.e., the impulse to sigh in relief, to smile in pleasure, to jump for joy in excitement, to attack in anger, to freeze or run away in fear, to vomit in disgust, to do nothing or punish oneself in depression.

Locating These Modules within the Brain

Evidence from a variety of sources—neurology, electrophysiology, and, most recently, the newly discovered brain-imaging techniques—makes it possible to propose a tentative identification of the modules shown on figure 11.2 with specific anatomically defined structures within the brain.

The Ventral and S-C to Dorsal Pathways

For the most part, I shall confine my remarks on this score to the upstream portion of figure 11.2, that which precedes the transition within consciousness from conscious experience to categorization, since this is the area to which the neurological evidence described under "The Ventral and S-C to Dorsal Visual Pathways" above relates. That evidence shows that in order to account for the visual functions that survive lesions of primary visual cortex (V1) and the consequent loss of visual conscious experience, the phenomenon known as 'blindsight', we must suppose that the residual visual functions are mediated by what we are calling the 'subcortical (S-C) to dorsal pathway', which proceeds by way of the superior colliculus and pulvinar to the posterior parietal cortex. This S-C to dorsal pathway bifurcates at the retina from the ventral pathway consisting of the lateral geniculate nucleus, the primary visual or striate cortex (V1), and the extrastriate visual areas (V2–V5) to the inferotemporal cortex. These two pathways, together with the intracortical dorsal and ventral streams distinguished by Ungerleider and Mishkin (1982) that bifurcate downstream of V1, are shown on figure 11.1.

Whereas all the structures composing the ventral pathway, with the doubtful exception of the inferotemporal cortex,[9] are exclusively visual in function, those composing the S-C to dorsal pathway (superior colliculus, pulvinar, and posterior parietal cortex) subserve all sensory modalities. This is consistent with Posner's (Posner & Petersen, 1990; Posner & Dehaene, 1994) hypothesis that the function of these structures, in their capacity as the "posterior attention system," is to control the focus of sensory attention as it switches from one modality to another or concentrates different modalities on the same area of environmental space. This concatenation of evidence allows us, in the case of the visual modality, to identify the bifurcation between consciousness and the zombie-within as shown on figure 11.2 with the bifurcation at the retina between a ventral pathway consisting of the lateral geniculate nucleus, the primary visual or striate cortex (V1), the extrastriate visual areas (V2–V5), and the inferotemporal cortex corresponding to the upstream portion of what I am calling "consciousness," and the S-C to dorsal pathway consisting of the superior colliculus and pulvinar, but almost certainly excluding its destination, the posterior parietal cortex, corresponding to the zombie. These relationships are shown on figure 11.4. It is a redrawing of Milner and Goodale's diagram (figure 11.1 above) which, for the sake of clarity, omits the dorsal stream properly so called (connecting V1 to the posterior parietal cortex) and is arranged in the same format as the upper part of figure 11.2 with the ventral pathway on the left and the S-C to dorsal pathway on the right.

Given the identification of the ventral pathway as the route whereby information is passed from the retina into consciousness and the S-C to dorsal pathway as the route into and through the zombie-within, what are we to say about the one exception, the posterior parietal cortex, which is the terminus of both the S-C to dorsal pathway and the intracortical dorsal stream? There would seem to be a connection here between the posterior parietal and the visual functions of reaching for objects (Weiskrantz, 1986; Cowey & Stoerig, 1995) and avoiding obstacles (Humphrey, 1974),[10] which are retained when visual conscious experience is abolished by lesions of the striate cortex (V1), thus occluding the ventral visual pathway and yielding the phenomenon of blindsight. Although it is clear from the performance of human subjects with lesions of the striate cortex (blindsight) that the functions of reaching for objects and avoiding obstacles do not require visual conscious experience of the relevant stimuli and are, to that extent, to be regarded on the present hypothesis as functions mediated by the zombie-within, the fact that the subject in such cases is induced to reach for an object he does not "see" by an appropriate instruction to guess where it was shows that conscious

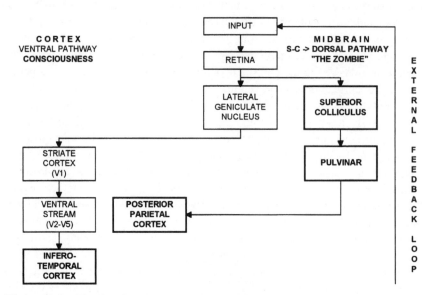

Figure 11.4.   The dorsal and ventral pathways. Multimodal modules in bold.

experience of some kind is involved in the production of such behavior. A plausible hypothesis would be that reaching and obstacle-avoiding behavior, though it does not require visual conscious experience, does require the integration of visual information supplied by the zombie along the S-C to dorsal pathway with conscious experience of the somesthetic feedback from the movements involved as they develop, and that this integration is the contribution to these functions made by the posterior parietal cortex. However, some recent evidence (Rossetti, Rode & Boisson, 1995; Rossetti, 2001) on the somesthetic counterpart of blindsight that the authors refer to as "numb-sense" shows that a patient (JA) with this condition can use his normal left hand to point accurately at the location of stimuli applied to the numb right hand, which he cannot consciously feel. This shows that, provided the blindsight or numb-sense subject can be induced to guess at the location of the target object by pointing at it, successful voluntary movement does not require conscious experience, whether visual or somesthetic, of the target toward which the movement is directed. What the evidence does not show is that such voluntary movement is possible without conscious experience of the feedback from the movement itself, whether visual, somesthetic, or both.

Although, as this evidence clearly demonstrates, the S-C to dorsal pathway has a secondary function in the visual control of voluntary movement, the fact that all its structures process information from all sensory modalities, when combined with the brain-imaging and neurophysiological data reviewed by Posner and Dehaene (1994) and the evidence of disorders of attention (such as unilateral neglect) resulting from lesions of these structures, suggests that its primary function is to integrate the involuntary alerting of conscious attention to problematic inputs from all sensory modalities mediated by the two midbrain structures, the superior colliculus and pulvinar, with the voluntary maintenance of the focus of attention on such inputs until an adequate categorization of them is achieved mediated by the posterior parietal cortex. On this hypothesis the posterior parietal is construed as having two functions: (1) a general function which is to maintain the focus of conscious attention within and between the different sensory modalities (acting on structures such as those in the ventral stream in the case of vision) on inputs to which the focus has been initially attracted by the zombie (in the shape of the superior colliculus and pulvinar) until such time as an adequate categorization of those inputs has been achieved,[11] and (2) a specific function to control voluntary movement by integrating, through the same mechanism of conscious attention-focusing, the visual and somesthetic feedback from such movements as they develop.

Provisional Anatomical Conclusions

Assuming that this analysis is approximately correct, we are in a position to make some tentative identifications of the modules shown on figure 11.2 with some of the actual structures that have been identified anatomically within the brain as laid out on figures 11.1 and 11.4. These tentative identifications are set out on figure 11.5 which is a reworking of figure 11.2 with the names of the neural structures substituted for the functional descriptions of the modules with which they have been provisionally identified in the preceding discussion in the special case of vision. Thus, in place of the senses, we have, in the case of the visual modality, the retina. In place of the sensory projection area, we have, in the case of the visual modality, the striate cortex. In place of the analyzer, we have, in the case of the visual modality, V2–V5. In place of the problematic input detector (PID), we have, for all modalities, the midbrain reticular formation.[12] In place of the automatic pilot, we have the cerebellum. In place of the involuntary attention focuser (peripheral), we have the superior colliculus.[13] In place of the involuntary attention focuser (central), we have the pulvinar.[14] In place of the voluntary attention focuser, we have the posterior parietal cortex. Finally, in place of conscious experience "evidence," we have, at least in the case of vision, the inferotemporal cortex.[15] You will notice that figure 11.5 omits the connection between the pulvinar and the posterior parietal cortex shown on figures 11.1 and 11.4 and which is needed to explain the visual control of reaching for objects and obstacle avoidance when the relevant parts of V1 have been destroyed (blindsight). This has been done in order not to obscure the functionally much more important connection between the pulvinar and the ingate controlling access to the inferotemporal cortex alias conscious experience. Further downstream the only identification to have emerged at all clearly from the preceding discussion is that between the feedback monitor and the dorsal stream.[16] However, two other identifications have been included on the basis of what has been known for a

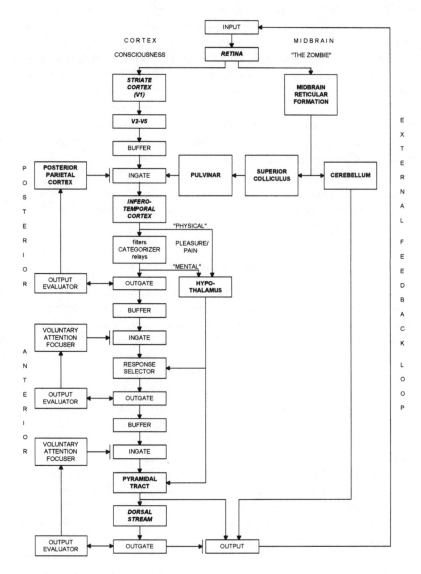

Figure 11.5 Consciousness and the "zombie-within." Tentative identifications in bold; visual structures in italics.

long time, that between response initiation and the pyramidal tract and between the emotion servo and the hypothalamus. Likewise the recent work on numb-sense mentioned above will doubtless soon make possible the identification of the somesthetic counterparts of the purely visual structures shown on figure 11.5. It may be that similar identifications can already be suggested for other sensory modalities. If not, future research will doubtless allow us to fill these gaps too.

But there, for the present, I shall let the matter rest. I hope I have said enough to persuade you that we are now in a position to answer the question, which has remained unanswered since my paper "Is consciousness a brain process?" (Place, 1956), namely, "If consciousness *is* a brain process, which of the various processes in the brain that we now identify neuroanatomically is it?" It turns out in the light of what has been said above that that question is too simplistic. But complicated though it is, I hope I have persuaded you that the rudiments of an answer are within our grasp.[17]

On the Social Relativity of Truth and the Analytic/Synthetic Distinction

The issue that I shall be addressing in this paper is a philosophical puzzle that confronts and is extensively discussed by specialists in such disciplines as the history of ideas, the history of science, the sociology of knowledge, and the sociology of science, but which with one or two honorable exceptions has tended to be neglected by professional philosophers. The puzzle is generated by a peculiarity of the verb 'to know,' which has been familiar to philosophers ever since it was first pointed out by Plato in the *Theaitetus*. If I say of some other person— let us call him Baralipton—that "Baralipton knows that *p*," I thereby commit myself to asserting the truth of the proposition to the truth of which I am claiming that Baralipton is committed. If I want to avoid that commitment to the truth of the proposition I am attributing to a third party, I have to say, in the case where I am uncertain as to whether *p* is true or false, that Baralipton thinks or believes that *p* or, where in my view *p* is false, that Baralipton thinks or believes that he knows that *p* but he doesn't.

This peculiarity of what Wittgenstein would have called the grammar of the verb 'to know', when used to characterize a propositional attitude, is very understandable if we consider a case where Baralipton and I share a common social environment. For in that case it is unlikely that I should find myself wanting to mention an opinion of Baralipton's without at the same time wanting to make clear my own view on the question at issue. But the situation is very different in the case where Baralipton belongs to a social environment far removed in space or time from our own. Suppose, for example, that Baralipton lived at a time when everyone accepted and would have said that they knew that the world is flat, that the whale is a very large fish, and that there is at least one known case of a whale swallowing a man. In this case not only is it very inconvenient to have to talk about these beliefs of Baralipton's as things he *thinks* he knows but doesn't really because, as we now know, they are actually false: it involves us in doing something that contravenes the canons of historical and sociological scholarship in that it commits us to judging a past or otherwise alien culture from the chauvinistic standpoint of our own particular time and cultural setting.

The standard response of sociologists and historians of ideas when confronted by this difficulty is to adopt some version of the doctrine of the social relativity of truth and knowledge according to which what is true and what is known to be true depends on the social context of the proposition whose truth is at issue. It is my belief that the charge of cultural chauvinism has to be taken seriously. I also believe that the charge of cultural chauvinism cannot be avoided without adopting *some* version of the social relativity thesis. But I am equally convinced that the two most widely accepted versions of the doctrine that truth is socially relative, which I shall call the 'naïve' and the 'sophisticated' versions of the doctrine respectively, must be rejected. I shall, therefore, proceed to an exposition of the two versions of the doctrine that I reject, together with my reasons for rejecting them, before going on to state the version that I endorse.

The Naïve Version of the Social Relativity Thesis

The naïve version of the doctrine of the social relativity of truth holds that what is true or false is what is believed to be true or false within a particular social group. This version of the doctrine is so obviously self-defeating that no self-respecting philosopher since Protagoras has taken it seriously. In recent years, however, it has become rather less easy to ignore by virtue of its adoption as an axiomatic principle by the Edinburgh-based so-called Strong Programme in the sociology of science led by David Bloor. Bloor's Strong Programme seeks to explain the historical development of science in sociological terms while remaining completely impartial with respect to the truth or falsity, rationality or irrationality of the beliefs and theories it discusses. It follows that, within the framework of such an enterprise, the only sense that can be given to the claim that a particular belief is true or false is that it is or was believed to be true or false, as the case may be, by a particular social group, in this case, a particular community of scientists. Since one of the principles included in the Strong Programme according to Bloor (1976, pp. 4–5) is the principle of reflexivity, which requires the principles constituting the Programme to have application to the Programme itself, it cannot be argued that this suspension of judgment is only a provisional attitude adopted for heuristic reasons, rather than a principle to which the Programme is seriously committed. The Programme, consequently, lays itself open to the following objection.

The minimal definition of a social group is the group that is constituted by any two human beings. You can, if you like, take a higher number than two as the minimum required to constitute a social group, but any proposed number will be arbitrary; and it doesn't, in any case, affect the logic of the argument what the precise number required to constitute a social group is taken to be. Nor is the logic of the argument affected by any further constraints that may be added as to the nature and possibility of social interaction between the members of the group thereby constituted.

Given this definition of a social group and given also the principle that a proposition is true, if and only if it is held to be true by all the members of a particular social group, it follows that any proposition that is held to be true by more than one person is true and any proposition that is held to be false by more than one person is false. Consequently if I want to show that this version of the thesis that truth is socially relative is false, all I need to do, according to this version of the thesis, is to find one other person who joins me in holding this version of the thesis to be false. Provided I can find such a person, and I anticipate no difficulty on that score, it follows that, for the social group so constituted, this version of the social relativity thesis is false. The fact that the same criterion also makes this version of the thesis true, by virtue of the fact that a social group consisting of at least two people holds it to be true, need be of no concern to me or any one who thinks like me. For my concern is with what is true for me rather than what is true for other people, assuming that we allow, as this theory must allow—but as I, along with most people, would not allow—that a proposition can be simultaneously true for one social group and false for another.

It follows that although this version of the social relativity thesis is not self-defeating, in the sense that it entails its own falsity in the strong sense that excludes the possibility of its also being true, it *is* self-defeating insofar as it excludes the possibility of *any* proposition's being true or false in this strong sense; and, since that must include the social relativity thesis itself, *that* thesis cannot be recommended as true to someone else without simultaneously conceding not just the listener's right to reject it as false but that insofar as there is disagreement about its truth value, it is just as much false as it is true.

Winch's Version of the Social Relativity Thesis

A more sophisticated version of the doctrine of the social relativity of truth, but one that I also reject, is the view that Peter Winch comes close to adopting, but does not quite adopt, in his paper "Understanding a primitive society" (Winch, 1964). This version of the doctrine differs from the naive version in that it does not claim *tout court* that if a proposition is accepted as true within a particular social group, then it is true. On this more sophisticated version of the theory, a proposition is true if and only if it satisfies certain fairly rigorous criteria that have to be satisfied before it can be accepted as true by the social group in question. While it is accepted that in many, if not most, cases the criteria for accepting the truth of a proposition in one social group do not differ substantially from those accepted in another, there are other cases where the criteria differ considerably from one society to another. In such cases, so it is alleged, we simply have to accept that what is true by the criteria that are accepted within one social group may be false by the standards accepted within another group.

I say that Winch "comes close to adopting" this version of the doctrine of the social relativity of truth and not that he actually does so, partly because he assures me[1] that he does not and never has subscribed to this view, and partly because a careful reading of the text confirms that what he is claiming is socially relative is not so much the method of truth determination as what it is and is not rational or sensible to believe, given the background assumptions shared by a particular social group. Nevertheless, because he focuses on an example, in which what is at issue is a particular method of determining the truth and falsity of certain propositions, it is not altogether surprising that he has been widely misinterpreted as holding the view that I have suggested he comes close to adopting. Moreover, since this is the conclusion someone might well be tempted to draw on the evidence he presents, and since there is no one else whom one can readily cite as subscribing to what I am calling the "sophisticated version of the doctrine of the social relativity of truth," it is in this sense, with suitable apologies for thereby distorting the author's intention, that I propose to interpret Winch's argument.

Winch develops his argument in relation to the example of the beliefs and truth determination practices of a Central African tribe, the Azande, as recorded in the late Professor E. E. Evans-Pritchard's book *Witchcraft and Oracles and Magic among the Azande* (1937). In Zande society, as Evans-Pritchard describes it, questions of the form "Is A being bewitched by B?" are asked and answered either affirmatively or negatively by consulting what is known as a 'poison oracle'. A poison oracle is consulted by asking leading questions, addressed to the oracle, of a kind to which a straight "Yes" or "No" answer can be given, while at the same time administering a special poison to a young chicken. Each question requires a new chicken that has not received the poison before. As each question is asked, the oracle is instructed to let the chick live if the answer is "Yes" and let the chick die if the answer is "No," or vice versa as the case may be.

The poison, which is a form of strychnine, is administered in a diluted form so that only about half the birds to whom it is administered actually die. But when it does act, it acts fast. Within a couple of minutes of the poison being administered, it will be clear either that the death agony has begun or that the bird has not been affected. Since the chances of the chicken dying or surviving are roughly 50/50, the poison oracle, considered as a decision making procedure, operates rather like tossing a coin; though it can, no doubt, be rather more easily fiddled, given that the questioner, who is always a different person from the operator who administers the poison, is a good judge of the chicken's chances of survival and adjusts his questions accordingly.

Now it is quite clear that in our culture a procedure such as this would not be acceptable as a way of determining the truth value of any proposition, although we frequently use analogous procedures like tossing a coin or running a horse race in order to decide issues such as which side shall bat first in a cricket match or who shall receive the lion's share of the bets laid with the bookmakers and the totalizator. But it is important to recognize that it is not just the procedure for answering the question that we would reject: we would also reject the question the procedure is designed to answer. For us, the question 'Is A bewitching B?' has no need of an answer. We just don't believe, as the Azande do, that people can influence each other's lives in this supernatural manner. Consequently for us, questions of the form "Who is bewitching B?" simply do not arise. No procedure is required for giving an answer to such questions. For us the issue is decided a priori in favor of the answer "No one," regardless of who the B in question is. Similarly we have a ready-made a priori answer to the question "Is A bewitching B?" which is invariably "No," regardless of what proper names are substituted for A and B in this sentence frame. But this is precisely the judgment that, as I interpret him, Winch thinks we are not entitled to make. On this view, we have no right to conclude that the Azande are mistaken in believing of some A and some B that A is bewitching B, precisely because we do not accept their criteria for deciding the truth or falsity of such statements, just as they presumably would not accept the criteria that lead *us* to conclude that witchcraft does not exist.

Now that argument might perhaps carry some weight if it were the case that the Azande use different criteria from those that we use for deciding the truth or falsity of *all* the propositions whose truth or falsity they acknowledge. But in fact, as Evans-Pritchard repeatedly emphasizes in his book, in relation to the kind of commonsense questions that arise for the Azande in the same way as they do for us, the criteria that a proposition must satisfy in order to be judged true by an Azande are no different from those required to satisfy us of the proposition's truth. To use one of Evans-Pritchard's examples (1937, pp. 69–70), when the Azande assert that the injuries suffered by a group of people on a particular occasion were due to witchcraft, they are not denying what is obvious to us— namely, that they were injured when the granary they were sitting under collapsed on top of them. Nor are they denying that the reason why the granary collapsed was that the termites had eaten the wooden poles that held it up, nor that the reason why the people were sitting under the granary was to shelter from the midday sun. All the Azande are doing is being good Leibnizians and demanding an answer to the question "Why did the granary fall down at the precise moment when those people were sheltering under it and not half an hour earlier or half an hour later, when they weren't or wouldn't have been?" This is a question that we would dismiss as a matter of pure coincidence but which for the Azande requires an answer in terms of the influence of witchcraft.

On our understanding of the matter, to say that some aspect of the event is a matter of chance or coincidence is to say that there is nothing in the causal factors that brought about the event in question that requires that the event should take that particular form rather than some other form—in this case, nothing that required that the event should occur at that precise moment. It follows that since the Azande are claiming that there is a causal factor, namely witchcraft, that *does* require that event to occur at that time, rather than at some other time, it is clear that in terms of the logical principles we accept, the law of the excluded middle requires that either they are right and we are wrong or that they are wrong and we are right. In other words, our criteria for deciding the truth of propositions, which include the law of the excluded middle, require us to come down on one side of the fence or the other on an issue such as this. Moreover, there is no reason to think that, in this respect, the criteria for the truth of a proposition that the Azande accept are any different from ours. It is just that they come down on a different side of this particular fence from the side we come down on.

But even if it could be shown that the Azande operate with a different set of criteria when they apply the terms that the Zande-English Lexicon translates as 'true' and 'false' from those we use in applying the English words 'true' and 'false', we would not, I think, be entitled to claim that the Azande decide truth and falsity by a different set of criteria from those that we apply. The conclusion we would have to come to, I suggest, is that the Zande-English Lexicon has got it wrong, that these Zande words are not in fact their words for 'true' and 'false' at all but, are at best, the nearest equivalent that their language possesses. I would go further than this and claim that no word in any other natural language can be regarded as the equivalent in that language of the English word 'true' unless one of the principles governing its application is the principle of noncontradiction.

The principle of noncontradiction rules out the possibility that for the same p, both p and not-p are true. Consequently, by that criterion, no word in any other natural language could be accepted as equivalent to the English word 'true' if, by applying the criteria for deciding whether or not the term in question applies to a particular proposition, we find ourselves compelled to conclude not just that what is believed in one language and culture is different from what is believed in another language and culture, but that the very same proposition is true by the standards of one language and culture and false by the standards of another. If *that* principle is accepted, as I am sure it must be, there is no room for what I am calling Winch's version of the doctrine that truth is socially relative. For if, by applying what are alleged to be procedures for establishing the truth of propositions in a given language and culture, the same proposition comes out true by those procedures and false by the procedures we accept as governing the application of the words 'true' and 'false' in English or any other natural language that uses the same conventions for its equivalent of "true," we should be forced to conclude either that the procedures have been misdescribed or that they are not, in fact, procedures for determining what in English is called "the truth of a proposition."

But if I am right in thinking that the principle of noncontradiction is an essential ingredient in *any* set of criteria for deciding between what is true and what is false, there is no avoiding the conclusion that it must either be the case that the Azande are correct in believing that witchcraft in their sense exists or that we are correct in believing that it doesn't.

Nor do we have to rely simply on an argument, based on the vast numerical superiority of those who reject Zande beliefs in this respect over those who accept them, in order to justify our belief in the nonexistence of Zande witchcraft influences. For we have the advantage that they do not have of being literate and of thus being able, with Evans-Pritchard's help, to commit their beliefs to paper. This enables us to detect internal inconsistencies within those beliefs that are not apparent when they are communicated solely by word of mouth and operated within a complex system of social practices. For those inconsistencies I refer you to Evans-Pritchard's (1937) book, particularly pages 24–29, where he discusses inconsistencies in Zande beliefs about the inheritance of witchcraft in relation to vengeance magic, and chapter 8, where he discusses the question "Are witches conscious agents?" (Evans-Pritchard, 1937, pages 118–133).

When confronted with such inconsistencies or other embarrassing consequences of the theory, an intelligent Zande theologian can easily devise some suitable piece of casuistry in order to wriggle out of the difficulty, just as our theologians do in similar circumstances. Indeed, Evans-Pritchard gives an example of just such a move on pages 24–25 where the relatives of a man who has been proved by the poison oracle to be a witch wriggle out of the uncomfortable implication of that conclusion when it is combined with the doctrine that witchcraft is inherited in the male line—namely, that they too are witches—by accusing the mother of the witch of having committed adultery. This accusation, if true, would make the witch a bastard and hence not a blood relative in the male line. Such ad hoc special pleading may satisfy those who already accept the basic assumptions of the belief system, but it is hardly likely to persuade the unbeliever. It is true that, as Kuhn (1962) has pointed out, scientists often put forward essentially similar ad hoc saving hypotheses when confronted by evidence inconsistent with existing theory; but at least, in this case, the scientific community is made uncomfortable by too frequent resort to devices of this kind and is ultimately stimulated to undertake a radical rethinking of the problem, which, in turn, leads to what Kuhn calls a "paradigm shift" and a "scientific revolution." The fact that scientists are eventually compelled to rethink their position in the light of repeated disconfirmation, whereas magicoreligious believers always find some way of reconciling the evidence with and thus retaining their original opinion, may provide some justification for preferring a scientific view to a magicoreligious one in cases where the two conflict; but the problem of chauvinism with respect to truth remains, especially in the context of the history of science itself.

Truth as Relative to Linguistic Convention

In attempting to devise a more plausible version of the doctrine that truth is socially relative, I shall take as my starting point the principle that the entities to which the adjectives 'true' and 'false' apply are what philosophers call 'propositions'. More controversial is the view I take of what a proposition is. I hold that a proposition, or 'thought', to use Frege's (1918) term, is a purely linguistic entity closely related to, but not identical with the sentence, which, for the time being, is used, as we say, to "express" it. It is not, as it has been represented by many writers in the so-called cognitive tradition (e.g., Fodor, 1987), an entity inside the heads of those who subscribe to or otherwise entertain it.

That propositions or thoughts are not identical with any one of the sentences used to 'express' them is not disputed. No one would deny that the English sentence "All men are mortal" expresses the same proposition or thought as its equivalent in other natural languages and as other equivalent English sentences, such as "Everybody dies sooner or later" or "In the long run we're all dead." Moreover, there is no reason to prefer any one of these sentences as a more apt or accurate way of expressing the proposition than any of the others.

What is controversial is the claim that although thoughts and propositions are not identical with any particular sentence, there is nothing to a proposition or thought over and above the actual and possible sentences that are or could be used to say the same thing in different ways on different occasions. The notion of a proposition or thought as something over and above the particular sentences that express it I take to be a reflection of the phenomenon to which Noam Chomsky (e.g., 1958; 1959) has repeatedly drawn attention, whereby sentences in natural language are seldom repeated word for word but are constructed anew on each occasion of utterance. It follows from this principle that when we say the same thing on different occasions, we seldom repeat ourselves word for word. The reasons for this are not difficult to understand. If we are called upon to repeat what we have just said when talking to the same listener, it is because our previous attempt to communicate what we wanted to say has failed. It makes sense, therefore, to put it rather differently on the second attempt. Likewise, when saying the same thing to another listener in another context, changes need to be made in the way the sentence is formulated in order to allow for the differences both in context and in the information available to the particular listener that are liable to affect the listener's ability to understand what is said. Consequently, when saying the 'same thing', both on the same and on different occasions, we almost invariably construct a slightly different sentence, and in some cases a very different sentence. Nevertheless, we are still saying the same thing in the sense that all these different sentences, when uttered in the appropriate context, "have the same meaning" and, if they are indicative sentences, the same truth conditions. In other words, if any one of these sentences expresses something true, then they all do.

In line with this notion I would propose to define a proposition or thought as what I propose to call an 'intensional' or 'modal class', that is to say, a class that includes possible instances as well as actual ones. This intensional or modal class comprises all possible sentence utterances in any natural language that now exists, may have existed in the past, or may exist in the future whose common feature is that they are all indicative sentences, all have the same truth conditions, and all identify the objects, states of affairs, or events to which they refer in the same or corresponding ways.

Now I don't want to spend too much time discussing the qualification at the end of this definition concerning the way in which objects, events, and states of affairs are referred to. The purpose of this qualification is to allow for the fact that sentences like "Ragusa is a port on the Adriatic" and "Dubrovnik is a port on the Adriatic" have the same truth conditions but occur as distinct propositions in an argument involving an identity statement that asserts that the two proper names involved have the same referent, viz. "Ragusa is a port on the Adriatic," "Ragusa is the old name for Dubrovnik," ERGO "Dubrovnik is a port on the Adriatic." It is also designed to allow the identification of a sentence like "My toe hurts," uttered by Arthur Jones on a particular occasion, the sentence "Your toe hurts," addressed to Arthur by someone else on that occasion, the sentence "Arthur's toe hurts" or "His [i.e., Arthur Jones's] toe hurts," addressed by someone else to another person on the same occasion, "Your toe will hurt," addressed to Arthur an hour or so earlier by the doctor, and "Your toe was hurting," addressed to Arthur by someone referring to the same occasion later, as all expressing one and the same thought or proposition.

The aspect of the definition I want to emphasize for our present purposes is the implication that what determines whether or not a given sentence is a member of the intensional or modal class, all of whose members have the same truth condition, is the operation of linguistic conventions, both semantic and syntactic, that govern both the kinds of sentence in which the words composing the sentence can occur in the natural language in question and the contexts in which the utterance of that particular sentence will have the relevant truth conditions.

They are conventions that, as far as our native language is concerned, we pick up unconsciously as we learn the language on our mother's knee.[2] They are never learned in the form of a verbally stated principle or rule. How could they be? We would have to have already learned the conventions before we could understand their verbal formulation. Many syntactic conventions still defy precise verbal formulation after much labor on the part of linguists and logicians, while in the case of semantic conventions, the nearest we can get to a verbal formulation is Tarski's (1930–1931) convention, according to which " 'It is snowing" is a true sentence if and only if it is snowing,' which only escapes being an empty tautology by using the device of quotation marks to draw a distinction between mentioning a sentence and using it.

This then is the version of the doctrine of the social relativity of truth that I want to defend. I maintain that whether or not a particular sentence in any natural language expresses something true, when uttered in a particular context, and what proposition or thought it expresses, when uttered in that context, is determined by the social conventions governing the putting together of words to form sentences of that language and the use of the sentences so formed to perform particular communicatory functions in particular contexts.

Some Implications of This Version
of the Social Relativity Thesis

Stated in this way the version of the social relativity thesis I am proposing appears reasonably innocuous and uncontroversial; but, as I interpret it, it has at least two highly controversial implications. One of these implications comes to light when the notion of what a proposition is, on which it is based, is incorporated into the notion of a 'propositional attitude', as when we say of someone that they believe the proposition in question to be true or false, as the case may be.

For on the view I am proposing, it only makes sense to say of a living organism that it knows or believes that a particular proposition is true or false if it has the ability under appropriate circumstances to understand and construct one or more sentences expressing the proposition in question in some natural language and is disposed either to assent to and assert or dissent from and deny the truth of the proposition so stated and to act accordingly.

I have been pursuing an implication of this view of the nature of propositional attitudes in a recent attempt (Place 1981a, 1981b, 1982, 1983) to rehabilitate and reconstruct the behaviorist account of language proposed by B. F. Skinner in his book *Verbal Behavior* (Skinner, 1957). This is the implication that it is illegitimate to attempt a serious scientific explanation of the behavior of animals, prelinguistic human infants, and human adults, insofar as the behavior in question is not in fact verbally controlled, in terms that involve attributing one or more propositional attitudes to the behaving organism. For to attribute a propositional attitude to an organism in such cases, given this definition of what a proposition is, implies either that the organism in question possesses linguistic skills that it manifestly does not possess or, if it does possess those skills, that they are being deployed in controlling behavior that does not in fact depend either directly or indirectly on the exercise of those skills.[3]

The second controversial implication of the doctrine that truth is relative to linguistic convention appears when it is viewed as a response to the problem of cultural chauvinism in the sociology of knowledge. For, unlike what I am calling the "naïve" and "sophisticated" versions of the doctrine that truth is socially relative, the doctrine that truth is relative to linguistic convention does not accept as true *any* proposition whose truth is accepted as a matter of common knowledge within a given culture, even if, as required by the sophisticated version of the doctrine, the proper truth determination procedures accepted by the culture have been followed. The only propositions whose truth is accepted as socially relative on this version of the doctrine are those that are *analytic* in the sense that their truth value (i.e., whether they are true or false) is determined completely and exclusively by the syntactic conventions governing the structure of the sentence used to express them and the semantic conventions governing its constituent terms. For although on this view the truth of *any* statement is, at least in part, determined by the linguistic conventions governing the use of the words making up the sentences used in its formulation, in the case of a factual or, as Kant (1781) would say, "synthetic" statement, the truth value is also partly determined by the accuracy with which, given those conventions, the sentence depicts the way things are, were, or will be in the universe of space and time that we all inhabit.

If a synthetic statement is false by the standards we currently accept, and that falsity is not a matter of using words in senses that are no longer current in contemporary culture but is due to the fact that no such event or state of affairs as that which it describes has existed in the past exists now or will exist in the future at the time and place indicated by the sentence, then no change in the linguistic conventions governing the words composing the sentence is going to make it true, unless the effect of those changes is to alter entirely the event or state of affairs depicted by the sentence.

An example of a statement that was once accepted as a matter of common knowledge but is now known to be factually false is the statement that the prophet Jonah was swallowed by a whale and lived to tell the tale. We know that this statement must be false, not only because no creature of the size and complexity of a human being could survive such an experience but also because it is inconsistent with what we know of the whale's diet and digestive system. In this case there are no conceivable changes in the conventions governing the words used to formulate the sentence that would render it true. It always did, does, and will express a false proposition. Though to say *that* is not to deny the obvious fact that the criteria we rely on to determine the truth value of statements such as this are different from those that applied in the past and that still apply in other cultural settings. Nor does it require us to reject the claim which might be made that the Jonah story, though factually false, expresses some deep spiritual truth in mythological form.

The situation with respect to a proposition or statement that is analytic is very different. An analytic statement may be defined as an indicative sentence whose truth value, when uttered in the appropriate context, is determined exclusively and a priori by the syntactic conventions governing the construction of the sentence and the semantic conventions governing the application of its terms. Such a sentence will express a true proposition at one time and place and a false proposition at another time and place, or vice versa, only by virtue of changes in the linguistic conventions on which its truth value depends. When such a change occurs, we cannot say, as we can in the case of a synthetic statement, that what was formerly thought to be true has now been shown to be false or vice versa. It is simply that the words that formerly expressed a true or false proposition, as the case may be, have ceased to do so.

However, this principle can be invoked as a way of avoiding cultural chauvinism in the history and sociology of science only if we are allowed to recognize that the fundamental principles of a science at any stage of scientific development are analytic, in the sense, already described, in which they are made true solely by virtue of the semantic conventions that currently govern the use of the words and symbols used to express them. On this view, when a scientific principle is abandoned as a result of what Kuhn (1962) calls a "paradigm shift," it is not that theoretical principles formerly thought to be true are now discovered to be false; it is simply that the conventions have changed so that sentences that previously expressed analytic truths no longer do so, while sentences that previously would have expressed analytic falsehoods, had they been formulated at all, or that were previously synthetic and subject to empirical determination, now express analytic truths.

Take for example the principle that whales are fishes. If we adopt the medieval definition of a fish as a creature that lives in the sea and propels itself through the water by means of fins and a characteristically paddle-shaped tail, the statement "Whales are fishes" is an analytic truth, since, on that usage, the criteria for assigning an object to the class 'whales' include those for assigning an object to the class 'fishes'. But once we adopt the modern convention according to which a fish has to be cold-blooded and reproduce itself by means of eggs fertilized outside the body and which precludes anything that is a mammal from also being a fish, the sentence "Whales are fishes" becomes an analytic falsehood. However, because of the changed conventions, the proposition that "Whales are fishes" used to express, given the previous conventions, is not the same proposition as that which the same sentence now expresses.

This view runs counter to a great deal of fashionable doctrine in logic and the philosophy of language. In particular it runs counter to Kripke's (1972) view, according to which natural kind terms like 'whale' and 'fish' "rigidly designate" the natural kinds they are the names of. It also runs counter to a great deal of Quine's philosophy, in particular to his well-known critique of the analytic/synthetic distinction in his "Two dogmas of empiricism" paper (Quine, 1951). It is, consequently, to the examination of the argument of that paper that the remainder of this paper is devoted.

The Analytic/Synthetic Distinction

The distinction between analytic and synthetic truth comes, needless to say, from Kant's (1781) *Critique of Pure Reason*. As it is stated by Kant, a sentence is analytic if the description occupying the predicate position in the sentence expresses what has already been expressed by a description that occupies the subject position in the same sentence. A sentence is synthetic if the description occupying the predicate position expresses something that has not already been expressed by the description that occupies the subject position. Not surprisingly, Quine begins his critique of the distinction in his "Two dogmas of empiricism" paper by pointing out that since Kant's formulation of the distinction presupposes the traditional view that all sentences are of subject and predicate form, this way of formulating the distinction is rendered obsolete by Frege's (1879) subsequent discovery that the very large category of relational sentences are not in fact of this form.

But as Quine's argument unfolds, it becomes apparent that his criticism is directed not just at Kant's formulation of the distinction nor just at Frege's revised formulation of it in terms of what is and is not true by definition. Quine's target, it turns out, is a whole family of closely related, if not actually coextensive, distinctions, including the grandfather of them all, Aristotle's distinction between 'necessarily true propositions' whose truth cannot be denied without self-contradiction and 'contingent propositions' whose denial involves no contradiction, the distinction drawn by Leibniz, and following him by Hume, between 'truths of reason' and 'matters of fact', and finally the other distinction drawn by Kant between propositions whose truth is established a priori and those whose truth is established a posteriori in the light of observation.

Since these other distinctions do not rely, as Kant's formulation of the analytic/ synthetic does, on the subject and predicate analysis of sentences, it is apparent that, in directing his attack on the analytic/synthetic distinction in the first instance, Quine is simply homing in on the weakest member of the family of alternative ways of formulating a single more fundamental distinction.

Quine himself puts the point as follows: "Hence the temptation to suppose . . . that the truth of a statement is somehow analyzable into a linguistic component and a factual component. Given this supposition, it next seems reasonable that in some statements the factual component should be null; and these are the analytic statements" (Quine, 1951, p. 34). Stated, in my view more perspicuously, in terms of the notion of linguistic conventions governing the construction and use of sentences, the thesis is that a statement is analytic, necessary, and true a priori if and only if, without being a statement *about* the meaning of words and expressions contained in it, its truth is determined completely and exhaustively by the linguistic conventions governing the construction and use of the sentence that is used to make it. By the same token, a statement is synthetic, contingent, and true a posteriori if and only if its truth is determined partly by the linguistic conventions governing the construction and use of the sentence used to make it and partly by virtue of a correspondence between the meaning of the sentence when uttered in a relevant context, as determined by those conventions, on the one hand and the way things actually are, were, might have been, or possibly will be in the aspect of the world to which the sentence relates on the other.

Quine's Critique of the Analytic/Synthetic Distinction

Quine's argument against the analytic/synthetic distinction, conceived in the broad sense that I have described, begins by drawing the traditional distinction between the meaning, or 'intension,' of a general term and its 'extension'. This distinction was first drawn in the seventeenth century by the Port Royal logicians Arnauld and Nicole (1662), who contrasted the extension of a general term with what they called its "comprehension." Quine, quite correctly, links this distinction both to Frege's (1892) distinction between the *Sinn* (usually translated as "sense") and *Bedeutung* (usually translated as "reference") of a singular term, and to Mill's (1843) distinction between the terms 'connotation' and 'denotation'.[4] The common feature of all these pairs of distinctions is that the extension, *Bedeutung*, reference, or denotation of a term consists, in the case of a singular term, in a single actually existing object that is picked out by the term in question and, in the case of a general term, in the class of such objects that fall under it. The meaning, comprehension, intension, *Sinn*, sense, or connotation of a term is that property of it that is grasped by someone who thereby understands it and is thus able to identify its *Bedeutung*, reference, or denotation or an instance belonging to its extension. Quine uses 'meaning' and 'extension' for the two sides of this family of distinctions. I prefer to use 'intension' in place of 'meaning', mainly because 'meaning' is the natural translation of Frege's word *Bedeutung*, which, as we have seen, is his word for the actually existing object picked out by a singular term (whence the more usual translation of the term in its technical uses as "reference").

According to Quine—and in this respect I cannot imagine that anyone would disagree with him—there is an intimate connection between the analyticity of a proposition and the intensions of its terms. He illustrates this connection by contrasting two universal statements:

(1) All creatures with hearts have kidneys.

(2) All bachelors are unmarried men.

In both these examples the truth of the statement is bound up with the fact that the extensions of the pair of terms involved in the sentence coincide. Every creature with a heart is a creature with kidneys and vice versa. Every bachelor is an unmarried man and vice versa. But in (1) the two general terms 'creature with a heart' and 'creature with kidneys' differ in meaning or 'intension'. It is a simple matter of fact, established by observation, that the two predicates have the same extension, that every known species of organism that possesses a heart also possesses kidneys. This, therefore, is an example of a synthetic truth. On the other hand, (2) is analytic. In this case the coincidence of the extensions of the predicates 'bachelor' and 'unmarried man' is determined without need of observation on the strength of a synonymy or equivalence of meaning or intension between the two predicates involved.

Quine's contention with respect to these examples is that whereas the notion of two expressions having the same or overlapping extensions is clear and precise, the notion that, in cases like that of 'bachelor' and 'unmarried man', this is due to coincidence or overlap between the intensions of the two expressions is totally obscure. In support of this conclusion, he cites four different criteria that have been proposed for deciding whether coextension and class inclusion arise analytically and necessarily or synthetically and contingently, and he concludes that none of them satisfy the requirement of helping us to decide a doubtful case, such as whether or not the statement 'Whatever is green is extended' is analytic or synthetic. There is no need, I think, to discuss these criteria in detail here, since I would not want to dispute Quine's judgment that they all rely on an unanalyzed notion of the synonymy of two linguistic expressions, a notion that is inseparable from the concept of 'analyticity,' which the criteria are intended to elucidate. From this he concludes that "for all its a priori reasonableness, a boundary between analytic and synthetic statements simply has not been drawn. That there is such a distinction to be drawn at all is an unempirical dogma of empiricists, a metaphysical article of faith" (Quine, 1980, p. 37).

A Rebuttal of Quine's Critique
of the Analytic/Synthetic Distinction

In order to rebut Quine's critique of the analytic/synthetic distinction, we need to recognize that Quine approaches the problem from what we may call an "extensionalist" standpoint. For our present purpose, an 'extensionalist' is someone who believes that classes/extensions exist independently of and prior to the classificatory activity of the human and, for that matter, the animal mind. Extensionalism in this sense contrasts with 'intensionalism' or 'conceptualism'. Intensionalism/ conceptualism, as here conceived, is the doctrine that while particulars exist independently of human and animal conception and resemble one another in ways that invite human beings and animals who interact with them to classify them in some ways rather than others, they are formed into classes only by virtue of the intensions or concepts imposed on them by the mind. It goes without saying that if you believe, as I have argued in this paper that we can and should believe, that the concepts of human language are social constructions maintained by social convention, you are ipso facto committed to the intensionalist/conceptualist position.

Since, as an extensionalist, Quine believes that classes exist independently of human and animal conception, it is not surprising that he should be unimpressed by the intensionalist/ conceptualist claim that the very existence of the classes that constitute the extension of a general term and the very possibility of making an identifying reference to the object picked out by a singular term depend on the intension of the general term and the sense of the singular term. We know, of course, from what Quine says elsewhere in his writings (e.g.1980, p. 14) that he is not favorably disposed toward this intensionalist/conceptualist position. But where, as in this passage, he explicitly discusses that view, he doesn't dismiss it as incoherent, as he seems to be doing in "Two dogmas." In that paper the intensionalist/conceptualist claim that there can be no extension without an intension or concept by which to sort members of the class from nonmembers is not even considered.

Of course to claim, as the conceptualist does, that there can be no extension without intension, no reference (*Bedeutung*) without sense (*Sinn*) is not by itself sufficient to explain how extension and reference are supposed to be generated by intension or sense. It may well be, therefore, that what Quine is claiming with respect to the intensionalist/conceptualist position, though he does not say so, is that no clear account has been given of how this result is supposed to be achieved. But if *that* is what he is claiming, he is surely mistaken. For suppose, as the intensionalist would encourage us to do, that we take the intension of a general term to consist in the criteria employed by a competent user of the term in deciding whether or not a given instance does or does not belong to its extension; and suppose also that the sense of a singular term consists in the criteria employed by a competent user of the term in identifying its reference; it is abundantly clear that in the case of the examples Quine discusses, the criteria by which we decide whether or not a creature has a heart are quite different from the criteria by which we decide whether or not it has kidneys; whereas it is equally clear that the criteria for deciding whether or not someone is a bachelor are indistinguishable from those we use in deciding whether or not someone is a man who has not been married before.[5]

We are now in a position to test the principle that a statement is analytic if the criteria for assigning an object to the extension of one predicate include or coincide with those for assigning an object to the extension of the other by applying it to the sentence 'Whatever is green is extended,' where, according to Quine, it is not clear whether the statement is true analytically or synthetically. If we do this, it at once becomes apparent why this is a difficult and puzzling case. For although it seems somehow self-contradictory to postulate an unextended green object, it doesn't seem right to say that whether or not an object is extended is among the criteria we use in deciding whether or not it is green in the way that whether or not a liquid satisfies the formula H_2O is, for the chemist at least, not just one of the criteria but the sole criterion for deciding whether or not it is water. Nevertheless, it seems right to say that there is a linguistic convention whereby the predicate 'green', when used as a color word, is restricted in its application to extended substances and their surfaces; and if we apply the principle that a statement that is true solely by virtue of linguistic convention is analytic, that makes the statement "Whatever is green is extended" an analytic proposition. Quine, of course, would retort that the notion of a linguistic convention is just as obscure as the notion of analyticity that it is supposed to illuminate. But if, as seems reasonable, it is accepted that conforming to a social norm or convention is a matter of avoiding behavior that the social group (the linguistic community in this case) rejects as unacceptably deviant, we can perhaps use, as positive evidence of the existence of such a norm or convention, the results of what I have called elsewhere (Place, 1992a) an "ethnomethodological thought experiment" in which the reader or listener is invited to imagine the consternation that would be provoked within the linguistic community by the suggestion (a) that a certain mathematical point is green, or (b) that a straight line, in the sense of the shortest distance between two such points on a plane, could likewise be green. However, to claim that there is evidence for the existence of a linguistic convention that forbids the ascription of color predicates to nonextended objects is not to deny that underlying that linguistic convention there is a contingent fact about the physics of light, namely, that, as far as we know, photons can only reach the eye of an observer if they are emitted from and/or reflected by some kind of extended object, and that, consequently, it is only such objects that can be distinguished by their color.

Conclusion: The Mutability of Analytic Truth

By way of conclusion I want to emphasize that in arguing for a rehabilitation of the analytic/synthetic distinction I am not arguing for the immutability of analytic truths. Indeed the whole object of the exercise is to be able to allow that, as semantic conventions change, so some of the sentences that previously expressed an analytic truth cease to do so and sentences that were previously synthetic become analytic. Moreover, I do not wish to deny that in the case of the concepts and theories of science these changes come about as a result of cumulative, empirical discoveries that render the old ways of talking no longer convenient and appropriate. But I still want to insist that, given the previous semantic conventions, the old sentences are still true, analytically, necessarily, and a priori. It is just that the conventions that make them true have been rendered obsolete by subsequent empirical discovery, just as the conventions that make many of our present scientific principles analytically true will no doubt be rendered obsolete by empirical discoveries in the future. But this process, whereby analytic principles that comprise the conceptual framework or paradigm within which scientific research is conducted are rendered obsolete by subsequent scientific discovery, should not be confused with the process whereby low-level hypotheses are falsified without disturbing the conceptual framework within which those hypotheses are formulated and without disturbing the analytic principles in terms of which the conceptual framework is itself formulated. There is nothing in this view that requires us to say either that the analytic principles of the past are now known to be false or to concede that our present analytic principles may be falsified in the future.

13

The Role of the Ethnomethodological Experiment in the Empirical Investigation of Social Norms and Its Application to Conceptual Analysis

The Liquidation of Philosophy

The idea behind this paper is one that has been with me since I was an undergraduate at Oxford in the period immediately following the end of the Second World War. I was studying philosophy and psychology in what was then the brand new honors school of Philosophy, Psychology and Physiology honors school. Those were heady days when philosophy at Oxford was undergoing a revolution from which emerged what came to be called 'ordinary language philosophy'.

To those of us who were caught up in that revolution, particularly those such as myself who were interested in the development of psychology as a hard-nosed empirical and experimental science, it seemed that we were witnessing the final act in a process that had been going on since the seventeenth century whereby one after another new empirical science had split off from philosophy. In the Middle Ages, philosophy encompassed any pursuit of knowledge for its own sake, as the institution of the degree of Doctor of Philosophy as the principal research degree in *any* academic discipline reminds us. In the seventeenth and eighteenth centuries, natural philosophy had separated out from its parent along the lines of fracture prescribed by Descartes's dualism of mind and matter and had evolved into the natural empirical sciences of physics, chemistry, and biology. Then in the nineteenth century it was the turn of the mental and moral sciences to break away. First economics, then sociology, anthropology, and finally psychology were established as independent sciences.

In the case of psychology the process of emancipation from philosophy had hitherto been regarded as incomplete—except by the behaviorists, who had bought their freedom from domination by philosophy at the expense of withdrawing from what had previously been regarded as the central issue of the discipline, the study of consciousness. Now ordinary language philosophy was attacking that last bastion of philosophy's claim to its own proprietary subject matter—the mind-body problem—and exposing it as conceptual confusion.

Conceptual Analysis

The foundation of Oxford ordinary language philosophy was the discovery of the technique known as 'conceptual analysis'. This discovery should probably be attributed to Wittgenstein during the phase of his thinking represented by the so-called *Blue and Brown Books* (Wittgenstein, 1958), typescript versions of which were widely circulated during the late 1930s and 1940s. Conceptual analysis may be described as a method of elucidating the meanings of words and expressions whose meanings are fixed by customary usage rather than by stipulative definition. Although it can in principle be applied to the elucidation of the words and expressions of any language or technical code in which the practitioner is fluent, it has in practice been applied only to the words and expressions of nontechnical natural language as they occur in everyday usage (ordinary language).

In essence, the idea of conceptual analysis is a simple deduction from Frege's (1884) principle that the meaning of a word or expression is the contribution that it makes to the various sentences of which it forms part. It is a consequence of Frege's principle that in order to throw light on the meaning of a word or expression we need to study the different kinds of sentence and the places within those sentences in which the word or expression in question can meaningfully occur. To do that is to do conceptual analysis. But though the idea is simple enough, like many simple ideas, its ramifications—in particular, its implications for the view that is taken of the nature of philosophical inquiry—are far reaching.

The view of the nature of philosophical inquiry that was characteristic of the Oxford ordinary language school took as its starting point the assumption that there are two kinds of intellectual issue: conceptual issues and empirical issues. Conceptual issues are issues concerning the meaning of words and are to be decided by conceptual analysis. Empirical issues concern matters of fact and are decided by making the appropriate observations. Conceptual issues are the concern of philosophers. Empirical issues are the concern of the relevant empirical science or textual research discipline. The traditional problems of philosophy, it was held, have two sources. They depend on (1) a confusion between conceptual and empirical issues; (2) conceptual confusions, in other words, confusions about the meaning of words. These confusions, it was thought, can always be cleared up by paying close attention to the way the words in question are used in ordinary language in everyday nonphilosophical contexts.

Finding Employment for Philosophers, Once Philosophy Is Liquidated

It is a consequence of this view that once the conceptual confusions involved in the traditional problems of philosophy have been dealt with in this way there will be nothing more for the philosopher to do, apart from tackling any new conceptual confusions as may arise in the future. This raised the urgent problem of how professional philosophers were to occupy themselves, once all the major philosophical issues of the past had been resolved in this way. The solution to this problem that recommended itself to those of us who thought about such matters at the time envisaged that once the traditional philosophical issues, such as the theory of knowledge, mind, and body, the freedom of the will, ethics, and so forth, had been dealt with, philosophers would have to use the skills they had acquired in exposing the conceptual confusions that had generated these problems in the service of what has since become known as 'empirical sociolinguistics'. Two prominent Oxford philosophers of the period who saw the need to take philosophy down this road were the late John Austin and my own tutor in philosophy at the time, the late Paul Grice. John Austin's (1962b) *How to Do Things with Words* is the source for what Searle (1969) was later to call "speech act theory," while Grice (1975; 1978) went on to develop the theory of conversational implicature. Needless to say, both of these theories have been enormously influential in the subsequent development of empirical research in fields such as pragmatics and sociolinguistics.

Conceptual Analysis as an Empirical Inquiry

Austin and Grice were well aware of the potential contribution of the conceptual analysis of ordinary language for empirical studies of the use of language in everyday life. What they were not prepared to recognize, at least not in public, was that conceptual analysis itself was a form of empirical investigation. Unfortunately I did not have or, perhaps I should say, did not make an opportunity to raise this issue with John Austin, although I was, of course, well aware of his interests in taking philosophy into the area of empirical linguistics. I did, however, discuss the issue with Paul Grice on more than one occasion. My recollections of those discussions are extremely sketchy, but, as I reconstruct them now, Grice employed three arguments in order to rebut my suggestion that conceptual analysis is an empirical investigation into the way language is used. His first argument was that philosophers are concerned with discovering propositions that are analytic and thus true necessarily and a priori, not with matters of synthetic, contingent, and empirical fact. Second, he argued that philosophers are concerned with linguistic universals, principles that are true of language and thought in general, not with the peculiarities of different natural languages that are the concern of the student of empirical linguistics. His third argument was that if philosophers were concerned with matters of linguistic fact, they would be interested in statistical studies of the frequency with which different locutions are used in everyday discourse; in fact such studies are of no philosophical interest whatsoever.

The first of these arguments can be rebutted relatively easily. It is true that what philosophers are concerned with are the kinds of relations between the meaning of words and expressions that render sentences like "All bachelors are unmarried men" or "Two is the only even prime" analytically true and their negations false. But what makes them analytically true are empirical facts about the meanings of those words in the relevant natural language, in this case English.[1]

The second argument is also fairly easily dealt with by pointing out that the features of language that are of interest to philosophers have no bearing one way or another on the question of whether the method that is used to investigate those features is or is not an empirical method. Nor is there any reason to think that the method of conceptual analysis, if it is applied in an indiscriminate and mechanical fashion, will always come up with linguistic features of the kind that are of interest to philosophers, rather than with peculiarities specific to a particular natural language. Indeed, I am conscious that I may be maligning Paul Grice's memory in even attributing this argument to him.

It is, however, with the problem of answering the third argument that I am concerned in this paper. This is a problem that I have been wrestling with on and off for the past forty years and it is only within the past five years when I started to take an interest in ethnomethodology that the answer began to dawn.

It is quite evidently true that statistical evidence about the frequency of occurrence of certain linguistic practices does not impinge one way or the other on the kind of linguistic issue that interests philosophers. What is less clear is why this should be. My suggestion is that philosophers are right to find no interest for them in the statistical frequency of different types of linguistic behavior for reasons that are closely related to those that lead ethnomethodologists to reject statistical frequency analysis as applied to all forms of social behavior. The ethnomethodologist's rejection of statistical frequency analysis differs from that of the philosopher in that it arises from an interest that the philosopher does not share in what people actually say and do on particular occasions. Measures of the statistical frequency of the occurrence of different varieties of behavior are rejected because such measures inevitably involve extracting particular instances from the context in which they occur, thereby ignoring those often crucial features of the situation that constrain what happens in the individual case. The most important of these features that are "written out of the story" by a statistical frequency analysis are the operative social norms and conventions; and it is in relation to the investigation of social norms and conventions—in the case of the philosopher, the norms and conventions of linguistic usage—that the concerns of the two groups coincide.

If what you are interested in are the norms and conventions governing a particular variety of social behavior, a statistical study of the frequency of that behavior is going to tell you very little. The frequency of incidence cannot by itself distinguish between behavior that has a high natural frequency of occurrence in the absence of social sanctions designed to constrain it and behavior that has a low natural frequency in the absence of social sanctions designed to promote it. The same statistical frequency can be generated in either way.

Garfinkel's Ethnomethodological Experiment

It is here that Harold Garfinkel's ethnomethodological experiment comes to the rescue. As is well known, the ethnomethodological experiment was first described by Professor Garfinkel in a paper entitled "Studies of the routine grounds of everyday activities" (Garfinkel, 1964). He describes the method as follows:

> Procedurally it is my preference to start with familiar scenes and ask what can be done to make trouble. The operations that one would have to perform in order to multiply the senseless features of perceived environments; to produce and sustain bewilderment, consternation, and confusion; to produce the socially structured affects of anxiety, shame, guilt and indignation; and to produce disorganized interaction should tell us something about how the structures of everyday activities are ordinarily produced and maintained. (Garfinkel, 1967, pp. 37–38)

Now I am conscious that in describing the procedure that Professor Garfinkel outlines in this passage as a method for determining the existence and nature of social norms and conventions, I am attributing to him, and through him to ethnomethodology, something that he has always insisted that ethnomethodology does not have and does not need, namely, a methodology. Ethnomethodology looks at other people's methodologies; it does not have a methodology of its own.

This is a view that I am afraid I cannot accept, not only because it seems to me that no inquiry can proceed without a methodology even if, as in most cases, the methodology is never explicitly stated, but also because I believe that the ethnomethodological experiment described by Garfinkel in this passage is the only methodologically sound empirical procedure for determining the existence and nature of social norms and conventions.

The ethnomethodological experiment so conceived is the procedure whereby the existence and nature of a social norm or convention is demonstrated by flouting the putative convention and observing what reaction that produces in the social group within which the convention is assumed to operate. If the reaction is one of consternation, indignation, and hostility toward the perpetrator, and if that reaction is calculated to produce feelings of guilt and shame in the perpetrator, it is a reasonable inference that an important convention has been isolated, conformity to which is maintained by the fear of provoking precisely those consequences.

Not surprisingly, examples of such ethnomethodological experiments carried out in vivo are relatively rare. In his paper Garfinkel gives only one clear-cut example: the case where he asked his students "to spend from fifteen minutes to an hour in their [own] homes imagining that they were boarders and acting out this assumption. They were instructed to conduct themselves in a circumspect and polite fashion. They were to avoid getting personal, to use formal address, to speak only when spoken to" (Garfinkel, 1967, p. 47). Typical reactions to this behavior on the part of the student are described as follows:

Family members were stupefied. They vigorously sought to make the strange actions intelligible and to restore the situation to normal appearances. Reports were filled with accounts of astonishment, bewilderment, shock, anxiety, embarrassment, and anger, and with charges by various family members that the student was mean, inconsiderate, selfish, nasty or impolite. (Garfinkel, 1967, p. 47)

Another example of an ethnomethodological experiment in vivo is described by Verplanck (1955). This experiment antedates ethnomethodology and was inspired by a quite different conceptual framework. It belongs to the literature on verbal conditioning, which had a brief vogue in social psychology in the late 1950s. It is of particular interest in that it illustrates the application of the convention-reversal procedure in demonstrating the existence of an important convention of ordinary conversation. This is the convention whereby the listener is constrained to supply an appropriate "continuer," as the conversation analysts call such things, in the form of an expression of agreement in response to an opinion voiced by the speaker. Because his concern is with the conventions governing the speaker's contribution rather than those that regulate the listener's response, this convention does not figure in Grice's (1975; 1978) theory of conversational implicature. It is, however, partly covered by Brown and Levinson's (1978) principle of politeness, which is presented by them as an addition to Grice's list of maxims.

In this experiment, Verplanck asked his students to select a fellow student or other suitable individual "who was not informed in any way that he was taking part in an experiment," and engage that person in normal conversation for a period of half an hour. This thirty-minute period was to be divided into three ten-minute periods. "During the first 10-minute period, once the conversation was under way, E [the experimenter] did not reinforce any statement made by S [the subject]," (Verplanck, 1955, p. 668). In other words, the experimenter did not respond to any statement made by the subject with an expression of agreement. I assume, though this is not explicitly stated, that other varieties of utterance were acknowledged by supplying the appropriate continuer. During this first phase of the experiment the number of expressions of opinion was counted so as to provide a baseline against which to measure the increase in the number of opinions expressed by the subject during the second ten-minute experimental period during which

E agreed with every opinion-statement by saying: "Yes, you're right," "That's so," or the like, or by nodding and smiling affirmation if he could not interrupt. . . . In the third 10-minute period, the Es attempted to extinguish the opinion-statements [in some cases] by withdrawing *all* reinforcement, that is, by failing to respond . . . in any way to S's speech, and [in other cases] by disagreeing with each opinion stated. (Verplanck, 1955, p. 668)

Verplanck describes the results of this experiment as follows:"Each of the 24 Ss showed an increase in his relative frequency of opinion during the reinforcement period over . . . his preceding . . . period. . . . Twenty one of the 24 showed a *reduced* RF$_{opin}$ [relative frequency of opinion] in the extinction or disagreement period below that of the preceding period of reinforcement" (Verplanck, 1955, p. 672). More significant for our present purpose is the following comment:

> No *S* ever gave any evidence that he was "aware" that he was serving as a subject in an experiment, that his behavior was being deliberately manipulated and recorded, or that he recognized that there was anything peculiar about the conversation. The only qualification that must be made is this: during extinction some *S*s got angry at *E* and commented on his disagreeableness, or noted his "lack of interest." (Verplanck, 1955, p. 671)

The Ethnomethodological Thought Experiment

Much more common than the ethnomethodological experiment in vivo is the *ethnomethodological thought experiment*. In this procedure, the investigator imagines or, more commonly, asks an audience to imagine the situation in which some putative norm or convention is contravened, and considers or asks the audience to consider how he or she in the capacity of a member of the social group in question would react to such behavior or how others might be expected to do so.

For an example of this kind of ethnomethodological thought experiment I quote from a recent book by Dorothy Smith.[2] She writes:

> When I take my dog for a walk in the morning, I observe a number of what we might call "conventions." I myself walk on the sidewalk; I do not walk on the neighbor's lawns. My dog, however, freely runs over the lawns. *My dog also, if I am not careful, may shit on a neighbor's lawn, and there are certainly some neighbors who do not like this.* (My italics) (Smith, 1987, pp. 154–155)

Smith (personal communication) points out that this is not, strictly speaking, an experiment in that both she and many of her readers have had personal experience of the actual reactions of neighbors in such a case. I would argue, nevertheless, that this case differs from the ethnomethodological experiment, properly so called, only in being restricted to evidence of what *actually* happens when a putative convention is contravened. The thought experiment proper has the advantage—which, as Professor C. B. Martin[3] (personal communication) points out, is much more significant from the standpoint of the philosopher than it is from that of the sociologist—of allowing the investigator to explore the way linguistic conventions extend or may with consistency be extended beyond the actual to the hypothetical case. It is this, moreover, rather than the opprobrium that the perpetrator of an ethnomethodological experiment in vivo is liable to incur, that accounts for and partly justifies the philosopher's preference for the thought experiment.

Needless to say, it is in the form of the thought experiment that the ethnomethodological experiment appears in the writings of the philosophers of ordinary language. In this case the object of the exercise is to throw light on the conventions governing the way words are put together to form intelligible sentences, by flouting the supposed convention and inviting one's reader to share the consternation that this produces in any competent speaker or interpreter of the language in question. Two examples of the use of the ethnomethodological thought experiment by philosophers for the purposes of the conceptual analysis of ordinary language must suffice. The first comes from Ryle's (1949) *The Concept of Mind*: "It would be absurd to speak of someone having a sensation, or a feeling, on purpose; or to ask someone what he had a twinge *for*" (Ryle, 1949, pp. 105–106). The second example comes from Austin's paper "The meaning of a word":

> Suppose that I ask "What is the point of doing so and so?" For example, I ask Old Father William "What is the point of standing on one's head?" He replies in the way we know. Then I follow this up with "What is the point of balancing an eel on the end of one's nose?" And he explains. Now suppose that I ask my third question "What is the point of doing *anything*—not anything *in particular*, but just *anything*?" Old Father William would no doubt kick me downstairs without the option. (Austin, 1970, p. 59)

It doesn't take much to see that in taking this action Old Father William is standing in for the linguistic community in general.

Distinguishing Varieties of Consternation

Professor J. J. C. Smart[4] (personal communication) raises an interesting objection to this use of consternation on the part of the listener as evidence that a linguistic convention has been transgressed. He points out that there are utterances that provoke consternation because of a purely empirical improbability of the information they purport to convey, rather than any semantic impropriety in the way the sentence is put together. Smart's example is the statement "I just saw a five-legged dog."

It is true that such a statement would cause as much if not more consternation than the examples cited by Ryle and Austin. Nevertheless, comparing the different cases suggests a difference in the kind of consternation involved. It would be natural to describe the consternation provoked by "I just saw a five-legged dog" as 'incredulity' or 'disbelief', whereas the consternation provoked by Ryle's "What did you have that twinge for?" and Austin's "What is the point of doing anything—not anything in particular, but just anything?" would be naturally described as 'bafflement', 'perplexity', or 'incomprehension'.

However, in order to sharpen this distinction, we need to do the kind of thing that professional philosophers by virtue of their training are very reluctant to do, namely, to switch from using ethnomethodological thought experiments to using ethnomethodological experiments in vivo, when they try to elucidate the conventions of linguistic usage. The reluctance of philosophers to do this does not stem from the kind of considerations that have deterred sociologists from exploiting the in vivo experiment. For the objections that can be raised against the use of in vivo experiments designed to elucidate the kinds of social convention of interest to the sociologist do not apply in the same way to their use as a way of elucidating the linguistic conventions that are of interest to philosophers. Flouting a convention governing a socially significant aspect of human conduct can cause serious social disruption and provoke anger and hostility against the perpetrator/experimenter. This does not apply in the same way to the case of in vivo experiments designed to elucidate the linguistic conventions that are of interest to the philosopher. No doubt, if a conceptual analyst were to make a practice of conducting in vivo experiments in ordinary social contexts, doubts might be raised about the experimenter's sanity, but a more serious consequence than that is hard to imagine.

Not only would it be possible to conduct in vivo experiments in which deviant sentences are inserted into appropriate slots in ordinary conversation and the reactions of the listener recorded; it would also be possible to conduct experiments that are a kind of halfway house between the pure in vivo experiment and the pure thought experiment. In this case, the experimenter interviews the subject and asks him or her how he or she would react if the experimenter were to utter the deviant sentence in an appropriate context in the course of ordinary conversation. By using either or both of these methods, it should be possible to differentiate clearly between the patterns of listener reaction typical of the incredulity provoked by utterances like "I just saw a five-legged dog" and those typical of the incomprehension provoked by Ryle's "What did you have that twinge for?" or Austin's 'What is the point of doing anything—not anything in particular, but just anything?'

Conclusion

If this account of the character and methodological affinities of conceptual analysis is correct, what consequences, if any, does it have for our view of interdisciplinary boundaries in this area? My own view, for what it is worth, is that simply because ethnomethodology and conceptual analysis use the same methodology to investigate social norms and conventions, we cannot say that they form a single discipline or that conceptual analysis is a branch of ethnomethodology concerned with the social conventions governing language. For while ethnomethodologists, qua sociologists, are interested in all kinds of social convention as phenomena in their own right, conceptual analysts, qua philosophers, are interested in *some* linguistic conventions for the sake of the light they throw on such traditional philosophical issues as the nature of linguistic communication, the character of moral and aesthetic judgments, the nature of truth and the manner of its determination (epistemology), and the kind of universe that is presupposed by those conventions and the process of linguistic communication that they make possible (metaphysics). However, since conceptual analysis is arguably the only methodological procedure, other than the representation of the structure of arguments in the symbolism of formal logic, that is available to the philosopher, the thesis that conceptual analysis is an empirical investigation of linguistic convention is in line with Quine's contention in "Epistemology naturalized" (Quine, 1969) that the issues of epistemology and, I would add, of philosophy in general arise within the body of science, rather than from some Olympian position outside it. But whereas for Quine epistemology is an offshoot of the psychophysiology of sensation, on this analysis philosophy in general, including epistemology, appears as an offshoot of empirical sociolinguistics.[5]

14

Linguistic Behaviorism as a Philosophy of Empirical Science

B. F. Skinner (1969; 1974) used to maintain that his radical behaviorism is a philosophy of science. It is a philosophy of science, however, that is restricted in its application to the science of psychology conceived as the empirical and experimental study of the behavior of living organisms. I shall argue in this chapter that what I call "linguistic behaviorism" is a philosophy of science that has application to every empirical science from physics to sociology. This claim rests on three premises:

1. Philosophy is the scientific study of the relation between language and the environmental reality it represents—the metaphilosophical thesis.
2. Science is the systematic attempt to increase the scope, generality, accuracy, and objectivity of linguistic representations of environmental reality—the metascientific thesis.
3. Language is a form of human social behavior that for scientific purposes needs to be studied and explained with the same methods and principles as are used in studying and explaining the other aspects of the instrumental (operant) behavior of free-moving living organisms (animals)—the metalinguistic thesis.

Differences from Other Philosophies of Science

Linguistic behaviorism differs from other approaches to the philosophy of science in maintaining

- that the philosophy of science is a linguistic inquiry, an investigation of scientific language using the technique known as 'conceptual analysis'; and
- that conceptual analysis and hence the philosophy of science, considered

as the application of conceptual analysis to scientific language, is an empirical sociolinguistic investigation of the norms or conventions governing the construction of intelligible sentences in natural language (Place, 1992a).

Differences from Other Behaviorist Approaches
to Language

It differs from other behaviorist approaches to language such as that of Skinner (1957), in that

- it treats the response of the listener/reader to verbal stimuli as being as important as, if not more important than, the verbal behavior of the speaker/writer;
- it identifies the sentence rather than the word as the functional unit of language, the unit that must be complete or whose completion must be predictable in order to be effective in controlling the behavior of the listener;
- it accepts and takes as axiomatic Chomsky's (1957) observation that sentences are seldom repeated word for word and are constructed anew on each occasion of utterance;[1]
- it accepts and takes as axiomatic Chomsky's claim that linguistic competence consists in the speaker's ability to construct and the listener's ability to construe indefinitely many sentences that are novel in the sense that the speaker has never previously constructed and the listener has never previously encountered that precise string of words before;
- it also accepts and takes as axiomatic Chomsky's further claim that novel sentences are made intelligible to the listener by their conformity to the rules (or "conventions," as I prefer to say) governing the way words are combined together to form such sentences in the natural language in current use.

Differences from Other Approaches
to Linguistic Theory

Linguistic behaviorism differs from other approaches within the science of linguistics such as that of Chomsky by

- its endorsement of the traditional empiricist thesis that linguistic competence is a skill the child learns initially and fundamentally on the proverbial 'mother's knee' but more significantly, as far as conformity to group norms are concerned, from interaction with the peer group;
- its insistence that linguistic competence is acquired by the same process of contingency shaping (error correction) as is observed in the acquisition of motor skills by prelinguistic organisms (animals and prelinguistic human infants); and

- the contention that the rules of syntax and semantics to which a speaker's sentence must conform if it is to be intelligible to the listener are embodied not as a kind of computer program in the brains of each party but as a set of social conventions that govern the error-correcting practices of a linguistic community.

Signs, Contingencies and Novel Sentences

The linguistic behaviorist account of the relation between sentences and the environmental reality they depict begins with the concept of a 'sign'. A sign is a type of stimulus event that, when it impinges on the sensorium of a living organism (the sign recipient), orientates the behavioral dispositions of that organism in a manner appropriate to an encounter with a particular type of contingency. A contingency is a relation—in most cases of causal dependence and in some cases of causal independence—whereby behaving in a certain way under certain antecedent conditions has or is liable to have a certain type of consequence. Most signs acquire the property of orientating the behavior of the organism toward an encounter with a particular contingency by virtue of having been associated with that sequence of events either, in the case of an innate behavioral disposition, in the history of the species or, in the case of an acquired disposition, in the course of the learning history of the individual concerned. It is the unique property of a sentence that it functions as a sign that can orientate the behavior of a competent listener toward an encounter with a contingency, the like of which neither speaker nor listener nor the ancestors from which they derive their genes need ever have encountered in their own case.

As a consequence of this ability to orientate the behavior of the listener toward an encounter with contingencies of the like of which he or she need have had no previous personal experience, the speaker is in a position to give instructions that will immediately induce the listener to do things she has never done before. As Goldiamond (1966) has pointed out, a prelinguistic organism, however intelligent, can be induced to perform such novel behavior only through a long process of progressive behavioral shaping. Not only does the ability to construct and construe novel sentences enhance the speaker's ability to control the behavior of the listener; it also enables the listener to receive from the speaker information about contingencies operating in the environment of which she (the listener) need have had no personal experience and of whose existence she would otherwise have been totally ignorant.

Contingency Semantics: A Picture Theory
of the Meaning of Novel Sentences

These remarkable properties of sentences are explained within linguistic behaviorism by invoking a version of Wittgenstein's (1971) "picture theory" of sentence meaning, which I have referred to in the past (Place, 1983; 1992b) as "behavioral contingency semantics," but which I am now inclined to call plain "contingency semantics." According to this theory a sentence acquires the property of orientating the behavior of the listener toward the impending presence of a contingency of a particular kind by virtue of an isomorphism between the structure and content of the sentence and the structure and content of one or more of the situations of which the contingency consists.

Sentences, like other signs, orientate the behavior of the listener/reader toward a complete contingency: antecedent condition, behavior, and consequence. Some (compound) sentences, to use Skinner's (1957; 1966) term, "specify" all three of the terms of which the contingency consists. An example of this is the sentence "If the baby cries (antecedent), give it a bottle (behavior) and it will go back to sleep (consequence)." This sentence is a compound of three atomic sentences, each of which specifies or depicts a different situation (event or state of affairs) corresponding to the three terms of the contingency (antecedent condition, behavior, and consequence). But you don't need to specify all three terms in order to orientate the behavior of the listener/reader toward the contingency. In an appropriate context, any one of these atomic sentences—the declarative "The baby is crying," the imperative "Give the baby a bottle," or the optative "I wish that baby would stop crying and go back to sleep"—can serve to alert the listener to that contingency. The same function can be performed by a compound conditional sentence or "rule," in Skinner's (1966) sense of that word, that combines two atomic sentences. Thus, the *prescriptive* rule "If the baby cries, give it a bottle" consists of two such sentences, one of which specifies the antecedent condition and the other the behavior to be performed under that condition, while the two sentences composing the *descriptive* rule "If you give it a bottle, it will go back to sleep" specify the behavior and its consequence.

Such incomplete specifications of the contingency for which the sentence, nevertheless, acts as a sign have their effect, either because the unspecified parts of the contingency have been specified so frequently that no repetition is needed on this occasion or, as in the case of the social consequences of compliance and failure to comply with a request, because this part of the contingency is never mentioned outside the early years of the parent-child relationship ("Mummy will be cross if you do that again"). Needless to say, it is only in the case of those parts of the contingency that *are* specified that the novel sentence can act as a sign for novelty on the side of the contingency.

The smallest unit that a sentence can specify, the segment of environmental reality that is specified by an atomic sentence, is the contingency term (antecedent condition, behavior to be performed, or consequence to be expected). A contingency term is what Barwise and Perry (1983) call a "situation." A situation in this sense is either

- an *event* whereby a change occurs at or over time in the properties of something and/or in its relations to other things; or

- a *state of affairs* whereby the properties of something and/or its relations with other things remain unchanged over a period of time.

Substituting Barwise and Perry's term "situation" for Russell's (1918–1919) term "fact" in this version of the picture theory has a number of advantages:

1. It avoids the systematic ambiguity of the term 'fact' as between
   - a true particular (existentially quantified) proposition;
   - the event or state of affairs (situation) that such a proposition describes and whose occurrence or existence makes the proposition true.
2. It avoids the implication that there is one and only one uniquely correct way of carving up reality into the facts of which it consists.
3. It allows us to recognize that events and states of affairs qua species of situation are segments of spatiotemporal reality, both of which involve the properties and relations between concrete particulars (Aristotle's "substances") and which differ only in that in the case of a state of affairs the properties and relations remain constant over a period of time, whereas in the case of an event they change either at a particular time (instantaneous event) or over time (process).
4. It allows us to draw a distinction between the situation that a sentence, any sentence, depicts and the *actual* situation to which, as I would say unlike Frege,[2] a true declarative sentence refers (*bedeutet*) and whose existence makes it true. What a sentence *depicts* is not an actual situation but *a range of possible situations*, any one of which, if it exists, will constitute the referent and truthmaker of a declarative, or, if it is brought into existence by the listener, will constitute compliance with an imperative.

The Intensionality of the Depicted Situation and the Correspondence Theory of Truth

The advantage of defining the situation depicted by a sentence intensionally, as a range of possible situations one of which may or may not actually exist, rather than extensionally as one that actually does so, is that the theory of sentence semantics is no longer restricted, as is Tarski's (1930–1931) truth conditional theory, to declarative sentences. On this view, imperatives depict situations just as declaratives do. In both cases the situation depicted is a range of possible situations that may or may not correspond to one that actually exists now, has existed in the past, or will exist in the future. The difference is that, in the case of an imperative, a situation corresponding to that depicted comes into existence if and when the listener complies with it, whereas in the case of a declarative, a situation corresponding to that depicted by the sentence exists at the time specified by the tense of the verb if and only if the sentence is true.

Both the relation between the sentence and the range of possible situations it depicts and the relation between the range of possible situations depicted by the sentence and the actual situation that exists if an imperative is complied with or a declarative is true are relations of isomorphism or correspondence.[3] The term 'isomorphism' is more appropriate as a description of the former relation, in that there is nothing in the situation depicted that is not contained in the sentence that depicts it. The term 'correspondence' is more appropriate as a description of the latter relation, in that any actual situation will have many other properties and involve many other relations beside those mentioned in the sentence. In both cases, however, there is a parallel between the structure and content of the situation depicted by the sentence and, on the one hand, the structure and content of the sentence itself and, on the other, the structure and content of those parts of the actual situation that are mentioned in the sentence.

The Function-and-Argument Analysis of Sentences and Its Ontological Consequences

The idea that the structure of the sentence mirrors the structure of the segment of environmental reality it depicts is one that goes back to Aristotle's notion that his subject and predicate analysis of the sentence mirrors a reality composed of substances or property-bearing entities and the properties they bear.

In the light of Frege's (1879) critique of the subject-predicate analysis of sentences, that analysis is replaced within contingency semantics by his function-and-argument analysis. In a simple atomic sentence such as "The cat is on the mat" or "Ascitel de Bulmer purchased Marton of King Henry I" (Whellan, 1859) the functions "is on/is under" and "purchased/sold" generate respectively two and three[4] "argument places" that in order to complete the sentence must be filled by singular terms designating a substance in Aristotle's sense of that term.

When incorporated into the picture theory of meaning, this more sophisticated analysis of the sentence allows the analysis of the situation that the sentence depicts to include changes in and persistence of complex relations between as many discrete substances as there are argument places in the sentence. It is no longer confined, as was the traditional analysis, to changes in and persistence of the properties of a single substance.

The Epistemological Problem as a Problem in Linguistic Communication

The repudiation of truth conditional semantics in order to give imperatives an equal status to that of declaratives within the picture theory of meaning should not be taken to imply any inclination to undervalue the importance of truth as a property of declarative information-providing sentences. For the colossal advantages that accrue to an organism able to both convey and receive this kind of information about otherwise inaccessible aspects of its environment a price has to be paid. The ability to receive information from other speakers and writers about contingencies whose existence and precise nature she is in no position to check exposes the listener to the danger of being misled by deliberate lies and other more innocent forms of misinformation supplied by others.

Despite the central role played by the argument from sense-perceptual illusion in the induction of skeptical doubts about the truth of our commonsense beliefs, the fact of the matter is that our senses very seldom deceive us; and when they do, it is seldom, if ever, for very long. That this should be so is hardly surprising when you consider the millions of years that our sensory apparatus and the capacity to learn sensory discriminations have had to evolve and adapt to life on this planet, since our remote ancestors first acquired the ability to respond to sensory stimulation. The epistemological problem is not a problem for prelinguistic organisms. It arises only when the listener's ability to respond to novel sentences gives to the speaker the power to mislead and thus presents the listener with the problem of discriminating between those items of information that are true—that accurately depict the way things really are out there—and those that do not—that are false and hence dangerously misleading.

Propositions as the Bearers of Truth

Consonant with, if not a corollary of, the view that the problem of distinguishing between the true and the false arises only in the context of linguistic communication is the thesis that *propositions*, the bearers of truth and falsity, are purely linguistic entities closely related to but not identical with the sentences that, as we say, "express" them. As I put it in a recent article,[5]

> The English sentence *All men are mortal* expresses the same proposition or thought as its equivalent in other natural languages, and as other equivalent English sentences, such as *Everybody dies sooner or later* or *In the long run we're all dead.* Moreover, there is no reason to prefer any one of these sentences as a more apt or accurate way of expressing the proposition than any of the others. (Place, 1991, p. 272)

In other words, the concept of a proposition respects the principle to which, as we have seen, Chomsky has drawn attention, whereby sentences are seldom repeated word for word and are constructed anew on each occasion of utterance. Not only does the speaker invariably construct a new and slightly different sentence when reporting what another speaker has said or written; she does the same when repeating what she herself has said on the same or on a previous occasion.

All these sentences constitute different ways of "saying the same thing." All of them, if they are declarative, have the same truth conditions. If one of them is true, they all are. If one of them is false, they all are. All of them, if they are declarative, "express the same proposition." A proposition is not a particular sentence. It is, rather,

> an 'intensional' or 'modal' class, that is to say, a class that includes possible instances as well as actual ones. This intensional or modal class comprises all possible sentence utterances in any natural language that now exists, may have existed in the past or may exist in the future whose common feature is that they are all indicative sentences, all have the same truth conditions and all identify the objects,

states of affairs or events to which they refer in the same or corresponding ways. (Place, 1991, p. 273)

Analytic and Synthetic Truth

To say that a proposition is true is to say that any proposition that contradicts it conflicts with the linguistic conventions governing the use of sentences expressing that proposition for descriptive purposes. In other words, given the semantic and syntactic conventions of the language, only a declarative sentence expressing that proposition will do as a description of the situation that the proposition describes. True propositions, however, are of two different kinds. On the one hand there are true propositions that are

- *universal,* in the sense that the description applies to any instance of a kind whether or not any such instance exists (this would exclude empirical generalizations);[6]
- *analytic,* in the sense that the application of the description is guaranteed by the relevant linguistic conventions regardless of whether or not a situation answering to the description actually exists;
- *a priori,* in the sense that no observation is required in order to determine whether or not the proposition is true; and
- *necessary,* in the sense that, given the relevant linguistic conventions, any denial of the proposition would be self-contradictory.

On the other hand, there are true propositions that are

- *particular,* in the sense that they apply to a particular instance or a finite class of particulars (as in the case of an empirical generalization);
- *synthetic,* in the sense that the proposition asserts the existence of something over and above what is implicit in the description given;
- *a posteriori,* in the sense that some kind of observational evidence is required in order to determine whether or not the proposition is true; and
- *contingent,* in the sense that the relevant linguistic conventions do not make it self-contradictory to deny that the proposition is true.

The view that the universal/particular, analytic/synthetic, a priori/a posteriori, and necessary/contingent distinctions are both coextensive and intensionally equivalent runs counter to so much currently accepted wisdom in contemporary philosophy that some discussion is called for of two well-known counterexamples:

1. Quine's (1951) example of a proposition that is universally quantified, yet arguably synthetic, true a posteriori, and contingent: "Any creature with a heart has kidneys."
2. The proposition "Two is the only even prime," which is arguably analytic, true a priori, and necessary but nevertheless existentially quantified and particular.

In the case of the first of these examples there are two distinct interpretations of the sentence that are possible depending on the criteria used to identify a heart and a kidney. Where the heart and kidneys are identified purely by their structural or anatomical characteristics, their external shape, their internal arrangement, and their relation to other organs such as the blood vessels and the gills or lungs as the case may be, the sentence "Any creature with a heart has kidneys" is an empirical generalization that records the fact that no instance has been observed of an intact living creature that has a heart by these criteria but lacks kidneys. This is no exception to our rule, since an empirical generalization summarizing the results of observation is not a universal proposition in the relevant sense. On the other hand, if the criteria for identifying hearts and kidneys are functional rather than structural, the meaning of those terms becomes inseparable from the function of the organs they stand for within the circulatory system as a whole. Using these criteria the proposition is genuinely universal; but it is also analytic, in that if what looked like a heart did not form part of a functioning system that includes a device for cleaning the blood of impurities (i.e., at least one kidney) it would not qualify as a heart. If that is correct then it also follows that the truth of the proposition has been decided a priori in advance of observation and is necessary in that its denial would involve a theoretical contradiction.

The claim that "Two is the only even prime number" is a particular proposition rests on the assumption that numbers are abstract objects and that this proposition mentions only one of them, namely the number two. The alternative view sees numbers as universals that exist only insofar as instances of them exist. This interpretation makes "Two is the only even prime" a universal proposition in the relevant sense. That it is also analytic is clear from the fact that its truth can be deduced a priori from the definitions of an even number and a prime number, which also makes it necessary in that to deny it would contradict one or the other of those definitions.

As we shall see later, it is an implication of this view that the universal law statements of empirical science are analytic, true a priori, and necessary. But it is also an implication that they only are so by virtue of current linguistic convention within the scientific community, and that may well change in the light of future empirical research. The fact that such laws have to fit the results of empirical research does not undermine either the claim that they are analytic, in the sense of being made true by the prevailing conventions for the use of the words involved, and true a priori, in the sense that, given those conventions, they remain true however subsequent research turns out. If subsequent research were to reveal cases of what by all other criteria is water that do not have the chemical composition H_2O, we would doubtless be compelled to give up the convention whereby only samples with that chemical composition are so classified. But given that the convention *has* been adopted, as shown by the fact that samples that do not have that composition are rejected as cases of water, such evidence would not falsify the hypothesis that water has the chemical composition H_2O, as it would have done before the convention was incorporated into the language and practice of science. Once the convention is in place, we either have to accept that what is not H_2O is not water or, if exceptions are repeatedly encountered, devise a new convention.

The Relativity of Synthetic Truth to Semantic and Syntactic Convention

An important feature of this version of the picture theory of meaning is the claim that it is not only analytic propositions whose truth depends on the semantic and syntactic conventions governing the context and structure of the sentences that express them. A synthetic proposition only depicts the situation it does depict by virtue of the semantic and syntactic conventions governing the content and structure of the sentences that express it.

This has two consequences. In the first place it means that there are no cases where we can straightforwardly observe a correspondence between a situation that exists and the situation depicted by a sentence. It might be supposed that a simple observation sentence like "There is a table here in front of me" would be such a case. But the correspondence between that sentence and the reality it purports to depict is uncertain, not because of traditional skeptical doubts concerning the very remote possibility that I might be suffering a hallucination, but because, in the absence of confirmation from other competent speakers of English, there is no assurance that that is the correct description of the situation according to the semantic and syntactic conventions of that language. Given that confirmation, however, not only do we exclude the already remote possibility that what we think we are confronted with is some sort of hallucination; we now have a declarative sentence that could only fail to constitute an accurate linguistic depiction of the situation confronting us in the extremely unlikely case where our fellow observers are engaged in a complex conspiracy to persuade us either that we are suffering from a hallucination or that the English sentence "There is a table here in front of me" has a different meaning from that which it actually has by virtue of the conventions of the language—a contingency that, if it were realized, would rapidly lead to a breakdown in the conditions necessary for interpersonal linguistic communication.[7]

Objective Observation Sentences as the Anchors of Empirical Knowledge

These objective observation sentences whose accuracy as a description of the state of affairs confronting them is agreed by a number of observers, all of whom are competent speakers of the language or code in use among them, are just the kind of incontrovertible empirical, synthetic, and contingent propositions that according to the intuitions of the epistemic foundationalist are needed as an anchor or foundation for empirical knowledge. Without such an anchor, I contend, there is no way that we can be assured that a system of propositions, however internally coherent it may be, actually corresponds to the extralinguistic reality it purports to depict. Moreover this empirical anchor is far superior to the private sensation protocols that have been cast in that role by traditional empiricist epistemologies. For, however salient my experience of what I call "my pain" may be, how can I be certain that this is really what they call "pain" in English, when I can't feel what you call "pain" and you can't feel what I call "pain"? I can only be satisfied on this point by observing that what you call "pain" in your case has the same kind of publicly observable causes and the same kind of publicly observable behavioral effects as what I call "pain" in my case.

Primitive Suggestibility and the Discrimination of Misinformation

Objective observation sentences are at best only an anchor attaching our linguistically formulated beliefs to the reality they purport to depict. That this is so becomes clear when we reflect that the primary function of the ability to construct and construe novel sentences is not to describe features of the current stimulus environment of a number of competent speakers and listeners. It is rather, as we have seen, to induce the listener to do things she has never done before and convey information to her about aspects of the environment to which she would otherwise have no access.

It is difficult to exaggerate the advantage that the ability to communicate this kind of novel information gives to the human species. Nevertheless, it is an advantage for which a price has to be paid: the danger of being deceived, either deliberately or involuntarily, by misinformation supplied by others.

The need to detect the lies and other false statements supplied by others is underlined by some evidence reviewed by Clark Hull in his book *Hypnosis and Suggestibility* (Hull, 1933, pp. 83–85). This evidence suggests that in order to understand the novel sentences it encounters in the speech of others a child must begin by acquiring

> a primitive habit tendency (of responding directly to verbal stimulations) which is useful in most situations but maladaptive . . . if a person responds positively and indiscriminately to all suggestions made by others, [in which case] he is likely to be taken advantage of by his associates in that the energies needed for his own welfare will be diverted to that of those giving the suggestions. (Hull, 1933, p. 85)

Holism and Cognitive Dissonance

Having acquired the initial propensity to accept as true everything that it is told by others, the child gradually learns to avoid these maladaptive consequences by discriminating between those statements made by others that demand further scrutiny and those that can be allowed to go through 'on the nod', as the saying goes. After rising steadily up to the age of eight, as the child gradually acquires what Hull calls "a working knowledge of the language," suggestibility, as measured by the postural suggestibility test, begins to decline, and continues to do so into adolescence.

But what does the child have to go on in making this discrimination? Clearly it does not do it by tracing every statement back to its source in observation. To do that would take far too long, even in those cases where it could be done; would be impossible in the case of statements about the past and other unobservables; and defeats the object of the exercise, which is precisely to get information from others to which one has no observational access oneself.

Since it is only in a minority of cases that its primitive tendency to accept everything it is told as true will let it down, what the child needs to do is to find some feature that will distinguish the odd piece of misinformation from the bulk of correct information that it can accept without further question.

For this purpose the only principle on which we can ultimately rely is the principle of the indivisibility of truth or "holism," as it is sometimes called. This is the principle according to which every true proposition must be consistent with every other true proposition. It is a straightforward consequence of the law of noncontradiction whereby if p is true, *not p* must be false and vice versa. It follows from this law that if q entails *not p*, p and q cannot both be true. Either one is true and the other false or both are false. It follows from this that in building up a stock of beliefs about the world on which to base one's action, one should be made uncomfortable by any apparent contradiction or "cognitive dissonance," as Leon Festinger (1957) calls it, within one's existing belief system and endeavor to ensure that any such contradiction is ironed out, before the relevant beliefs are accepted as reliably true. The effect of this endeavor should be to ensure that by and large an individual's beliefs will constitute a coherent system and, provided most of the constituent beliefs are true, will thereby constitute a body of knowledge whose reliability will be confirmed by its overall utility as a guide to action (the pragmatic principle) and its conformity to the opinions of others (Wittgenstein's, 1953, "agreement in judgments").

Given such a coherent body of beliefs whose overall correspondence with reality is guaranteed by its consistent reliability as a guide to action, the individual, whether child or adult, has a standard against which to evaluate any new piece of putative information presented to it by another speaker. If there is no obvious dissonance or contradiction between the new item and the existing stock, it can be allowed to go through on the nod. Only when a contradiction or dissonance is detected between the new item and the existing stock will alarm bells ring and all the armory of logical argument be brought to bear in order either to justify the new item's rejection or find some way of resolving the contradiction and incorporating the new item into the system.

Building a coherent body of propositions representing environmental contingencies, anchored to reality by objective observation and confirmed by its utility as a guide to action is not just a strategy designed to resolve the epistemological problem as it confronts the individual. It is a cooperative social process in which every member of the linguistic community is involved in the process of adding to, correcting, and transmitting what Binswanger (1947) has called the *"Mitwelt,"* the body of coherent and validated knowledge and belief that is the shared property of that community. It is a process, however, that before the advent of what we now call "science" proceeds by an unself-conscious process of progressive behavioral shaping. This process ensures that where adequate evidence is available to the unaided human sensorium and contingencies are ones that are of importance for the survival and welfare of the individual and the social group, the linguistic specification of those contingencies within the system of commonsense practical belief will accurately represent the actual contingencies that obtain.

Commonsense Knowledge and Supernatural Belief

Where the ability to predict the contingencies is vital, but the evidence on which to base such prediction is lacking, beliefs and practices based on those beliefs develop within the linguistic community that, while they are not contradicted by the available evidence, postulate "supernatural" contingencies whose formulation is not shaped by experience of the actual contingencies involved as are the beliefs that constitute the body of practical commonsense knowledge. Since they are not constrained by the actual contingencies involved, such supernatural belief systems tend to vary from one social group to another. Moreover, in a world in which law and morality does not extend to interactions between members of different social groups, sanctions based on the fear of supernatural retribution become an essential part of intertribal trade. In these circumstances differences between groups in their supernatural beliefs are a serious barrier to such trade.

The Origins of Philosophy and Science

Philosophy, in the Western tradition at least, began in Ancient Greece as an attempt to resolve the problem of differences in supernatural belief as it presented itself in the circumstances of the Greek colonies in Asia Minor and elsewhere. Cities like Miletus, where Greek philosophy first appeared lived by trading with peoples of other faiths among whom they had settled but on whom, unlike a conqueror, they were unable to impose their own belief system by force. Instead, they sought to resolve the problem by the method of argument and debate, in a manner that did not prejudge the issue as to who was right and who was wrong. As time went on, part of philosophy developed into what we now call "science" as it was gradually realized that such debates could sometimes be resolved by systematically subjecting the propositions in question to the kind of systematic shaping by the actual contingencies to which the practical belief of commonsense knowledge are subjected in the natural course of events. This is the experimental method.

Science and the Problem of Universals

Using the method of systematic observation and experiment allows the replacement of supernatural belief with the knowledge that results from shaping by rigorous exposure to the actual contingencies. Systematic observation and experiment, however, are not by themselves sufficient to yield the new ways of understanding the universe that are the characteristic products of scientific research. What is also needed is a restructuring of the concepts that are used to classify the particulars we encounter in the world around us as instances of the different universals or kinds of thing.

The dependence of knowledge on a preexisting ability on the part of the organism to classify features of its environment into instances of the same and different kinds is not confined to scientific knowledge, nor, indeed, to propositional knowledge generally. It is an implication of Darwin's theory of evolution by variation and natural selection that the survival and reproduction of complex, free-moving living organisms—animals, in other words—depends on their ability to change the spatial relations between themselves and other objects, including other organisms of the same and of different species, and so bring about the conditions necessary for that survival and reproduction. In order to do that, the organism requires a system, its nervous system, whose function is to match output both to the current stimulus input and to the organism's current state of deprivation with respect to conditions required for its survival and successful reproduction.

Matching behavior to the conditions required for survival and reproduction is the function of the motivational/emotional part of the system. Matching behavior to current stimulus input is the function of the sensory/cognitive part of the system. The sensory/cognitive system cannot perform its function successfully without the ability to group inputs together in such a way that every actual and possible member of the class or category so formed is a reliable indicator of the presence of a particular contingency, an environmental situation in which a particular behavioral strategy or set of such strategies is going to succeed. In other words the survival and reproduction of an organism of this kind depends crucially on its having a conceptual scheme—a conceptual scheme, moreover, that reliably predicts the actual behavior-consequence relations operating in the organism's environment.

Whether it is built into the organism's genetic constitution or acquired by some process of abstraction learning or, as seems most likely, develops through some combination of the two, this Darwinian perspective predicts that an organism's conceptual scheme will follow what Skinner (1938, p. 33) calls "the natural lines of fracture along which behavior and environment actually break."

Some recent evidence (Catania, Shimoff & Matthews, 1989), however, suggests that once contingencies are specified by a linguistic formula or rule, the precise matching of expectations to the actual contingency, which is characteristic of the contingency-shaped behavior of prelinguistic organisms, disappears. There are three possible explanations of this phenomenon. One explanation proposes that where, as in these experiments, the contingency specification is supplied by the experimenter, the contingencies controlling the subject's behavior are those involving the supply of social reinforcement by the experimenter, rather than those involved in the task itself. Another is that the expectation that is set up by a sentence is much more open and, consequently, less easily disconfirmed than one based only on previous encounters with the actual contingency. A third is that the consequences of failing to adapt behavior to minor changes in the contingency are not drastic enough for those changes to impress themselves on the behavior and prompt a reconsideration of how the contingency should be specified. Whatever the reason, there is evidently a connection between this insensitivity of a verbal specification to disconfirmation by subsequent experience of the actual contingency and the ease with which supernatural explanations reinforced by the verbal community can survive what in other circumstances would be regarded as manifest disconfirmations.

But outside the domain of the supernatural, where the interest of the community is to ensure an *exact* correspondence between the linguistic specification and the actual contingency, we can be more satisfied that "the natural lines of fracture" are being followed, and that practical commonsense knowledge is what it purports to be, genuine knowledge of the contingencies it depicts. However, this accurate following of "the natural lines of fracture" extends only as far as the immediate concerns of human beings and the evidence available to the unaided human sensorium. The function of science is to extend the kind of verbally and mathematically formulated knowledge that can yield precise and accurate predictions of outcome into areas, such as the causes of disease and natural disaster, where traditionally only supernatural explanations and ritual practices have been available. In order to do this, many of the time-honored conceptual boundaries of common sense are redrawn with the result that sentences like "Whales are fishes" that once expressed propositions that were analytic, true a priori, and necessary cease to do so, while sentences like "Water is H_2O," that were once synthetic, true a posteriori, and contingent become analytic, true a priori, and necessary.

From Contingencies to Causation

The concepts of common sense and those of science have it in common that they both group together things that have the same kinds of cause or same kinds of effect. They differ in that the causal relations that define the boundaries of the concepts of common sense are anthropocentric in the sense that they are viewed as contingencies confronting a human agent. By contrast the causal relations that define the boundaries of the concepts of science are viewed, in Spinoza's phrase *sub specie aeternitatis* as they are in themselves, regardless of how they impinge on human affairs.[8] To take an obvious example, the commonsense concept of 'animal' excludes human beings. In science, homo sapiens is just one among many species of free-moving living organisms. Needless to say, this scientific repudiation of anthropocentrism does not extend to the technological exploitation of the scientific discoveries that the adoption of the objective standpoint makes possible.

Empirical Science as the Study of Behavior

It might be supposed that in moving away from anthropocentrism toward a more objective perspective, the scientific attitude would require the abandonment of the concept of the three-term contingency with the behavior (of a living organism) as its middle term in favor of some less specifically biological and action-orientated conception of the causal relation. From the standpoint of linguistic behaviorism it is accepted that the concept of behavior in traditional behaviorism, in which its application is restricted to the molar aspects of the behavior of living organisms, is too narrowly parochial to satisfy the kind of universality and objectivity that the scientific attitude demands. The remedy, however, is not to abandon the concept of behavior but to follow what is already a widespread linguistic practice in all branches of science and recognize that it is not just whole living organisms who behave. So do their constituent parts, and so does every entity in the universe that interacts causally with some other entity. Following that usage allows us to say that every empirical science uses the methods of systematic objective observation, measurement, recording, and wherever possible experimental manipulation, in order to study the behavior of some variety or kind of concrete particular or body extended in three dimensions of space and one of time.

The Causal Relation

In studying behavior in this general sense, the scientist is studying causation—the causal action of one thing on another. Moreover, it is because and insofar as they behave in the same way, because and insofar as the same consequences follow when the same causes impinge that we can be sure that our scientific conceptual scheme follows Skinner's "natural lines of fracture." It follows that without an understanding of the causal relation, we cannot hope to understand the scientific enterprise.

Viewed from the standpoint of linguistic behaviorism a proper understanding of the causal relation requires acceptance of the following (analytic) principles.

1. Causation is the relation between situations (events and/or states of affairs). It is not and should not be represented as a relation between propositions (such as the relation of material implication "if p then q").
2. Causation is primarily a relation between particular actually existing situations.
3. Nevertheless all causal relations have two aspects:
   - a categorical aspect whereby two causally related situations are juxtaposed in space-time, and
   - a modal aspect which links the causally related situations to other possible situations that might have existed if circumstances had been different.
4. Causes are always multiple. The belief in a single cause has more to do

with the human urge to pin the blame for what has happened on a single scapegoat than it has with any reality.

5. The causes of a state of affairs are all themselves states of affairs, all of which exist so long as their effect exists.

6. All but one of the causes of an event are states of affairs (standing conditions) that are in position before the event occurs and persist at least until it begins to do so.

7. Every event has a single triggering event that when combined with the standing conditions completes the set conditions that are jointly sufficient for the coming about of the effect. The onset of the effect event coincides with the occurrence or termination of the triggering event.

8. In its categorical aspect, every causal relation involves some kind of direct or indirect contact between at least two concrete particulars, the *causal agent* and the *causal patient*.

9. The *causal agent* is the concrete particular ("substance," in Aristotle's sense) whose continued direct or indirect contact with the causal patient maintains the effect, where the effect is a state of affairs, or whose coming into direct or indirect contact with the causal patient triggers the effect, where the effect is an event.

10. The *causal patient* is the concrete particular, the persistence of or change in whose properties and relations with other things constitutes the effect.[9]

11. In its modal aspect, to say that the existence or occurrence of one situation is a cause or causally necessary condition for the occurrence or existence of another independently existing situation (its effect) is to say that, other things being as they were, if the cause had not existed or occurred, the effect would not exist or have occurred as and when it does or did (the *causal counterfactual*).

12. Since we can never observe what would exist or would have occurred if the situation had been different from that which actually existed or occurred, we can only establish the truth of this causal counterfactual by deducing it from some kind of law statement.

13. A law statement that 'supports' a causal counterfactual is a statement to the effect that, *if at any time* during a period that includes the duration or moment of onset of the effect all other relevant conditions are as they were when the effect actually existed or occurred and a situation of the cause type existed or occurred, a situation of the effect type would exist, or occur, or would have a high probability of existing or occurring.

14. Law statements in this sense are of three kinds:
    - individual law statements that describe the dispositional properties of particular individuals (e.g., "this piece of glass is particularly brittle");
    - universal law statements that describe the dispositional properties of things of a kind (e.g., "glass is brittle");
    - scientific law statements that describe in quantitative terms the causal

relation between the dispositional properties of things of a kind and the effect they produce (e.g., Ohm's Law).

15. Individual law statements, though universally quantified over (restricted periods of) time, are synthetic, determined as true or false by observation (a posteriori), and contingent. Universal law statements and scientific law statements, if true and generally accepted as such, are analytic, true a priori, and necessary. If something proves not to have the dispositional properties that are conventionally and analytically ascribed to things of the kind of which it has hitherto been taken to be an instance, we conclude not that the universal law statement is false but that the individual in question has been misclassified.

16. The analyticity of scientific law statements, the fact that they are made true a priori by linguistic convention within the scientific community, explains the phenomenon of the scientific revolution as described by Kuhn (1962), whereby difficulties in describing observations in terms of the existing conventionally established conceptual scheme or "paradigm" leads eventually to its replacement by another set of conventions that because of the change in conceptual boundaries are "incommensurable" with those of the previously dominant paradigm.

17. The linguistic conventions that make scientific law statements analytic survive only insofar as they facilitate the formulation of individual law statements describing the dispositional properties of concrete particulars that despite their universal quantification over restricted periods of time are synthetic, true (if they are true), a posteriori, and contingent.

18. Since causes are always multiple, the individual law statements that support causal counterfactuals are true only insofar as they contain a ceteris paribus clause stipulating that a situation of the cause type will be effective only if all other causes that together are jointly sufficient for the coming about or existence of a situation of the effect type are in place.

19. It follows from this that the only way to determine the truth of an individual law statement, and hence the truth of the causal counterfactuals it supports, is to use what Mill (1843) calls the method of "concomitant variation"—in other words, the experimental method. This is the procedure whereby each "variable" whose causal efficacy is suspected is systematically varied while all other factors whose causal efficacy in relation to the "dependent variable" or effect in question is suspected are held as far as possible constant. Any change that occurs in the dependent variable under these conditions and fails to occur in its absence can then be attributed with some confidence to the only "independent variable" whose value has been changed.

20. This method of concomitant variation relies, in order to validate the conclusions based upon it, on the assumption that like causes produce like effects. Though requiring some qualification to allow for those phe-

nomena to restricted random variation, the principle that like causes invariably produce like effects is an analytic principle that differs from the laws of empirical science in that its analyticity, a priori truth determination, and necessity is not simply a matter of existing linguistic conventions within the scientific community, conventions that are liable to change in the light of the results of future empirical research. *This* convention, like the arithmetical conventions that make "Two is the only even prime number" an analytic truth, is one that could not conceivably be other than it is. This is partly because if like causes did not produce like effects, no free-moving living organism that relies on its brain to select an output appropriate to current input could survive and reproduce. Its brain could never anticipate what outcome is probable, given the current input. But it is also because, if like causes did not produce like effects, no ordered universe could have emerged from the primeval chaos.

The Ontological Independence of Dispositional Properties from Their Structural Basis

Based on this account of causation, Linguistic Behaviorism has a distinctive view on the issue of microreductive explanation. This takes as its starting point the view that a dispositional property depends for its existence on some feature or set of features of the structure of the entity whose property it is. This is to reject H. H. Price's claim that "There is no *a priori* necessity for supposing that *all* dispositional properties must have a 'categorical basis'. In particular, there may be mental dispositions which are ultimate" (Price, 1953, p. 322; quoted by Armstrong, 1968, p. 86). However, the present view differs from that of Armstrong (1968), who likewise rejects Price's claim in that the principle that every dispositional property must have its "categorical basis" is seen as a special case of the (analytic) principle whereby there are no situations (events or states of affairs) for which some kind of causal story cannot be told. In other words, the relation between a dispositional state and its "categorical basis" is a causal relation. But if that is so, the dispositional state and its "categorical basis" must, in Hume's words, be "distinct existences," not one and the same thing, as proposed by Armstrong (1968, pp. 85–88).

Another consequence of the view that a disposition depends causally on its "categorical basis" is that the "categorical basis" cannot be purely categorical. For, as we have seen above, every causal relation has both a categorical aspect whereby two causally related situations are juxtaposed in space and time, and a modal aspect whereby the causally related situations are linked to other possible situations that might have existed, if circumstances had been different. In other words, the structural features that give an entity a dispositional property must include dispositional properties of the structure alongside its categorical spatiotemporal features.

These relationships can be illustrated by the example of the sharpness of a knife or needle. The adjective 'sharp' is systematically ambiguous as between the disposition to cut or pierce soft objects on which the property bearer impinges and those features of the property bearer, the fineness of its edge or point and the hardness/rigidity of the material of which it is composed, that give it that dispositional property. Once that ambiguity is recognized, however, it becomes apparent that the relation between the dispositional property and the features that give it that property is a causal relation and that, of the two causes of the disposition, one, the fineness of the edge or point, is categorical while the other, the hardness or rigidity of the material, is modal or dispositional.

Considered as a dispositional property, the sharpness of something such as a knife or needle is remarkable in that the structural features on which its existence depends are features of the *macrostructure* of the property bearer and are, consequently, accessible to our commonsense understanding of the matter. In most other cases—for example, in the case of the dispositional property of hardness/ rigidity on which the existence of the dispositional property of sharpness in part depends—the existence of the dispositional property depends on categorical and modal features of the *microstructure* that are accessible only to scientific scrutiny and understanding. Indeed, so successful has been the strategy of searching in the microstructure for a basis for the dispositional properties distinctive of natural kinds that it is often seen as the hallmark of the scientific enterprise. So much so that it has become very difficult to get a hearing for behaviorists such as B. F. Skinner, who have insisted that the scientific study of the environmental conditions governing the acquisition of the molar behavioral dispositions of living organisms should precede and be conducted independently of the study of the microstructural basis of those dispositions in the brain. Yet if, as is argued here, the relation between a dispositional property and its microstructural basis is a causal relation between "distinct existences," that is precisely the strategy demanded by the experimental method, the method of concomitant variation. For unless the environmental factors can be held constant or their effect on the resultant behavioral dispositions allowed for, there can be little hope of disentangling the complex microstructural changes in the brain by which those effects are mediated.

Appendix
Publications of U. T. Place

Book

1996. (With D. M. Armstrong and C. B. Martin). *Dispositions: A Debate*, edited by Tim Crane. Routledge, London.

Journal Articles

1954. The concept of heed. *British Journal of Psychology,* 45, 234–255.

1955. (with J. J. C. Smart). Contradictories and entailment. *Philosophy and Phenomenological Research,* 15, 541–544.

1956. Is consciousness a brain process? *British Journal of Psychology,* 47, 44–50.

1960. Materialism as a scientific hypothesis. *The Philosophical Review,* 69 (1), 101–104.

1966. Consciousness and perception in psychology II. *Proceedings of the Aristotelian Society, Supplementary Volumes,* 40, 101–124.

1969. Burt on brain and consciousness. *Bulletin of the British Psychological Society,* 22, 285–292.

1971. The infallibility of our knowledge of our own beliefs. *Analysis,* 31, 197–204.

1971. Understanding the language of sensations. *Australasian Journal of Philosophy,* 49 (1), 158–166.

1972. Sensations and processes—a reply to Munsat. *Mind,* 81, 106–112.

1973. The mental and the physical—a reply to Dr. Meynell. *Heythrop Journal,* 14, 417–424.

1977. Twenty years on—"Is consciousness still a brain process?" *Open Mind,* 6, 3–10.

1978. Psychological paradigms and behaviour modification. *De Psycholoog,* 13, 611–621.

1981. Skinner's *Verbal Behavior* I—Why we need it. *Behaviorism,* 9, 1–24.

1981. Skinner's *Verbal Behavior* II—What is wrong with it. *Behaviorism,* 9, 131–152.

1982. Skinner's *Verbal Behavior* III—How to improve parts 1 and 2. *Behaviorism,* 10, 117–136.

1983. Comments on Mark Burton's theses. *Behavior Analysis,* 4, 1, 22–31.

1983. Skinner's *Verbal Behavior* IV—How to improve part 4, Skinner's account of syntax. *Behaviorism*, 11, 163–186.

1983. Disposicijska svojstva i argument *virtus dormitiva* [Dispositional properties and the *virtus dormitiva* argument]. *Filozofska Istrazivanja*, 3, 7, 77–84.

1985. A response to Sundberg and Michael. *The Analysis of Verbal Behavior*, 3, 41–47.

1985. Three senses of the word "tact." *Behaviorism*, 13, 63–74.

1987. Causal laws, dispositional properties and causal explanations. *Synthesis Philosophica*, 2 (3), 149–160.

1988. Thirty years on—Is consciousness still a brain process? *Australasian Journal of Philosophy*, 66 (2), 208–219.

1988. Skinner's distinction between rule-governed and contingency-shaped behaviour. *Philosophical Psychology*, 1, 225–234.

1989. Towards a connectionist version of the causal theory of reference. *Acta Analytica* 4 (5), 71–97.

1989. Concept acquisition and ostensive learning: a response to Professor Stemmer. *Behaviorism*, 17 (2), 141–145.

1990. Intensionalism, connectionism and the picture theory of meaning. *Acta Analytica*, 6, 47–63.

1990. E. G. Boring and the mind-brain identity theory. *The British Psychological Society, History and Philosophy of Psychology Newsletter*, 11, 20–31.

1991. On the social relativity of truth and the analytic-synthetic distinction. *Human Studies*, 14, 265–285.

1992. Eliminative connectionism and its implications for a return to an empiricist/behaviorist linguistics. *Behavior and Philosophy*, 20 (1), 21–35.

1992. The role of the ethnomethodological experiment in the empirical investigation of social norms and its application to conceptual analysis. *Philosophy of the Social Sciences*, 22 (4), 461–474.

1992. Two concepts of consciousness: The biological/private and the linguistic/social. *Acta Analytica*, 8, 53–72.

1992. Holism and cognitive dissonance in the discrimination of correspondence between sentences and situations. *Acta Analytica*, 8, 143–155.

1993. A radical behaviorist methodology for the empirical investigation of private events. *Behavior and Philosophy*, 20, 25–35.

1994. Connectionism and the resurrection of behaviourism. *Acta Analytica*, 12, 65–79.

1995. The Searle fallacy: A reply to John Beloff (and in passing to John Searle). *The British Psychological Society, History and Philosophy of Psychology Newsletter*, 21, 5–18.

1995/1996. Symbolic processes and stimulus equivalence. *Behavior and Philosophy*, 23 (3)/24 (1), 13–30.

1996. The picture theory of meaning and its implications for the theory of truth and its discrimination. *Communication and Cognition*, 29 (1), 5–14.

1996. Intentionality as the mark of the dispositional. *Dialectica*, 50, 91–120.

1996. Mental causation is no different from any other kind. *The British Psychological Society, History and Philosophy of Psychology Newsletter*, 23, 15–20.

1996. Metaphysics as the empirical study of the interface between language and reality. *Acta Analytica*, 15, 97–118.

1997. Linguistic behaviorism and the correspondence theory of truth. *Behavior and Philosophy*, 25 (2), 83–94.

1997. Rescuing the science of human behavior from the ashes of socialism. *Psychological Record*, 47, 649–659.

1997. On the nature of conditionals and their truthmakers. *Acta Analytica*, 18, 73–87.

1997. *De re* modality without possible worlds. *Acta Analytica*, 19, 129–143.

1998. Sentence and sentence structure in the analysis of verbal behavior. *The Analysis of Verbal Behavior*, 15, 131–133.

1998. Behaviourism as a standpoint in the science of language. *Connexions*, 4. [http://www.shef.ac.uk/~phil/connex/issue04/place1.html]

1998. Evidence for the role of operant reinforcement in the acquisition and maintenance of linguistic competence. *Connexions*, 4. [http://www.shef.ac.uk/~phil/connex/issue04/place2.html]

1999. Intentionality and the physical—a reply to Mumford. *Philosophical Quarterly*, 49 (195), 225–231.

1999. Token- versus type-identity physicalism. *Anthropology and Philosophy*, 3 (2), 21–31.

1999. Connectionism and the problem of consciousness. *Acta Analytica*, 22, 197–226.

1999. Vagueness as a mark of dispositional intentionality. *Acta Analytica*, 23, 91–109.

2000. The role of the hand in the evolution of language. *Psycoloquy*, January 23. [http://www.cogsci.soton.ac.uk/psyc]

2000. The two factor theory of the mind-brain relation. *Brain and Mind*, 1, 29–43.

2000. The causal potency of qualia: its nature and its source. *Brain and Mind*, 1, 183–192.

2000. (with Noam Chomsky). The Chomsky-Place correspondence 1993–1994, edited by Ted Schoneberger, *The Analysis of Verbal Behavior*, 17, 7–38.

2002. A pilgrim's progress? From mystical experience to biological consciousness. *Journal of Consciousness Studies*, 9 (3), 34–52.

Chapters/Contributions to Edited Collections

1967. Comments on Hilary Putnam 'Psychological predicates." In *Art, Mind and Religion: Proceedings of the 1965 Oberlin Colloquium in Philosophy*, edited by W. H. Capitan and Daniel D. Merrill, pp. 55–68. Pittsburgh University Press, Pittsburgh, Pennsylvania.

1977. Filosofie, psychologie en filosofische psychologie. In *Ontwikkelingen in de Psychologie* [Developments in Psychology], edited by Karel Soudijn and Henk Bergman, pp. 23–38. Boom/Intermediaire, Amsterdam.

1986. Ethics as a system of behavior modification. In *Psychological Aspects of Language: The West Virginia Lectures*, edited by Linda J. Parrott and Philip N. Chase, pp. 157–178. Charles C. Thomas, Springfield, Illinois.

1987. Skinner re-skinned. In *B. F. Skinner, Consensus and Controversy*, edited by Sohan Modgil and Celia Modgil, pp. 239–248. Falmer Press, Lewes, Sussex.

1987. Skinner re-placed. In *B. F. Skinner, Consensus and Controversy*, edited by Sohan Modgil and Celia Modgil, pp. 253–256. Falmer Press, Lewes, Sussex.

1989. Low claim assertions. In *Cause, Mind and Reality: Essays Honoring C. B. Martin*, edited by John Heil, pp. 121–135. Kluwer, Dordrecht.

1989. Thirty-five years on—Is consciousness still a brain process? In *The Mind of Donald Davidson*, edited by Johannes Brandl and Wolfgang L. Gombocz, *Grazer Philosophische Studien*, 36, 17–29. Radopi, Amsterdam.

1991. Conversation analysis and the analysis of verbal behavior. In *Dialogues on Verbal Behavior: The First International Institute on Verbal Relations*, edited by Linda J. Hayes and Philip N. Chase, pp. 85–109. Context Press, Reno, Nevada.

1992. Behavioral contingency semantics and the correspondence theory of truth. In *Understanding Verbal Relations: The Second and Third International Institute on Verbal Relations*, edited by Steven C. Hayes and Linda J. Hayes, pp. 135–151. Context Press, Reno, Nevada.

1995. "Is consciousness a brain process?" Some misconceptions about the article. In *Consciousness at the Crossroads of Cognitive Science and Philosophy: Selected Proceedings of the Final Meeting of Tempus Project "Phenomenology and Cognitive Science," Maribor, Slovenia, 23–27 August, 1994*, pp. 9–15. Imprint Academic, Thorverton, Devon.

1996. Linguistic behaviorism as a philosophy of empirical science. In *The Philosophy of Psychology*, edited by William O'Donohue and Richard F. Kitchener, pp. 126–140. Sage, London.

1996. Folk psychology and its implications for psychological science: Introduction. In *The Philosophy of Psychology*, edited by William O'Donohue and Richard F. Kitchener, pp. 243–244. Sage, London.

1996. Folk psychology and its implications for psychological science: Folk psychology from the standpoint of conceptual analysis. In *The Philosophy of Psychology*, edited by William O'Donohue and Richard F. Kitchener, pp. 264–270. Sage, London.

1997. Contingency analysis applied to the pragmatics and semantics of naturally occurring verbal interactions. In *Context and Communication Behavior*, edited by James L. Owen, pp. 369–385. Context Press, Reno, Nevada.

1998. From mystical experience to biological consciousness: A pilgrim's progress? In *Current Trends in History and Philosophy of Psychology*, edited by Man Cheung Chung, Volume 1, pp. 43–48. British Psychological Society, Leicester.

1998. Behaviourism and the evolution of language. In *Current Trends in History and Philosophy of Psychology*, edited by Man Cheung Chung, Volume 2, pp. 55–61. British Psychological Society, Leicester.

1999. Ryle's behaviorism. In *Handbook of Behaviorism*, edited by William O'Donohue and Richard F. Kitchener, pp. 361–398. Academic Press, San Diego, California.

2000. Consciousness and the "zombie-within": A functional analysis of the blindsight evidence. In *Beyond Dissociation: Interaction between Dissociated Implicit and Explicit Processing,* edited by Yves Rossetti and Antti Revonsuo, pp. 295–329. John Benjamins, Amsterdam.

Lesser Publications

1959. The phenomenological fallacy—a reply to Smythies. *British Journal of Psychology,* 50, 72–73.

1979. Review of K. V. Wilkes, *Physicalism*. London: Routledge & Kegan Paul, 1978. *Philosophy*, 54, 423–425.

1979. Essay review of Karl R. Popper and J. C. Eccles, *The Self and its Brain: An Argument for Interactionism, Annals of Science*, 36, 403–408.

1984. Logic, reference and mentalism. *The Behavioral and Brain Sciences,* 7, 565–566.

1985. Semi-covert behavior and the concept of pain. *The Behavioral and Brain Sciences*, 8, 70–71.

1985. Three senses of the word "tact"—a reply to Professor Skinner. *Behaviorism*, 13, 155–156.

1988. What went wrong?—Comments on B.F. Skinner's 'Whatever happened to psychology as the science of behavior?' *Counselling Psychology Quarterly,* 1, 307–309.

1992. Behaviorism and behavior analysis in Britain. *The Association for Behavior Analysis Newsletter*, 15, 4, 5–7.

1996. Names as constituents of sentences: An omission. *Journal of the Experimental Analysis of Behavior*, 65, 302–304.

1996. The properties of conscious experiences: A second reply to John Beloff. *The British Psychological Society, History and Philosophy of Psychology Newsletter*, 23, 31–33.

1998. In praise of the breadth of British philosophers. Letter to the Editor, *The Observer*, 6 December, 30.

Published Abstracts of Unpublished Conference Papers

1983. Behavioural contingency semantics. In *Abstracts of the 7th International Congress of Logic, Methodology and Philosophy of Science,* edited by Peter Simons, vol. 2, sections 5 and 12, pp. 342–345. J. Huttegger OHG, Salzburg.

1985. Conversation analysis and the empirical study of verbal behaviour. Abstract of paper presented at the Annual Conference of the Experimental Analysis of Behaviour Group, University of Sussex, April 1984. *Behavioural Processes*, 10, 196–197.

1988. Consciousness as an information processing system. *The British Psychological Society 1988 Abstracts*, 58.

1989. Contingency analysis of naturally occurring verbal interactions. *The British Psychological Society 1989 Abstracts,* 67.

1991. The problem of error-correction in connectionist networks: a new perspective on the law of effect. *Proceedings of the 17th Annual Convention of the Association for Behavior Analysis—May 24–27, 1991, Atlanta, Georgia,* p. 148. Society for the Advancement of Behavior Analysis, Kalamazoo, Michigan.

1992. Is there an operant analysis of animal problem-solving? *Proceedings of the 18th Annual Convention of the Association for Behavior Analysis—May 25–28, 1992, San Francisco, California,* p. 155. Society for the Advancement of Behavior Analysis, Kalamazoo, Michigan. Abstract reprinted in *Behavioral Development*, 3 (3), (1993) 5.

1993. A behavioral view of language. *Proceedings of the 19th Annual Convention of the Association for Behavior Analysis, Chicago, Illinois, May 27–30,* p. 550. Society for the Advancement of Behavior Analysis, Kalamazoo, Michigan.

1993. Psychologism and anti-psychologism: An historical overview. *Proceedings of the British Psychological Society 1993*, 37.

1994. Philosophical fashion and scientific progress [in the theory of universals]. *Proceedings of the British Psychological Society 1994*, 87.

1995. Conceptual analysis as the empirical study of linguistic convention. *Proceedings of the British Psychological Society 1995*, 143.

Unpublished Conference Presentation

Place, U. T. 1968. The use of operant responding as a measure of mood fluctuation in periodic psychoses. Paper presented at the Annual Conference of the Experimental Analysis of Behaviour Group. Nottingham, England.

1999. (with J. A. Wheeler Vega). An anticipation of reversal theory from within a conceptual-analytic and behaviorist perspective. Paper presented at the 9th International Conference on Reversal Theory, June 28–July 2, University of Windsor, Ontario.

Obituaries and Memorial Articles in Honor of U. T. Place

Dickins, Thomas E. 2002. A behaviourist's perspective on the origins of language. *History & Philosophy of Psychology*, 4 (1), 31–42.

Dickins, Thomas E. and Dickins, David W. 2001. Symbols, stimulus equivalence and the origins of language. *Behavior and Philosophy, Ullin Place Special Issue*, 29, 221–244.

Graham, George. 2000. Ullin Thomas Place: 24 October 1924–2 January 2000. *Brain and Mind*, 1, 181–182.

Graham, George. 2000. Ullin Thomas Place, 1924–2000. *Proceedings and Addresses of the American Philosophical Association 74–77, Memorial Minutes*, 116–117.

Holth, Per. 2001. The persistence of category mistakes in psychology. *Behavior and Philosophy, Ullin Place Special Issue*, 29, 203–219.

Leigland, Sam. 2000. Remembering Ullin Place. *The Behavior Analyst*, 23(1), 99.

Leslie, Julian C. 2001. Broad and deep, but always rigorous: Some appreciative reflections on Ullin Place's contributions to behaviour analysis. *Behavior and Philosophy, Ullin Place Special Issue*, 29, 159–165.

Lewis, Harry. 2000. Ullin Thomas Place (1924–2000). *Pelican Record*, 41, 1, 124–127.

Lewis, Harry. 2001. Ullin Place and mind-brain identity. *History & Philosophy of Psychology*, 3 (1), 32–38.

Martin, C. B. 2000. A remembrance of an event: Foreword to "The two factor theory of the mind-brain relation" by Ullin T. Place. *Brain and Mind*, 1(1), 27.

Moore, J. 2001. On psychological terms that appeal to the mental. *Behavior and Philosophy, Ullin Place Special Issue*, 29, 167–186.

Palmer, David C. 2000. Ullin Place: 1924–2000. *The Behavior Analyst*, 23(1), 95.

Palmer, David C. 2001. Behavioural interpretations of cognition. *History & Philosophy of Psychology*, 3(1), 39–45.

Reed, Phil. 2001. Editorial: Ullin Place, 1924–2000. *Behavior and Philosophy, Ullin Place Special Issue*, 29, 155–157.

Smart, J. J. C. 2000. Ullin Thomas Place (1924–2000). *Pelican Record*. Corpus Christi College, Oxford, 41, 123–124.

Smart, J. J. C. 2000. Ullin Thomas Place (1924–2000). *Australasian Journal of Philosophy*, 78, 432.

Stemmer, Nathan. 2001. The mind-body problem and Quine's repudiation theory. *Behavior and Philosophy, Ullin Place Special Issue*, 29, 187–202.

Valentine, Elizabeth. 2000. Ullin Place (1924–2000). *History & Philosophy of Psychology*, 2 (1), 72–74.

Wetherick, N.E. 2000. U. T. Place (1924–2000). *The Psychologist*, 13, 233.

Notes

Editorial Introduction

1. Place (1956); Feigl (1958); Smart (1959).

2. Of 151 citations to Place's work since 1984, fifty are to ICBP.

3. For detailed accounts of the history and variants of, and the objections to, identity theory, see Ullin T. Place, Identity theories, Http://www.host.uniroma3.it/progetti/kant/field/mbit.htm (accessed September 27, 2002).

Steve Schneider, Identity Theory, *International Encyclopedia of Philosophy,* Http://www.utm.edu/research/icp/i/identity.htm (accessed September 14, 2002).

J. J. C. Smart (2000), The identity theory of mind, *Stanford Encyclopedia of Philosophy,* Http:///setis.library.usyd.edu.au/stanford/entries/mind-identity (accessed February 14, 2000).

Chapter 1

Shortened versions of this paper were delivered to the "Mind and Brain" symposium, organized by Dr. Peter Fenwick at the Institute of Psychiatry, London, in November 1996 and to the Eleventh Annual Conference of the British Psychological Society, History and Philosophy Section, York, in March 1997. It was published in abridged form in *Current Trends in History & Philosophy of Psychology*, edited by Man Cheung Chung, pp. 43–48, British Psychological Society, Leicester, 1998 and with an editorial introduction and footnotes by Anthony Freeman in *Journal of Consciousness Studies*, 9 (3), 34–52, 2002.

1. That is, the twentieth century—Eds.

2. Rugby, Warwickshire, a well-known English public school—Eds.

3. He also discusses emergentism, but as that does not lend itself to diagrammatic representation, this section left no lasting impression. I rediscovered it only on re-reading chapter 2 of the book from a copy of volume 1 kindly supplied to me by Mr. Clive Hicks in response to my having mentioned that I had mislaid my copy of that volume when I presented a version of this paper at a conference on "Mystical Experience" organized by Dr. Peter Fenwick at the Institute of Psychiatry in London, in November 1996.

Chapter 2

This paper is reprinted from the *British Journal of Psychology*, 45, 243–255, 1954.

Chapter 3

This classic paper is reprinted from the *British Journal of Psychology*, 47, 44–50, 1956, and has subsequently been reprinted many times.

1. I am greatly indebted to my fellow participants in a series of informal discussions on this topic, which took place in the department of philosophy, University of Adelaide—in particular to Mr. C. B. Martin for his persistent and searching criticism of my earlier attempts to defend the thesis that consciousness is a brain process; to Professor D. A. T. Gasking, of the University of Melbourne, for clarifying many of the logical issues involved; and to Professor J. J. C. Smart, for moral support and encouragement in what often seemed a lost cause.

Chapter 4

This paper is reprinted from *Philosophical Review*, 69, 101–104, 1960, © 1960 Cornell University, by permission of the publisher.

1. I should say that I am in substantial agreement with the remainder of Smart's paper.

2. This problem is discussed in more general terms in two papers by Feigl. The relevant passage will be found in Feigl (1953), from the bottom of p. 621 to the top of p. 623. See also pp. 438–445 of Feigl (1958).

3. Feigl (1953), p. 623, top, gives another example, that of temperature and molecular movement, which brings out the same point, although Feigl's interpretation of it differs from my own. He distinguishes between the identity of things observed under different conditions, as in the case of the same mountain observed from different viewpoints by different observers (p. 622, near top), and the identity of concepts, as in the case of 2^3 and $\sqrt{64}$ (p. 622, bottom). The identity of things is established empirically, while the identity of concepts is established either deductively, as in the case of 2^3 and $\sqrt{64}$, or empirically, as in the case of temperature and molecular motion, by the empirical verification of a scientific theory within which it is possible to define one concept in terms of the other. I prefer to regard the temperature, lightning, and sensation-brain-process cases as examples of a special variety of the identity of things in which an identity is asserted between a state, process, or event and the microprocesses of which it is composed. I suspect, however, that the difference between Feigl's position and my own on this point is not as fundamental as it appears at first sight.

4. We certainly cannot say that a process has been discovered that satisfies the criteria I have suggested, that is, a process an understanding of which enables us to explain the peculiarities of sensations, mental images, and dreams as reported by the individual in whom they occur. We can, of course, explain a great many of the peculiarities of sensation in terms of the stimulus pattern impinging on the receptors, the anatomy and physiology of receptor organs, and the cerebral projection of afferent nerve fibers; but what we want, if I am right, and what we have not yet got, is the clear identification of a process in the brain that "incorporates" a relatively small part of the total stimulus pattern impinging on the receptors at any one moment in the way that the sensation process does, that is, capable of assuming forms determined by factors endogenous to the brain as in dreams and mental imagery, and that has the sort of function in the individual's thought processes

and his adaptation to his environment that his sensations and mental imagery appear to have.

Chapter 5

This chapter comprises sections 3 through 6 from a paper constituting U. T. Place's reply to A. J. Watson, presented in a symposium, "Consciousness and Perception in Psychology," at a meeting of the Aristotelian Society, July 1966, and published in the *Proceedings of the Aristotelian Society, supplementary volumes*, 40, 101–124, 1966. Reprinted by courtesy of the Editor of the Aristotelian Society © 1966.

1. That is, the twentieth century—Eds.
2. That is, the twentieth century—Eds.

Chapter 6

This paper is reprinted from *Analysis*, 31, 197–204, 1971.

1. I am indebted to Professor P. T. Geach and Mr W. J. Rees for drawing my attention to this objection.
2. I am indebted to Professor P. T. Geach for drawing my attention to this principle and for his criticisms of an earlier draft of this section of my paper.

Chapter 7

This paper is reprinted from the *Australasian Journal of Philosophy,* 66, 208–219, 1988, by permission of the Australasian Association of Philosophy and Oxford University Press.

1. In an unpublished paper titled "Intentionality and materialism" presented to the Department of Philosophy at the University of Sydney, c.1969.
2. Used by Burnheim.
3. Both used by Martin and Pfeifer.
4. In the light of an argument developed by Richard Garrett (1985) which in turn derives from an argument developed by Donald Davidson (1982), I am now inclined to think that it is only what Searle (1979) calls "intentionality-with-a-t" that is invariably the mark of the dispositional. I would, however, want to argue that any open-ended predicates that are intensional-with-an-s (Searle), referentially opaque (Quine), or non-Shakespearean (Geach), by the criterion of failure of substitutability *salva veritate* are being used nonreferentially as a linguistic device for characterizing the scope of a disposition. But, in the case of proper names and definite descriptions used to characterize a particular individual toward whom or which behavior is directed, it appears, in the light of the Davidson-Garrett argument, that a different explanation of the failure of substitutability *salva veritate* is required. The suggestion is that in these cases failure of substitutability is evidence that the name or description in question is being used as an indirect quotation of the name or description by which the individual is known to the agent whose behavioral dispositions are being described. On this account the "transparency" of the names and definite descriptions used in characterizations of the behavioral dispositions of animals, to which Davidson and Garrett draw attention, is explained by the fact that where, as in the case of animals, there is *no* name or description by which a particular individual is known to the agent, there is no reason for singling out *any* one name or description as the "correct" way to characterize the agent's behavioral orientation toward that individual.

5. *Treatise on Human Nature*, book 1, Section 14.

6. I am indebted to my colleague Dr. Tony Galton for this example.

7. I am indebted to my colleague Dr. Harry Lewis for this example.

Chapter 8

This paper is reprinted from *Anthropology and Philosophy*, 3, 21–31, 1999, by permission.

1. See Place (1997) for a fuller exposition of this distinction and Place (1999a) for its application to refute C. B. Martin's (1994) electro-fink argument.

2. Davidson (1980, p. 210) dismisses this important distinction with this sentence: "The theory under discussion is silent about processes, states, and attributes if these differ from individual events." But later on the same page he makes it clear that what he is really talking about are those mental verbs that (sometimes) take as their grammatical object an embedded declarative sentence in oratio obliqua or indirect reported speech, i.e., a clause of the form "that *p*." Of the examples of such verbs that he lists, only two, 'notice' and 'perceive', are invariably used to refer to a "clockable" mental event. Of the others 'remember' is sometimes so used, but not always. The remainder ('believe', 'intend', 'desire', 'hope', 'know') invariably refer to dispositional mental states, as does 'remember' in many of its uses. Furthermore, as I pointed out in "The mental and the physical—a reply to Dr. Meynell" (Place, 1973), mental events are constituted by the interface between an antecedent mental process and a subsequent and consequent dispositional state; and it is the subsequent and consequent dispositional mental state that is characterized by the "that *p*" clause.

3. For a more extensive discussion of this point, see my "Intentionality as the mark of the dispositional" (Place, 1996b, pp. 114–115).

4. In Place (1999b) I made the mistake of suggesting that Medlin had borrowed the concept of central state materialism from Armstrong. In fact it appears that Medlin has as much if not more claim to have originated the doctrine than has Armstrong. I hope this acknowledgement will go some way to correcting a mistake that, since the book is now published, I am not in a position to retract.

5. See Goodman (1965, pp. 34–49) for the view that causal counterfactuals are sustained by dispositional statements ascribed to tokens as well as types, i.e., they need to be universally quantified over occasions within the period over which the disposition obtains but not over dispositional property bearers. See Place (1977; 1999a) for the view that such law statements are not properly represented by the formula "If *p* then *q*" and are invariably subject to a ceteris paribus or "other things being equal" clause.

6. In Place (1988) I offered a different reconstruction of Davidson's argument. Though it turns Davidson's on its head by taking as its conclusion what for him is evidently a premise ("There are no psycho-physical bridge laws"), I would stand by the 1988 reconstruction as representing one strand in Davidson's somewhat convoluted thinking on this issue. The present reconstruction, however, is undoubtedly much closer to the original.

7. As stated elsewhere (Place, 1987; 1988; Armstrong et al., 1996), I reject this premise on the grounds that, as Nelson Goodman (1965, pp. 34–49) points out, all that is required to "sustain" a causal counterfactual is a dispositional statement that is restricted in its scope to the behavior of a single individual and that is universally quantified only over occasions during the lifetime of the disposition.

8. For a discussion of Boring's contribution and of the case for the view that the kind of perfect correlation Boring has in mind is never found in a causal relation between distinct existences, see Place, 1990, pp. 28–29.

Chapter 9

This paper is reprinted from *Brain and Mind,* 1 (1), 29–43, 2000, © 2000 Kluwer Academic Publishers, with kind permission of Kluwer Academic Publishers.

1. I speak of the "structural basis" of a disposition rather than, as others have done, of its "categorical basis." This is because careful analysis of the examples shows that while the underlying basis consists in part of the categorical spatiotemporal arrangements of the parts, there are also the dispositional properties of the parts that hold the structure together.

2. I have given a detailed account of this view as applied to the concept of "believing" in "The infallibility of our knowledge of our own beliefs" (Place, 1971) (chapter 6 in the present volume—Eds.)

Chapter 10

An earlier version of this paper with the title "Are qualia dispositional properties?" was presented at a workshop on "Consciousness Naturalized" at the Center di Pontignano, University of Siena, May 1999. A shortened version was presented at the Annual Meeting of the European Society for Philosophy and Psychology, University of Warwick, July 1999. It was also read by George Graham at an invited lecture in honor of Place's memory at the Society for Philosophy and Psychology, Barnard College, Columbia University, June 2000. The full version, published in *Brain and Mind*, 1, 183–192, 2000, © 2000 Kluwer Academic Publishers, is reprinted here with kind permission of Kluwer Academic Publishers.

1. Chapter 7, this volume—Eds.

2. There is evidence from a study by Marcel (1983) that a written word presented to the "blind" part of the field in blindsighted patients can influence the interpretation of a simultaneous auditorily presented word with more than one meaning. But there is no evidence that such stimuli are ever positively identified.

3. I first made this point in my discussion of the "phenomenological fallacy" in the final two paragraphs of "Is consciousness a brain process?" (Place, 1956). Smart (1959) made the same point in presenting his notion of "topic neutrality" in "Sensations and brain processes." As I pointed out in my contribution to *Cause, Mind and Reality: Essays Honoring C. B. Martin*, edited by John Heil (Place, 1989), both these contributions were influenced by an unpublished paper, now lost, by our then colleague C. B. Martin titled "Low-claim assertions."

4. Chapter 9, this volume—Eds.

Chapter 11

Earlier versions of this paper were presented under the title "Consciousness and the zombie-within" at the Inaugural Conference of the Association for the Scientific Study of Consciousness, Claremont, California, June 1997, and under the title "Connectionism and the problem of consciousness" at a conference on "T. Horgan and J. Tienson, *Connectionism and the Philosophy of Psychology*," Ljubljana, Slovenia, August 1997, which paper was subsequently published in *Acta Analytica*, 22, 197–226, 1999. This chapter is reprinted from *Beyond Dissociation: Interaction between Dissociated Implicit and Explicit Processing*, edited by Yves Rossetti and Antti Revonsuo, pp. 295–329, John Benjamins, Amsterdam, 2000, by permission of the publisher.

1. "Dorsal' here only in the sense that, like the dorsal stream properly so called, it terminates in the posterior parietal cortex.

2. The evidence described in notes 9 and 10 suggests that the function of the superior colliculus is to control the orientation of the relevant sense organs toward the location of a problematic input in environmental space, and that the function of the pulvinar is to control the access of such inputs into consciousness.

3. See note 8.

4. There is reason to think that in the human brain there are two more limited-capacity channels, one that selects the name assigned to the concept or category in question by the natural language spoken by the individual concerned and another that constructs a syntactically articulated sentence appropriate to the "thought" that emerges from a further stage in the categorization process.

5. I am indebted to Pim Haselager of the University of Nijmegen for drawing my attention to the need to emphasize this point.

6. The "nonobjects" used by Vanni, Revonsuo, and Hari (1997) in their experiments are another example.

7. The inhibition of the skeletal musculature during this phase of sleep makes sense only as a device whose function is to prevent the massive and obviously maladaptive somnambulism that would otherwise occur in response to such imagery.

8. Tim Shallice (1988; Burgess & Shallice, 1996) has drawn my attention to a hypothesis proposed by Schank (1982), which suggests that the original function of mental imagery was to allow the organism to remind itself of the past consequences of the various courses of action suggested by the current stimulus situation as possible solutions to the problem that situation presents.

9. There is evidence (Gibson & Maunsell, 1997) of cells in IT that respond to cross-modal associations between visual and auditory stimuli in a delayed match-to-sample memory task.

10. There is at present no evidence that human blindsighted subjects can learn to negotiate obstacles in the absence of visual stimulation routed via V1, as Humphrey's monkey subject Helen learned to do. But all the human blindsighted subjects studied thus far have been able to rely on the unaffected portion of the visual field to do this. If, like Helen, they had been compelled to rely on visual information arriving from the retina via the subcortical route, my guess is that they too would have learned to avoid obstacles in the absence of V1.

11. Evidence confirming the suggestion that the posterior parietal cortex performs this function is provided by a recent study by Vanni, Revonsuo and Hari (1997), which shows that the magnetic alpha rhythm generated in the parietooccipital sulcus (POS) is suppressed by object targets to a much greater degree than nonobjects, a finding that is readily interpreted as showing the persistence of activity in this area when a stimulus is *not* readily categorized, as compared with the rapid shutdown when it is.

12. As shown by Moruzzi and Magoun (1949).

13. For the role of the superior colliculus in coordinating, at a preconscious level, the position and sensitivity of the different sense organs in relation to particular locations in environmental space, see Stein and Meredith (1993). For the role of the superior colliculus in controlling the reflexive orienting response whose absence on the affected side of the body is characteristic of the phenomenon of unilateral neglect, see Rafal and Robertson (1995).

14. A study by Vanni, Revonsuo and Hari (1997) provides evidence suggesting that the pulvinar is involved in modulating activity in the ventral stream (V2–V5), where object recognition, or, as I would think, the preparation of the evidence for it, occurs and that the effect of such modulation is to "select the next target for ventral processing." If this may be interpreted to mean that the pulvinar controls whichever parts of the total visual input

are currently subject to ventral processing and hence in the focus of conscious attention, it supports the suggestion that the function of this structure is to regulate the involuntary attraction of the focus of conscious attention to problematic inputs by processes that are themselves necessarily preconscious, i.e., part of what I am calling the "zombie-within."

15. Evidence confirming this identification is provided by Sheinberg and Logothetis (1997). They showed that in a binocular rivalry experiment 90 percent of the cells in a monkey's IT respond to whichever of the two rival stimuli is currently in the focus of attention; whereas in V1, V4, and V5 only 20–25 percent of cells do so. But, apart from that cited in note 9 above, there is no evidence of the involvement of other sensory modalities beside the visual in IT. It is, therefore, unlikely that the unity of consciousness across sensory modalities that is demanded, as much by functional considerations as by phenomenology, is secured by concentration in a single anatomical location. For this a better candidate is the synchronous firing of cells in different parts of the cortex.

16. Needless to say, this identification rides roughshod over a number of complexities. The dorsal stream is a body of linked cortical modules connecting the (visual) projection area (V1) with the posterior parietal cortex. It is of similar complexity to that of the ventral stream that appears on figures 11.2 and 11.5 as the (visual) analyzer (V2–V5) connecting V1 to the inferotemporal cortex. The posterior parietal cortex appears to have two functions: (a) the function emphasized on figures 11.2 and 11.5, where it is identified as the voluntary attention focuser and (b) the function that it presumably shares with the dorsal stream as a whole and which is the basis for this identification of providing the integration of visual and somesthetic information required for the feedback monitoring of voluntary movement. A further complexity is added by recent evidence (Gallese, 1998; Rizzolatti & Arbib, 1998) the role of the premotor cortex (the counterpart of the posterior parietal on the anterior side of the fissure of Rolando), not only in the visual feedback control of voluntary movement but in the visual interpretation of the movement of others. As in the case of the role of mental imagery in response selection, to do justice to these complexities on a diagram such as that on figures 11.2 and 11.5 would seriously detract from the sense of a flow of information within consciousness from input to output.

17. For the courage to embark on this attempt to explore the neuropsychological implications of my 1956 paper "Is consciousness a brain process?" and for their individual contributions to giving it such merits as it has, I am indebted above all to the late Donald Broadbent and, in the temporal order of their contributions, to Larry Weiskrantz, Rodolfo Llinás, Gerald Edelman (and members of the staff of the Neurosciences Institute, then in New York, while I was a Visiting Fellow at the Institute in 1991), Kathleen Taylor, Alan Cowey, Colin Blakemore, and Yves Rossetti and Antti Revonsuo, editors of the volume in which this paper first appeared.

Chapter 12

This paper is reprinted from *Human Studies,* 14, 265–285, 1991, © 1991 Kluwer Academic Publishers, by kind permission of Kluwer Academic Publishers.

1. Personal communication.

2. The traditional empiricist view that as children we learn to speak and to understand what is said to us has been out of favor in recent years, due mainly to the impact of the serial digital computer as a model for the functioning of the human brain. With the advent of the alternative parallel distributed processor (PDP) model (Rumelhart, McClelland and the PDP Group, 1986), the empiricist theory of language acquisition is beginning to make a comeback, to the relief of those of us who have remained faithful to it.

3. It should be noted that, for the purpose of this argument, a propositional attitude is

what is naturally expressed in ordinary language by an embedded indicative sentence in oratio obliqua, typically introduced by means of the pronoun 'that' and its equivalents in other languages. By this criterion 'wanting something' and 'intending to do something' do not describe propositional attitudes.

4. Mill's distinction applies to both general and singular terms. The only exception is in the case of a proper name that denotes its bearer but lacks connotation.

5. It should be emphasized that in speaking of 'criteria' in this connection there is no implication that such criteria are always or even commonly specifiable in some kind of verbal formula or definition. On that point Quine is entirely right. But the notion that we can and frequently do use criteria we cannot specify in words is not an incoherent notion. It is precisely the kind of thing that a parallel distributed processor (PDP) learns to do (see note 2 above).

Chapter 13

This paper is a revised and extended version of a paper presented at the First International Conference on "Understanding Language Use in Everyday Life," University of Calgary, August 1989. It is reprinted from *Philosophy of the Social Sciences*, 22, 461–474, 1992, © Sage Publications, by permission.

1. For a defense of this view of analyticity, see Place (1991). Chapter 12, this volume—Eds.

2. Of the Department of Sociology, Ontario Institute for Studies in Education, Toronto, Ontario, Canada. (Place's sister—Eds)

3. Of the Department of Philosophy, University of Calgary, Alberta, Canada.

4. Of the Research School of Social Sciences, Australian National University, Canberra, Australia.

5. I should like to acknowledge my debt to the former Wilde Reader in Mental Philosophy at Oxford, Brian Farrell, both for alerting me to the implications of ordinary language philosophy for empirical psychology, sociology, and linguistics and, more specifically, for the observation (personal communication) that ordinary language philosophers were using a form of introspection to throw light on their own linguistic habits, which, it was assumed, mirrored those endorsed by the linguistic community as a whole. I am indebted to an anonymous reviewer for suggesting the topic addressed in the concluding section of the paper.

Chapter 14

This chapter is reprinted from *The Philosophy of Psychology*, edited by William O'Donohue and Richard F. Kitchener, pp. 126–140, Sage, London, 1996.

1. It should be emphasized that this construction is a matter of combining a ready-made and oft-repeated function or verb phrase with one or more equally ready-made and oft-repeated arguments or noun phrases, rather than a matter of assembling the sentence from its individual constituent words.

2. According to Frege, the referent (*Bedeutung*) of a sentence is its truth value. For an exposition and discussion of this aspect of Frege's thought, see Dummett (1973), pp. 180–186.

3. Since, as Brentano (1874; 1995, p. 272) points out, you cannot have a relation one of whose terms does not exist, it should be emphasized that the phrase "range of possible situations that a sentence depicts" refers to a dispositional orientation that is induced in a listener who understands the sentence and which is confirmed if it subsequently transpires that a situation falling within that range of possible situations either already exists, has

come into existence, or has existed in the past within the range of times and places indicated in the sentence.

4. In discussing the "Ascitel de Bulmer" example in "Behavioral contingency semantics and the correspondence theory of truth" (Place, 1992b), I point out that there are another three argument places potentially generated by the function 'purchase/sold' that specify the price paid, and the place where and the date on which the transaction took place, making a total of six argument places. But although they are filled by singular terms, those singular terms do not straightforwardly designate particular substances as do those occupying the three "substantive" argument places, those occupied in the example by, "Ascitel de Bulmer," "Marton," and "King Henry I."

5. Chapter 12, this volume—Eds.

6. I first drew attention to the phenomenon whereby sentences that invariably turn out true become analytic because of a change in the conventions of the language, whereby the situation depicted by the sentence becomes a criterion for the application of the terms it contains, in my discussion of the "His table is an old packing case" example in "Is consciousness a brain process?" (Place, 1956, p.46). For a more recent exposition of this view, together with a defense of the analytic/synthetic distinction against well-known Quinean objections (Quine, 1951), see Place (1991).

7. For a more extensive presentation of this argument and that of the following section, see Place (1993).

8. I owe this Spinozistic conception of science to my old friend and former colleague Professor J. J. C. Smart. See his *Our Place in the Universe* (1989), p. 111.

9. Since in every causal interaction both parties are changed as a consequence, the distinction between the causal agent and the causal patient is a matter of which of the two is changed most (the patient) and which comes off relatively unscathed (the agent). In a case where the changes are more or less equal, as when a cube of salt is dissolved in a bowl of water, it is a matter of which effect, the disappearance of the cube or the water's becoming salty, is of interest to the speaker. I am indebted to Professor C. B. Martin of the University of Calgary for this point.

References

Anscombe, G. E. M. 1965. "The intentionality of sensations." In *Analytical Philosophy*, edited by R. J. Butler, pp. 158–180. Second Series. Blackwell, Oxford.

Apter, Michael J. 1982. *The Experience of Motivation: The Theory of Psychological Reversals*. Academic Press, London.

Apter, Michael J. 1989. *Reversal Theory: Motivation, Emotion, and Personality*. Routledge, London.

Armstrong, D. M. 1968. *A Materialist Theory of the Mind*. Routledge & Kegan Paul, London.

Armstrong, D. M. 1997. *A World of States of Affairs*. Cambridge University Press, Cambridge.

Armstrong, D. M., Martin, C. B., and Place, U. T. 1996. *Dispositions: A Debate*, edited by Tim Crane. Routledge, London.

Arnauld, A., and Nicole, P. 1662. *La Logique, ou L'Art de Penser: Contenant outre les Règles Communes, Plusiers Observations Nouvelles, Propres a Former le Jugement*. Paris.

Austin, J. L. 1962a. *Sense and Sensibilia*. Oxford University Press, Oxford.

Austin, J. L. 1962b. *How to Do Things with Words*, edited by J. O. Urmson. Oxford University Press, Oxford.

Austin, J. L. 1970. *Philosophical Papers*, edited by J. O. Urmson and G. J. Warnock. Second edition, Clarendon, Oxford.

Ayer, Sir Alfred Jules. 1936. *Language, Truth and Logic*. Victor Gollancz, London.

Baker, Lynne Rudder. 1997. "Why constitution is not identity." *Journal of Philosophy*, 94, 599–621.

Barwise, Jon, and Perry, John. 1983. *Situations and Attitudes*. MIT Press, Cambridge, Massachusetts.

Binswanger, Ludwig. 1947. *Ausgewälte Vorträge und Aufsätze*. Francke, Bern.

Bloor, David. 1976. *Knowledge and Social Imagery*. Routledge & Kegan Paul, London.

Boring, Edwin G. 1933. *The Physical Dimensions of Consciousness*. Century, New York.

Brentano, Franz. 1874. *Psychologie vom empirischen Standpunkt*. Duncker und Humblot, Leipzig. English translation as *Psychology from an Empirical Standpoint*, edited by Oskar Kraus and Linda L. McAlister. Routledge & Kegan Paul, London, 1995.

Broadbent, Donald E. 1958. *Perception and Communication*. Pergamon, Oxford.

Broadbent, Donald E. 1971. *Decision and Stress*. Academic Press, London.

Brown, Penelope, and Levinson, Stephen. 1978. "Universals in language use: Politeness phenomena." In *Questions and Politeness: Strategies in Social Interaction*, edited by Esther N. Goody, pp. 56–289. Cambridge University Press, Cambridge.

Burgess, Paul W., and Shallice, Tim. 1996. "Confabulation and the control of recollection." *Memory*, 4, 359–411.

Cartwright, Nancy. 1989. *Nature's Capacities and Their Measurement*. Clarendon, Oxford.

Catania, A. C., Shimoff, E., and Matthews, B. A. 1989. "An experimental analysis of rule-governed behavior." In *Rule-Governed Behavior: Cognition, Contingencies and Instructional Control*, edited by Steven C. Hayes, pp. 119–150. Plenum Press, New York.

Chalmers, David J. 1996. *The Conscious Mind*. Oxford University Press, New York.

Chisholm, Roderick M. 1957. *Perceiving: A Philosophical Study*. Cornell University Press, Ithaca, New York.

Chomsky, Noam. 1957. *Syntactic Structures*. Mouton, s'Gravenhage.

Chomsky, Noam. 1959. Review of B. F. Skinner's *Verbal Behavior*. *Language*, 35, 26–58.

Cowey, Alan, and Stoerig, Petra. 1995. "Blindsight in monkeys." *Nature*, 373 (6511), 247–249.

Cowey, Alan, and Stoerig, Petra. 1997. "Visual detection in monkeys with blindsight." *Neuropsychologia*, 35, 929–939.

Davidson, Donald. 1969. "Individuating events." In *Essays in Honor of Carl G. Hempel: A Tribute on the Occasion of His Sixty-Fifth Birthday*, edited by Nicholas Rescher, pp. 216–234. Reidel, Dordrecht.

Davidson, Donald. 1970. "Mental events." In *Experience and Theory*, edited by Lawrence Foster and J. W. Swanson. Duckworth, London.

Davidson, Donald. 1980. *Essays on Actions and Events*. Oxford University Press, Oxford.

Davidson, Donald. 1982. "Rational animals." *Dialectica*, 36, 317–327.

Dennett, Daniel C. 1978. *Brainstorms: Philosophical Essays on Mind and Psychology*. Bradford Books, Montgomery,Vermont.

Dretske, Fred. 1995. *Naturalizing the Mind*. MIT Press, Cambridge, Massachusetts.

Dummett, Michael. 1973. *Frege: Philosophy of Language*. Duckworth, London.

Edelman, Gerald M. 1987. *Neural Darwinism: The Theory of Neuronal Group Selection*. Basic Books, New York.

Evans-Pritchard, Sir Edward. 1937. *Witchcraft, Oracles and Magic among the Azande*. Clarendon Press, Oxford.

Farah, Martha J. 1990. *Visual Agnosia: Disorders of Object Recognition and What They Tell Us about Normal Vision*. MIT Press, Cambridge, Massachusetts.

Feigl, H. 1953. "The mind-body problem." In *Readings in the Philosophy of Science*, edited by Herbert Feigl and May Brodbeck, pp. 612–626. Appleton-Century-Crofts, New York. (Originally published in *Revue International de Philosophie*, 4, 1950.)

Feigl, Herbert. 1958. "The 'Mental' and the 'Physical," in *Concepts, Theories and the Mind-Body Problem. Minnesota Studies in the Philosophy of Science*, volume 2, edited by Herbert Feigl, Michael Scriven, and Grover Maxwell, pp. 370–497. University of Minnesota Press, Minneapolis.

Festinger, Leon. 1957. *Cognitive Dissonance*. Stanford University Press, Stanford, California.

Fodor, Jerry A. 1975. *The Language of Thought*. Crowell, New York.

Fodor, Jerry A. 1987. *Psychosemantics*. MIT Press, Cambridge, Massachusetts.

Frege, Gottlob. 1879. *Begriffschrift*. Nebert, Halle. English translation by P. T. Geach in *Translations from the Philosophical Writings of Gottlob Frege*, edited by Peter Geach and Max Black. Second edition. Blackwell, Oxford, 1960.

Frege, Gottlob. 1884. *Die Grundlagen der Arithmetik: Eine logisch mathematische Unter-suchung über den Begriff der Zahl*. Breslau. Edition with English translation by J. L. Austin as *The Foundations of Arithmetic: A Logico-Mathematical Enquiry into the Concept of Number*. Oxford University Press, Oxford, 1950.

Frege, G. 1892. Uber Sinn und Bedeutung. *Zeitschrift für Philosophie und Philosophische Kritik*, 100, 25–50. English translation "On sense and reference" by Max Black. In *Translations from the Philosophical Writings of Gottlob Frege*, edited by Peter Geach and Max Black. Blackwell, Oxford, 1960.

Frege, Gottlob. 1918. Der Gedanke: Eine logische Untersuchung. *Beiträge zur Philoso-phie des Deutschen Idealismus*, 1, 58–77. English translation as "The thought: a logical enquiry" by A. M. Quinton and Marcelle Quinton. *Mind*, 65, 289–311, 1956.

Gallese, V. 1998. "From neurons to meaning: Mirror neurons and social understanding." Paper presented to the Second Annual Conference of the Association for the Sci-entific Study of Consciousness, Bremen, Germany, June 21.

Garfinkel, Harold. 1964. Studies in the routine grounds of everyday activities. *Social Problems*, 11, 225–250. Reprinted with revisions in *Studies in Ethnomethodology*, edited by H. Garfinkel. Prentice-Hall, Englewood Cliffs, New Jersey, 1967.

Garrett, Richard K. 1985. Elbow room in a functional analysis: freedom and dignity re-gained. *Behaviorism*, 13, 21–36.

Geach, P. T. 1957. *Mental Acts: Their Content and Their Objects*. Routledge & Kegan Paul, London.

Geach, P. T. 1962. *Reference and Generality: An Examination of Some Medieval and Mod-ern Theories*. Cornell University Press, Ithaca, New York.

Gibson, Jay R., and Maunsell, John H. R. 1997. "Sensory modality specificity of neural activity related to memory in visual cortex." *Journal of Neurophysiology*, 78 (3), 1263–1275.

Goldiamond, Israel. 1966. "Perception, language and conceptualization rules." In *Problem Solving: Research, Method and Theory*, edited by Benjamin Kleinmuntz, pp. 183–224. Wiley, New York.

Goodman, Nelson. 1965. *Fact, Fiction and Forecast*. Second edition. Bobbs-Merrill, Indianapolis.

Graham, George, and Horgan, Terence. 2002. "Sensations and grain processes." In *Con-sciousness Evolving*, edited by James H. Fetzer, pp. 63–86. John Benjamins, Amsterdam.

Grensted, L.W. 1930. *Psychology and God: A Study of the Implications of Recent Psy-chology for Religious Belief and Practice; Being the Bampton Lectures for 1930*. Longmans, London.

Grice, H. P. 1975. "Logic and conversation." In *Syntax and Semantics 3: Speech Acts*, edited by Peter Cole and J. L. Morgan. Academic Press, New York.

Grice, H. P. 1978. "Further notes on logic and conversation." In *Syntax and Semantics 9: Pragmatics*, edited by Peter Cole. Academic Press, New York.

Hebb, D. O. 1949. *The Organization of Behavior: A Neuropsychological Theory*. John Wiley, New York.

Hill, Christopher S. 1991. *Sensations: A Defense of Type Materialism*. Cambridge Univer-sity Press, Cambridge.

Hügel, Baron Friedrich, Freiherr von. 1908. *The Mystical Element in Religion as Studied in St Catherine of Genoa and her Friends*. Dent, London.

Hull, Clark L. 1933. *Hypnosis and Suggestibility: An Experimental Approach*. Appleton-Century, New York.

Hume, David. 1978. *A Treatise of Human Nature*, edited by L. A. Selby-Bigge and P. H. Nidditch. Second edition. Clarendon Press, Oxford.

Hume, David. 1902. *Enquiries Concerning the Human Understanding and Concerning the Principles of Morals*, edited by L. A. Selby-Bigge. Second edition, Oxford, Clarendon Press.

Humphrey, N. K. 1974. "Vision in a monkey without striate cortex: A case study." *Perception*, 3, 241–255.

Inge, William Ralphe. 1899. *Christian Mysticism: Considered in Eight Lectures Delivered before the University of Oxford*. Methuen, London.

Inge, William Ralphe. 1918. *The Philosophy of Plotinus: The Gifford Lectures at St Andrews, 1917–1918*. Longmans, Green, London.

Inge, W. R. 1935. *Protestantism*. Revised edition, Nelson, London.

Jordan, M. I. 1986. "Attractor dynamics and parallelism in a connectionist sequential machine." *Proceedings of the Eighth Annual Conference of the Cognitive Science Society*. Erlbaum, Hillsdale, New Jersey.

Kant, Immanuel. 1781. *Kritik der Reinen Vernunft*. Hartknoch, Riga. English translation by Norman Kemp Smith as *Immanuel Kant's Critique of Pure Reason*. Macmillan, London, 1929.

Kim, Jaegwon. 1992. "Multiple realization and the metaphysics of reduction." *Philosophy and Phenomenological Research*, 52, 1–26.

Kosslyn, Stephen M., Thompson, William L., Kim, Irene J., and Alpert, Nathaniel M. 1995. "Topographical representations of mental images in primary visual cortex." *Nature*, 378, 496–498.

Kripke, Saul. 1972. "Naming and necessity." In *Semantics of Natural Language*, edited by Donald Davidson and Gilbert Harman. Reidel, Dordrecht.

Kripke, Saul. 1980. *Naming and Necessity*. Blackwell, Oxford.

Kuhn, Thomas S. 1962. *The Structure of Scientific Revolutions*. Chicago: University of Chicago Press.

Lewis, David. 1973. "Causation." *Journal of Philosophy*, 70, 556–567.

Luck, Steven J., and Beach, Nancy J. 1998. "Visual attention and the binding problem: A neurophysiological perspective." In *Visual Attention*, edited by Richard Wright, pp. 455–478. Oxford University Press, Oxford.

Lewis, Harry. 2000. Ullin Thomas Place (1924–2000). *Pelican Record*, 41, 1, 124–127.

Lycan, W. G. 1969. "On 'intentionality' and the psychological." *American Philosophical Quarterly*, 6, 305–311.

Lycan, W. G., ed., 1999. *Mind and Cognition*. Second edition. Blackwell, Oxford.

Mackie, J. L. 1962. "Counterfactuals and causal laws." In *Analytical Philosophy*, edited by R. J. Butler, pp. 66–80. First Series. Blackwell, Oxford.

Mackie, J. L. 1974. *The Cement of the Universe: A Study of Causation*. Clarendon, Oxford.

Marcel, A. J. 1983. "Conscious and unconscious perception: Experiments on visual masking and word recognition." *Cognitive Psychology*, 15, 197–237.

Marcel, A. J. 1988. Phenomenal experience and functionalism. In *Consciousness in Contemporary Science*, edited by A. J. Marcel and E. Bisiach. Clarendon Press, Oxford.

Martin, C. B. 1994. "Dispositions and conditionals." *Philosophical Quarterly*, 44, 1–8.

Martin, C. B., and Pfeifer, Karl. 1986. "Intentionality and the non-psychological." *Philosophy and Phenomenological Research*, 46, 531–554.

McCauley, Robert, and Bechtel, William. 2001. Explanatory pluralism and heuristic identity theory. *Theory and Psychology*, 11, 736–760.

Medlin, Brian. 1967. "Ryle and the mechanical hypothesis." In *The Identity Theory of Mind*, edited by C. F. Presley, pp. 94–150. University of Queensland Press, St Lucia, Brisbane.

Mill, John Stuart. 1843. *A System of Logic, Ratiocinative and Inductive, Being a Connected View of the Principles of Evidence and the Methods of Scientific Investigation*. John W. Parker, London.

Milner, A. David, and Goodale, Melvyn A. 1995. *The Visual Brain in Action*. Oxford University Press, Oxford.

Moruzzi, G., and Magoun, H. W. 1949. "Brain-stem reticular formation and activation of the EEG." *Electroencephalography and Clinical Neurophysiology*, 1, 455–473.

Pashler, Howard E. 1991. "Shifting visual attention and selecting motor responses: distinct attentional mechanisms." *Journal of Experimental Psychology: Human Perception and Performance*, 17, 1023–1040.

Pashler, Harold E. 1998. *The Psychology of Attention*. MIT Press, Cambridge, Massachusetts.

Patmore, Coventry. 1877. *The Unknown Eros and Other Odes*. George Bell, London.

Patmore, Coventry. 1895. *The Rod, the Root and the Flower*. George Bell, London.

Phelips, Vivian. 1931. *The Churches and Modern Thought: An Inquiry into the Grounds of Unbelief and an Appeal for Candour*. Watts, London.

Place, U. T. 1954. "The concept of heed." *British Journal of Psychology*, 45, 243–255.

Place, U. T. 1956. "Is consciousness a brain process?" *British Journal of Psychology*, 47, 44–50.

Place, U.T. 1960. "Materialism as a scientific hypothesis." *Philosophical Review*, 69, 101–104.

Place, U. T. 1967. "Comments on Hilary Putnam Psychological predicates." In *Art, Mind and Religion: Proceedings of the 1965 Oberlin Colloquium in Philosophy*, edited by W. H. Capitan and Daniel D. Merrill, pp. 55–68. Pittsburgh University Press, Pittsburgh, Pennsylvania.

Place, U. T. 1969. "Burt on brain and consciousness." *Bulletin of the British Psychological Society*, 22, 285–292.

Place, U. T. 1971. "The infallibility of our knowledge of our own beliefs." *Analysis*, 31, 197–204.

Place, U. T. 1973. "The mental and the physical—a reply to Dr. Meynell." *Heythrop Journal*, 14, 417–424.

Place, U. T. 1977. "Twenty years on—Is consciousness still a brain process?" *Open Mind*, 6, 3–10.

Place, U. T. 1981a. "Skinner's *Verbal Behavior* I—why we need it." *Behaviorism*, 9, 1–24.

Place, U. T. 1981b. "Skinner's *Verbal Behavior* II—what is wrong with it." *Behaviorism*, 9, 131–152.

Place, U. T. 1982. "Skinner's *Verbal Behavior* III—how to improve Parts I and II." *Behaviorism*, 10, 117–136.

Place, U. T. 1983. "Skinner's *Verbal Behavior* IV—how to improve Part IV, Skinner's account of syntax." *Behaviorism*, 11,163–186.

Place, U. T. 1987. "Causal laws, dispositional properties and causal explanations." *Synthesis Philosophica*, 2, 3, 149–160.

Place, U. T. 1988. "Thirty years on—Is consciousness still a brain process?" *Australasian Journal of Philosophy*, 66, 208–219.

Place, Ullin T. 1989. "Low claim assertions." In *Cause, Mind and Reality: Essays Honoring C. B. Martin*, edited by John Heil, pp.121–135. Kluwer, Dordrecht.

Place, Ullin T. 1990. "E. G. Boring and the mind-brain identity theory." *The British Psychological Society, History and Philosophy of Psychology Newsletter*, 11, 20–31.

Place, U. T. 1991. "On the social relativity of truth and the analytic/synthetic distinction." *Human Studies*, 14, 265–285.

Place, Ullin T. 1992a. "The role of the ethnomethodological experiment in the empirical investigation of social norms, and its application to conceptual analysis." *Philosophy of the Social Sciences*, 22, 461–474.

Place, U. T. 1992b. "Behavioral contingency semantics and the correspondence theory of truth." In *Understanding Verbal Relations*, edited by Linda J. Hayes and Steven C. Hayes, pp. 135–151. Context Press, Reno, Nevada.

Place, U. T. 1993. "A radical behaviorist methodology for the empirical investigation of private events." *Behavior and Philosophy*, 20, 25–35.

Place, Ullin T. 1996a. "Linguistic behaviorism as a philosophy of empirical science." In *The Philosophy of Psychology*, edited by William O'Donohue and Richard F. Kitchener, pp. 126–140, Sage, London.

Place, U. T. 1996b. "Intentionality as the mark of the dispositional." *Dialectica*, 50, 91–120.

Place, Ullin T. 1997. "On the nature of conditionals and their truthmakers." *Acta Analytica*, 18, 73–87.

Place, Ullin T. 1999a. "Intentionality and the physical—a reply to Mumford." *Philosophical Quarterly*, 49, 225–231.

Place, U. T. 1999b. "Ryle's behaviorism." In *Handbook of Behaviorism*, edited by William O'Donohue and Richard F. Kitchener, pp. 361–398. Academic Press, San Diego, California.

Place, Ullin T. 2000a. "The two-factor theory of the mind-brain relation." *Brain and Mind*, 1, 29–43.

Place, Ullin T. 2000b. "The causal potency of qualia: Its nature and its source." *Brain and Mind*, 1, 183–192.

Place, Ullin T. 2000c. "Consciousness and the 'zombie-within.'" In *Beyond Dissociation: Interaction between Dissociated Implicit and Explicit Processing*, edited by Yves Rossetti and Antti Revonsuo. John Benjamins, Amsterdam.

Place, Ullin T. 2002. "From mystical experience to biological consciousness: A pilgrim's progress?" *Journal of Consciousness Studies*, 9 (3), 34–52.

Place, U. T., and Wheeler Vega, J. A. 1999. "An anticipation of reversal theory from within a conceptual-analytic and behaviorist perspective." Paper presented at the 9th International Conference on Reversal Theory, June 28–July 2, University of Windsor, Ontario.

Popper, Karl R. 1963. *Conjectures and Refutations: The Growth of Scientific Knowledge.* Routledge & Kegan Paul, London.

Posner, Michael I., and Dehaene, Stanislaus. 1994. "Attentional networks." *Trends in Neuroscience*, 17, 75–79.

Posner, Michael I., and Petersen, Steven E. 1990. "The attention system of the human brain." *Annual Review of Neuroscience*, 13, 25–42.

Price, H. H. 1953. *Thinking and Experience*. Hutchinson, London.

Putnam, Hilary. 1973. "The nature of mental states." In *Art, Mind, and Religion*, edited by W. H. Capitan and D. D. Merrill. University of Pittsburgh Press, Pittsburgh, pp. 37–48.

Putnam, Hilary. 1975. "The meaning of 'meaning.'" In *Language, Mind, and Knowledge. Minnesota Studies in the Philosophy of Science,* volume 7, edited by Keith Gunderson, pp. 131–193. University of Minnesota Press, Minneapolis.

Quine, W. V. 1951. "Two dogmas of empiricism." *Philosophical Review*, 60, 20–43.

Quine, W. V. 1969. "Epistemology naturalized." In *Ontological Relativity and Other Essays*, pp. 26–68. Columbia University Press, New York.

Quine, W. V. (1980) "Reference and modality." In *From a Logical Point of View*, pp. 139–159. Second revised edition, Harvard University Press, Cambridge, Massachusetts.

Rafal, R., and Robertson, L. 1995. "The neurology of visual attention." In *The Cognitive Neurosciences*, edited by Michael S. Gazzaniga, pp. 625–648. MIT Press, Cambridge, Massachusetts.

Raichle, Marcus E., et al. 1994. "Practice-related changes in human functional anatomy during non-motor learning." *Cerebral Cortex*, 4, 8–26.

Reed, Phil. 2001. Editorial: "Ullin Place, 1924–2000." *Behavior and Philosophy, Ullin Place Special Issue*, 29, 155–157.

Rizzolatti, G., and Arbib, M. A. 1998. "Language within our grasp." *Trends in Neuroscience*, 21, 188–194.

Rorschach, Hermann. 1932. *Psychodiagnostik: A Diagnostic Test Based on Perception*. Hans Huber, Berne. English translation as *Psychodiagnostics*, by Paul Lemkau and Bernard Kronenberg, edited by W. Morganthaler. Grune & Stratton, New York, 1942.

Rossetti, Yves. 2001. "Implicit perception in action: Short-lived motor representations in space." In *Finding Consciousness in the Brain: A Neuropsychological Approach*, edited by Peter G. Grossenbacher. John Benjamins, Amsterdam.

Rossetti, Yves, Rode, Gilles, and Boisson, Dominique. 1995. "Implicit processing of somesthetic information: A dissociation between Where and How?" *Neuroreport*, 6 (3), 506–510.

Rubin, E. 1915. *Synsoplevede Figurer*. Gyldendalska, København.

Rumelhart, David E., McClelland, James L., and the PDP Research Group. 1986. *Parallel Distributed Processing: Explorations in the Microstructure of Cognition*. Two volumes. MIT Press, Cambridge, Massachusetts.

Russell, B. 1918–1919. "The philosophy of logical atomism." *The Monist*, 28, 495–527; 29, 32–63, 190–222, 345–380.

Ryle, Gilbert. 1949. *The Concept of Mind*. Hutchinson, London.

Ryle, Gilbert. 1954. *Dilemmas*. Cambridge University Press, Cambridge.

Schank, Roger C. 1982. *Dynamic Memory: A Theory of Reminding and Learning in Computers and People*. Cambridge University Press, New York.

Searle, John R. 1969. *Speech Acts: An Essay in the Philosophy of Language*. Cambridge University Press, Cambridge.

Searle, John R. 1979. "What is an intentional state?" *Mind*, 88, 74–92.

Searle, John R. 1983. *Intentionality: An Essay in the Philosophy of Mind*, Cambridge University Press, Cambridge.

Searle, John. 1984. *Minds, Brains and Science: The 1984 Reith Lectures*, British Broadcasting Corporation, London.

Shallice, Tim 1988. *From Neuropsychology to Mental Structure*. Cambridge University Press, Cambridge.

Sheinberg, David L., and Logothetis, Nikos K. 1997. "The role of temporal cortical areas in perceptual organization." *Proceedings of the National Academy of Sciences, USA*, 94, 3408–3413.

Sherrington, Sir Charles. 1947. *The Integrative Action of the Nervous System*. Cambridge University Press, Cambridge.

Skinner, B. F. 1938. *The Behavior of Organisms: An Experimental Analysis*. Appleton-Century-Crofts, New York.

Skinner, B. F. 1957. *Verbal Behavior*. Appleton-Century-Crofts, New York.

Skinner, B. F. 1966. "An operant analysis of problem solving." In *Problem Solving: Re-*

search, Method and Theory, edited by Benjamin Kleinmuntz, pp. 225–257. New York: Wiley.

Skinner, B. F. 1969. *Contingencies of Reinforcement: A Theoretical Analysis*. Appleton-Century-Crofts, New York.

Skinner, B. F. 1974. *About Behaviorism*. Knopf, New York.

Skinner, B. F. 1989. "The behavior of the listener." In *Rule-Governed Behavior: Cognition, Contingencies and Instructional Control*, edited by Steven C. Hayes, pp. 85–96. Plenum, New York.

Smart, J. J. C. 1959. "Sensations and brain processes." *Philosophical Review*, 68, 141–156.

Smart, J. J. C. 1989. *Our Place in the Universe: A Metaphysical Discussion*. Blackwell, Oxford.

Smith, Dorothy E. 1987. *The Everyday World as Problematic: A Feminist Sociology*. North Eastern University Press, Boston, Massachusetts.

Snowdon, Paul. 1995. "Perception and attention." Paper presented to a one-day conference on "Attention and Consciousness: Psychological and Philosophical Issues," Department of Philosophy, University College London, 26th May.

Stapledon, Olaf. 1939. *Philosophy and Living*. Penguin, Harmondsworth, Middlesex.

Stein, Barry E., and Meredith, M. Alex. 1993. *The Merging of the Senses*. MIT Press, Cambridge, Massachusetts.

Stoerig, Petra, and Cowey, Alan. 1997. Blindsight in man and monkey. *Brain*, 120, 535–559.

Tarski, Alfred. 1930–1931. O pojeciu prawdy w odniesieniu do sformalizowanych nauk dedukcyjnych [On the notion of truth in reference to formalized deductive sciences], *Ruch Filozoficzny* 12. English translation of the German text by J. H. Woodger as "The concept of truth in formalized languages." In *Logic, Semantics, Metamathematics: Papers from 1923 to 1938*, pp. 152–278. Clarendon Press, Oxford, 1956.

Tolman, Edward C. 1932. *Purposive Behavior in Animals and Men*. University of California Press, Berkeley, California.

Tranel, Daniel, and Damasio, Antonio R. 1985. "Knowledge without awareness: An autonomic index of facial recognition by prosopagnosics." *Science*, 228, 1453–1455.

Treisman, Anne. 1988. "Features and objects: The Fourteenth Bartlett Memorial Lecture." *Quarterly Journal of Experimental Psychology*, 40, 201–237.

Treisman, Anne, and Gelade, G. 1980. "A feature integration theory of attention." *Cognitive Psychology*, 12, 97–136.

Treisman, Anne, and Gormican, Stephen. 1988. "Feature analysis in early vision: Evidence from search asymmetries." *Psychological Review*, 95, 15–48.

Tye, Michael. 1995. *Ten Problems of Consciousness: A Representational Theory of the Phenomenal Mind*. MIT Press, Cambridge, Massachusetts.

Underhill, Evelyn. 1911. *Mysticism: A Study in the Nature and Development of Man's Spiritual Consciousness*. Methuen, London.

Ungerleider, Leslie G., and Mishkin, Mortimer. 1982. "Two cortical visual systems." In *Analysis of Visual Behavior*, edited by David J. Ingle, Melvin A. Goodale, and Richard J. W. Mansfield, pp. 549–586. MIT Press, Cambridge, Massachusetts.

Vanni, S., Revonsuo, A., and Hari, R. 1997. "Modulation of the parietooccipital alpha-rhythm during object-detection." *Journal of Neuroscience*, 17 (18), 7141–7147.

Verplanck, William S. 1955. "The control of the content of conversation: Reinforcement of statements of opinion." *Journal of Abnormal and Social Psychology*, 51, 668–676.

Weiskrantz, L. 1986. *Blindsight*. Clarendon Press, Oxford.

Whellan, T. 1859. *History and Topography of the City of York and the North Riding of Yorkshire*. Volume 2. John Green, Beverley, Yorkshire.

Winch, P. 1964. "Understanding a primitive society." *American Philosophical Quarterly*, 1, 307–324.

Wittgenstein, Ludwig. 1953. *Philosophical Investigations*. English translation by G. E. M. Anscombe. Blackwell, Oxford.

Wittgenstein, Ludwig. 1958. *The Blue and Brown Books*. Blackwell, Oxford.

Wittgenstein, Ludwig. 1971. *Tractatus Logico-Philosophicus*. English translation by D. F. Pears and B. F. McGuinness. Second edition, Routledge & Kegan Paul, London.

Zihl, J., Tretter, F., and Singer, W. 1980. "Phasic electrodermal responses after visual stimulation in the cortically blind hemifield." *Behavior and Brain Research*, 1, 197–203.

Index

action, 73
activity verb, 36
analysis. *See* conceptual analysis; ordinary
    language philosophy
analytic/synthetic distinction, 149–150,
    157, 172
    Quine's critique of, 150–151
    rebuttal of Quine's critique, 152–153
animals, nonhuman, 61, 86, 106, 165,
    178
anomalous monism (Davidson's theory),
    72–74, 84, 87–89
Aristotle, 149–150, 169, 170
Armstrong, D. M., 5–7, 71–72, 87, 91,
    96–97, 183. *See also* central state
    materialism; dispositions
attention, concept of, 16, 31, 34–43, 119,
    135
    and consciousness, 31
    disorders of, 134
    as paying attention, 31, 34–36, 39
    posterior attention system, 120, 133
    and skill, 35
    types of, 119–120
    See also heed
Austin, John L., 4, 27, 157, 162
Azande, Central African tribe, 141
    and social relativity of truth, 141–
    144
    See also social relativity of truth

behavior, 180
behaviorism, 6, 27–28, 92
    influence of on U. T. Place, 27–28
    linguistic, 165–184
    See also Ryle, Gilbert; Skinner, B. F.

belief, 63–69
    and assertion, 64, 66
    and dispositions, 6, 8, 64
    and infallible knowledge, 63–69
    not a brain state, 8, 64
    in supernatural, 177
    and truth, 147
    See also lying; speaker and audience
blindsight, 105, 114, 117, 122, 127, 128,
    133
Bloor, David, 139
Boring, E. G., 4, 15, 89
brain, neuroanatomy of, 118–137
    modular design of, 132–135
    ventral and dorsal pathways, 118,
    132–135
Brentano, Franz, 71
Broadbent, Donald, 105, 113, 115–116,
    121, 128, 131

Cartesian dualism, implausibility of, 59,
    76–78
    and interactionism, 76
    See also Descartes, René
Cartwright, Nancy, 101
categories, types of, 85, 90
categorization, 105–107, 115–116, 121,
    125, 130, 131, 178–183
causal judgment, 74
causal laws, 73, 88, 100, 181
causal potency of consciousness, and
    identity, 77–80, 104–112
causal relations, 78, 87, 102, 107, 180
    agents and patients, 181
    spatio-temporal structure, 107–109, 180
    See also causation

causation, 73, 77, 79, 179
  primary cause, 107
  relata of, 77, 79
  structured in space-time, 180
central state materialism, 4, 6, 87, 96, 101.
    See also Armstrong, D. M.; Melden,
    David
Chalmers, David, 112
children, learning in, 65, 166, 176
Chomsky, Noam, 145, 166, 171
class independence, and conceptualism,
    152
cognitive dissonance, 175–176
(*The*) *Concept of Mind*, 16, 27, 30, 63, 92,
    95, 113, 162. *See also* Ryle, Gilbert
conceptual analysis, 11, 28, 92, 166
  and conceptual issues, 156
  as empirical work, 155–164
  See also ordinary language philosophy
confirmation, contrast with disconfirma-
    tion, 179
consciousness, 31, 35, 39, 41, 62, 127,
    128
  as brain process, 80
  contrasted with dispositions, 45
  functions of, 12, 16–17, 29, 121
  and input-output transformation, 121
  scientific investigation of, 57–59, 61
consternation, varieties of, 162–163
constitution (composition), 5, 46–47, 49,
    81
  and identity thesis, 49, 98–99
contemplative theory of head, 31, 40
  Ryle's objections to, 32
contingency, three-term, 131–132, 168
contingency semantics, 167–169, 178
convention, 8–9, 11, 12, 144, 147–148,
    158–159, 166, 173–174, 182
correlation, 49
correspondence theory of truth, 169–170
counterfactual theory of causation,
    108–109. *See also* causation
Cowey, Allan, 29, 106, 116, 117, 133

Davidson, Donald, 72, 76, 84, 86–88, 102,
    194n.2. *See also* anomalous monism
de dicto versus de re, 81
Dennett, Daniel, 72

Descartes, René, 3, 4, 15, 75–76. *See also*
    Cartesian dualism.
dichotic listening experiments, 115
dispositional statements, 74
dispositional theory of heed, 34–39
dispositions, 6, 63, 97–99, 183
  and action or behavior, 64
  as hypotheticals, 33, 43, 72, 91, 96
  and laws, 181
  structural versus categorical basis for,
    92, 94–95, 99, 183
divided account of mental, 7, 12, 91
  and two-factor theory, 90–103
Dretske, Fred, 7
dual aspect theory, 80
dualism. *See* Cartesian dualism

emotional responses, 10, 121, 131–132
epiphenomenalism, 17, 54, 74, 76, 79–80
  why false, 79, 104
epistemological, asymmetry, as privileged
    access, 93
ethnomethodological thought experiment,
    153, 161–162
ethnomethodology, as research program,
    155
  as experimental, 159, 161
Evans-Pritchard, E. E., 141–144
events, contrasted with states, 5–7, 85,
    169
experience. *See* consciousness

fact, and situation, 169
feature detection, 125
Feigl, Herbert, 5, 70, 192n.3
Festinger, Leon, 176
figure-ground organization, 29, 109–111,
    127–128, 129
Fodor, Jerry, 72, 144
Frege, Gottlob, 81–82, 86, 144, 149, 150,
    156, 170
function and argument analysis, of sen-
    tences, 170
functionalism, 5

Garfinkel, Harold, 159
Gasking, D. A. T., 5
Geach, Peter, 72, 85, 86, 91, 96

Goodman, Nelson, 100–101, 108, 194n.5, 194n.7
Grice, Paul, 4, 157, 160

hallucination, 43
hard problem, 112
heed, 16, 31–43. *See also* attention
Helen, the monkey, 105
holism, 175–176
Hull, Clark, 65, 175
Hume, David, 7, 77, 111, 108, 129, 183
Humphrey, Nicholas, 105, 114, 116, 133

identity
  contingent, 8–9
  logical conditions for, 49–54, 81–82, 87
  type versus token, 81–89
identity theory, 3
  developments of, 4–7, 14, 70–80
  Feigl's formulation, 192n.3
  objections to, 55
  scientific hypothesis of, 6, 10, 14, 45–46, 54, 56, 72, 114
impotence, causal, 77
infallible knowledge of beliefs, 63–69. *See also* mental self-knowledge
Inge, Dean, 22
inner events and processes, 30, 31, 33, 40, 45, 61
input filter, and output relay, 131
intensionalism versus extensionalism, 152, 171
intentionality, 71–72
introspection, 30, 50, 57–58, 63–69, 112
  as empirically indecisive, 58
  and internal monitoring, 16, 40
  and introspective reports, 17, 35, 57–60
  See also epiphenomenalism
"is," uses of, 46–47

Kant, Immanuel, 129, 147, 149–150
knowledge, 63–69, 176
Kripke, Saul, 84, 149
Kuhn, Thomas, 144, 148, 182

language, 147, 165
  and ontology, 47–48
laws, of nature, 101, 173, 181–182

learning, 69
Leibniz's law, 5, 80, 95, 99, 102
Lewis, David, 108
limited capacity channel, 105, 115, 121, 125
linguistic behaviorism, 11
  as philosophy of science, 11, 165, 183
linguistics, 61
liquidation of philosophy, 155–56
  and conceptual analysis, 156
localization, of conscious activity in brain, 113–137
logical behaviorism, 5. *See also* Ryle, Gilbert
logical positivism, 4, 26–27
lying, and believing, 63–64, 66, 170

Mackie, John, 74, 108
Martin, C. B. (Charlie), 5, 71, 96, 98, 101, 109, 161
materialism, as science, 4–6, 14–15, 45, 70, 54, 72. *See also* physicalism
meaning
  picture theory, 12, 167
  and sentence contribution, 156
  and verbal behavior, 151, 156
Medlin, Brian, 5, 87, 91, 96, 104
mental, no distinguishing mark of, 85, 90
mental imagery, 128, 196n.8
mental propensities, 93
mental self-knowledge, 94
mind-body (brain) identity theory, 4, 45–52
  not for mental dispositions, 99, 102
  as scientific hypothesis, 46, 74, 53–55
  See also identity theory
mind-body problem, 3
mind's eye, 45
modules, within brain, 123, 132
  within consciousness, 125
mood and motivation, 10
multiple realizability, 5–6
mutability of analytic truth, 153–154
mysticism, 21
  and ethical transformation, 17, 22
  as lesson about consciousness, 29
  personal appeal of to Place, 17, 21

neuroanatomy, in localizing consciousness, 118–137
noncontradiction, principle of, 143, 149, 176
  and holism, 176
novel sentences, 167

observation, 48–50, 174, 177, 180
  of single events, 49–50, 53–54, 84, 89
Ockham's Razor (parsimony), 48–49, 53–54, 58–59, 97, 174–175
ordinary language philosophy, 4, 11, 26–27, 28, 161. *See also* conceptual analysis
overdetermination, 77–78

pain, 94
Pashler, Harold, 120–121
Phelips, Vivian, 24
phenomenological fallacy, 51–52
philosophical problems, 10, 59–60, 156, 177
  physicalism, 45
  as resisting solution, 15, 25–26, 60, 72
  solving them, 26, 157
  See also materialism
picture theory of meaning, 12, 167, 169–170
Place, U. T.
  empirical work of, 10–11
  life, mission in, 19, 24, 26
  parents, 17–21
poison oracle, 141
Posner, Michael, 120–133
Price, H. H., 95–96, 183
problematic input detection, 126
properties, 109, 111
propositional attitudes, 71, 73, 85, 146
  as dispositional, 85
  and truth, 138, 143
propositions, 67–69, 138, 140, 171
  as intensional classes, 145–146, 169
  as restricted to language users, 147
  as sentences, 144
privileged access, 92–94
  as privacy, 45
psychoneural identity thesis. *See* central state materialism; identity theory

psychophysical bridge-laws, 103
psychophysical parallelism, 17, 53, 55
  difficulties with, 76, 79–80
Putnam, Hilary, 5, 84

Quakerism, 4, 19, 23
qualia, 15, 104, 106, 110–111
  biological function of, 104
  not dispositional, 110–111
  as evidence for categorization, 106
Quine, W. V., 86, 87, 149–153, 163–164, 172

rationality, 67, 69, 139
  versus irrationality, 68–69
reciprocal disposition partner, 109
reductionism, 84
  and reductive explanation, 183
reference, and sense, 152
referential opacity, 86, 193n.4
religion, 18, 19, 23–24, 26
  and supernatural, 177
representation, 7–8
representational content, phenomenal, 7
representationalism, 7
response, execution of, 107, 121
  selection of, 107, 121
rigid designation, 84
Ryle, Gilbert, 4, 25, 30–43, 60, 63, 70, 85, 86, 90, 91, 95. *See also* behaviorism; *Concept of Mind*

science, 177, 179
  contrast with philosophy, 177
  evolution of, 178
  and problem of universals, 177–179
Searle, John, 71
self-knowledge, 94
semantics, 9, 168
sensation, bodily, 9
  brain process, 45–52, 70–80
sentences
  observation sentences, 174
  as signs, 168
  and situations, 168–169
  structure of and world mapping, 168–170
Sherrington, Sir Charles, 50

sign, as stimulus type, 167
simplicity. *See* Ockham's razor
Skinner, B. F., 6, 10, 11, 12, 130, 147,
    165–166, 168, 178, 180, 184. *See
    also* behaviorism
sleep, 130
Smart, J. J. C., 5, 15, 53–55, 72–75, 110,
    162, 183
Smith, Dorothy, 161
Snowdon, Paul, 119
social relativity of truth, 8, 138–154, 174
    naïve and sophisticated, 139, 147
    See also truth
sociolinguistics, 8, 164, 166
speaker, and audience (listener), 66, 145,
    166–167, 170, 175
    as cooperative truth seeking, 176
state, contrasted with event and process, 6,
    90–91
stimulus, internal, 17. *See also* categoriza-
    tion
Stoerig, Petra, 29, 106, 116–117, 123, 133
striate cortex, lesions of, 105–106, 116,
    133
strong programme, in sociology, 139–140
suggestibility, 175

three term contingency. *See* contingency,
    three term
token identity, 87–89, 103
    as typically contingent and synthetic,
    82–84, 87
Triesman, Anne, 125
triggering event, 77–78, 181. *See also*
    causation

truth, 146, 153–154, 169–170, 182
    analytic versus synthetic, 8, 83–84,
        138–154, 172–174
    contingent versus necessary, 9, 46, 60,
        84, 172–173
    as modal class, 171
    propositions as bearers of, 171
    Tarski's convention, 146, 169
    See also social relativity of truth
truth makers, 101
two parallel processing streams, 106
two-factor theory, 90–103
Tye, Michael, 7
type identity, 8, 87, 98
    as typically necessary and analytic, 9,
        82–84, 87
type-token distinction, 8, 82–83

Underhill, Evelyn, 21–22
universals. *See* science

Verplanck, William, 160–161

Watson, A. J., 56–61
Weiskrantz, Lawrence, 29, 105, 116, 117,
    127, 133. *See also* blindsight
What it is like, 41
Winch, Peter, 140–141
Wittgenstein, Ludwig, 6, 27, 85, 91, 94,
    156, 167, 176
    influence of on Place, 11, 91

zombies-within, 106, 114–116
    modular design of, 123
    as sub-conscious, 29, 122